THE
PROFESSIONS
in Early Modern England

Edited by Wilfrid Prest

CROOM HELM
London • New York • Sydney

© 1987 Wilfrid Prest
Croom Helm Ltd, Provident House, Burrell Row,
Beckenham, Kent BR3 1AT
Croom Helm Australia, 44–50 Waterloo Road,
North Ryde, 2113, New South Wales

British Library Cataloguing in Publication Data

The Professions in early modern England.
  1. Professions—England—History
  2. Professions—Social aspects—England
  I. Prest, Wilfrid R.
    305.5'53'0942   HT687

  ISBN 0-7099-2051-2

Published in the USA by
Croom Helm
in association with Methuen, Inc.
29 West 35th Street
New York, NY 10001

Library of Congress Cataloging in Publication Data
applied for:

Phototypeset by Sunrise Setting, Torquay, Devon
Printed and bound in Great Britain by Mackays of Chatham Ltd, Kent

Contents

Tables

Preface

The social history of the professions has begun to attract considerable attention in recent years. But most work published to date deals with particular occupations or the professions in general from the nineteenth century onwards. This volume aims to help correct that deficiency by bringing together contributions from scholars who have made a close study of various professional and quasi-professional occupations in England during the early modern period (*c*. 1500–1750).

By drawing on the expertise of a number of individual specialists, it becomes feasible to cover a much wider range with more authority than any one historian on his or her own could reasonably contemplate. But while that is all very well in theory, the obvious practical problem is to find experts both able and willing to contribute to a project such as this. Although I have been fortunate in recruiting a team of contributors whose research interests extend well beyond the three traditional learned professions, some particular gaps do remain. True, public administrators and architects are both already covered to some extent in the published writings of Gerald Aylmer and H. M. Colvin. But university dons have not so far received similar attention, and I much regret that it has proved impossible to include the fruits of Christopher Brooks's important recent comparative work on early modern guilds and professions.[1]

What counts as a profession for the purposes of this volume, and what was distinctive or important about the early modern professions? The noun 'profession', derived from the Latin *profiteri* ('to avow or confess'), was by the mid-seventeenth century conventionally applied to what Addison later called 'the three great professions of divinity, law and physic', besides being used more generally as a synonym for calling, occupation or vocation.[2] In addition to clergymen, lawyers and medical practitioners, the following chapters deal with school-teachers, military and naval officers and estate stewards. All these are examples of what would now be conventionally regarded as professional occupations, even though their early modern predecessors were on the whole less highly trained or tightly organised than is the case today. The sixteenth, seventeenth and (to a slightly lesser extent) the first half of the eighteenth century saw considerable expansion across the professional sector as a whole. The fundamental background causes were demographic and economic growth, combined with the evolution of a steadily more ambitious and complex state apparatus. The impact of these forces was by no means identical across the entire occupational spectrum, since not all professions were able to exploit the opportunities created. But those which did flourished, and thereby made a significant contribution to the heightened cultural and intellectual diversity of urban life in particular during the second half of our period. In the revolutionary decades of the mid-seventeenth century, hostility towards the monopolistic pretensions of the three learned professions — 'the grand remoras and forest incumbrances' of the republic, according to an anonymous pamphleteer of 1652, was a common radical rallying-cry, and one which by no means died with the Good Old Cause.[3] Its persistence and vigour are backhanded testimony to the prominence which the professions had achieved in early modern English society.

For help at the latter stages of assembling this book, I am most grateful to James Hogg and, especially, Jonathan Rée. I should also like to thank my fellow contributors for their co-operation and patience.

W.R.P.

Notes

(Books referred to here and below are published in London unless otherwise indicated.)

1. G. E. Aylmer, *The King's servants: the civil service of Charles I, 1625–1642* (1961); G.E. Aylmer, *The state's servants: the civil service of the English Republic 1649–1660* (1973); H. M. Colvin, *A biographical dictionary of English architects 1660–1840* (1954), pp. 10–25. There is a useful bibliography in G. Holmes, *Augustan England: professions, state and society, 1680–1730* (1982).

2. *The Spectator*, no. 21 (24 Mar. 1711); see also *OED*, under 'profession'.

3. 'Dalepater mendemus', *Lex exlex* (1652), pp. 4–5; cf. C. Hill, *Change and continuity in seventeenth-century England* (1974), ch. 7; W. A. Speck, 'Social status in later Stuart England', *P & P*, no. 34 (1966), pp. 127–9.

Contributors

David Cressy teaches at the Long Beach campus of California State University. He is currently preparing a book about the experience of migration to the New World in the seventeenth century.

Roger Hainsworth, Reader in History at the University of Adelaide, has worked extensively on the archives of later seventeenth- and early eighteenth-century landed estates; he is the editor of two published volumes of Lowther family papers.

Rosemary O'Day lectures in history at the Open University. Her latest book is *The Debate on the English Reformation* (Methuen, 1986).

Margaret Pelling, a member of the Wellcome Unit for the History of Medicine, University of Oxford, is the author of *Cholera, fever, and English medicine 1825–1865* (Oxford University Press, 1978). She is writing a monograph on barber-surgeons and social conditions in London before 1640.

Wilfrid Prest teaches at the University of Adelaide and has written *The rise of the barristers: a social history of the English bar, 1590–1640* (Clarendon Press, 1986).

Ian Roy, of King's College, University of London, is a former Literary Director of the Royal Historical Society; his main research interest is the English Civil War.

Abbreviations

DNB:	*The Dictionary of National Biography*
Econ. Hist. Rev.:	*Economic History Review*
HMC:	Historical Manuscripts Commission
OED:	*Oxford English Dictionary*
P & P:	*Past and Present*
RO:	Record Office
Trans. Roy. Hist. Soc.:	*Transactions of the Royal Historical Society*

All books referred to are published in London, unless otherwise stated. Punctuation and spelling have been modernised in quotations, but not in the titles of books.

1

Introduction: The Professions and Society in Early Modern England

Wilfrid Prest

Historiography

The history of the professions in England is a relatively new and unexplored field. In 1666 the antiquary William Dugdale published his *Origines juridiciales, or historical memorials of the English laws* . . ., which with its documentary extracts and descriptive accounts of serjeants at law and inns of court and chancery, plus appended 'Cronologie' listing judges, crown law officers and serjeants from the Conquest onwards, has some claim to be considered the first history of an English profession. But Dugdale had no immediate successors and it was not until the later nineteenth century that a body of historical writing on the legal and medical professions began to accumulate.[1] Mostly pious compilations by men who were or had been practitioners themselves, even the best of this work tends to a narrow antiquarianism focused on the development of particular disciplines, making little effort to relate the domestic annals of any one professional occupation to the rest, let alone to a wider social world.[2]

The first attempt to draw some coherent general themes out of these parochial chronicles was the work not of historians but of social scientists. In their classic study *The professions* (1933), Alexander Carr-Saunders and P. A. Wilson provided what is still the standard general history of the professions in England. Primarily concerned with contemporary policy issues, Carr-Saunders and Wilson nevertheless found themselves 'compelled to widen our survey and to include some account of the origin and development of existing professions'. Accordingly they gave summary accounts of the evolution of the tradi-

tional learned professions (the church, law and medicine), and
the rise of 'new' professions (such as accountancy, engineering,
nursing, surveying, etc.), with their distinctive organisational
form, the 'qualifying association', during the nineteenth and
early twentieth centuries. These part-historical, part-contem-
porary sketches of the functions and organisation of a large
number of occupations take up the first half of *The professions*.
They are followed by a brief general account of the emergence
or 'segregation out' of professions from early medieval times.
'Professions before the industrial revolution' are said to have
grown up either within the church or the craft guilds; by the
eighteenth century some half-dozen had established
themselves and were 'regarded first and foremost as gentlemen's occupations'. Most attention is given, however, to
'professions since the industrial revolution', and their proliferation in step with the practical application of scientific
knowledge, the growing complexity and scale of economic and
social organisation, and the introduction of systematic
methods for training and testing would-be entrants to the
professions.[3]

The framework of interpretation and periodisation established by Carr-Saunders and Wilson, particularly the
dichotomy between professions before and after the industrial
revolution, with its stress on the limited and socially dependent
character of the former, proved remarkably durable. Indeed it
was accepted virtually without question by historians and
sociologists almost down to the present day. Carr-Saunders
and Wilson themselves were well aware of the fragile foundations on which they built, pointing out that 'No adequate
history of any one of the professions exists . . . We possess no
more than a brief outline of the history of one or two professions and a few studies of special periods.'[4] But these caveats
were easily ignored or overlooked. Readers found that *The
professions* gave them a relatively brief, clear, straightforward
and apparently authoritative summary of complex historical
facts, besides conforming very well to a basic operating
assumption of most sociologists and many historians, who see
the economic and social changes of the late eighteenth and
early nineteenth centuries as *the* crucial watershed between
'traditional' or 'pre-industrial' and 'modern' society.

The continuing influence of the Carr-Saunders and Wilson
paradigm is most apparent in the work of sociologists

interested in the general historical development of the professions as background to their primary concern with the role of the professional sector today. Thus one recent study includes a chapter on 'The development of the professions in Britain' which contrasts pre-industrial 'status professionalism', when professions were 'relatively unimportant . . . but occupied a niche high in the system of social stratification', with 'the rise of occupational professionalism, based on specialisation of knowledge and task'. According to another, the eighteenth-century professions provided the English 'gentryman' with 'effete, aristocratic, protective coloration'.[5] A far more ambitious enterprise, the first sustained attempt at a systematic general history of professions in the West within a broadly Marxist or at least Weberian framework, was undertaken by Magali Sarfatti-Larson in her influential *The rise of professionalism: a sociological analysis* (1977). Yet Larson's elegant and apparently subversive three-stage model, which relates successive professional formations to the dominant mode of production (feudal, capitalist, monopoly capitalist), is also grounded on the 'general point' that 'professions are typical products of modern industrial society', and 'professionalization . . . an instance of the complex process of "modernization" . . . The continuity of older professions with their "pre-industrial" past is therefore more apparent than real.' Needless to say, Larson's chief reference 'on the pre-industrial "professions" [sic] in England' is Carr-Saunders and Wilson.[6]

The impression that before the nineteenth century the professions were mere genteel parasites, lacking any distinctive social identity and entirely dependent on the patronage of the landed elite is rather reinforced than contradicted by the relatively few historians of later modern England who have addressed the topic. Thus W. J. Reader's *Professional men: the rise of the professional classes in Victorian England* (1966), the first and until recently the only survey of the professions in any discrete period of English history written by a practising historian, highlights the discontinuities between modern professions 'as we know them', which are 'very much a Victorian creation, brought into being to serve the needs of an industrial society' and their eighteenth-century precursors, whose members are said to have derived status and material rewards from their aristocratic associations rather than from any sense of corporate solidarity or the exercise of socially useful expertise.[7] A complementary view from a not dissimilar vantage point is provided by Harold Perkin's account of *The origins of modern English society 1780–1880*, where we are told that although the professions 'fitted snugly into the old dependency society', they were 'emancipated' by the industrial revolution, when 'urbanization and the rise of living standards' created an increased demand for the services of doctors, lawyers, writers and clergymen, 'which reduced their dependence on the few rich' and gave them 'a greater measure of self-respect'.[8]

The dichotomy between 'traditional' or 'pre-industrial' professions and the 'modern' professions which emerged in late eighteenth- and nineteenth-century England pervades not only general and synoptic accounts by sociologists and historians, but also the numerous chronicles celebrating the 'professionalisation' of particular occupations which actually constitute the bulk of what at present passes for the history of the professions. As the titles of some typical examples suggest, this genre essentially continues the tradition of nineteenth-century antiquarianism, celebrating the 'rise', 'growth', 'evolution' or 'development' of, in these instances, the accounting, chartered surveying, architectural and teaching professions, from inchoate and undifferentiated obscurity to fully realized professionalism.[9] Of course such institutional and organisational transformations have occurred with increasing frequency over the past century or so; but authors face an almost irresistible temptation to dramatise the contrast and heighten the achievement by highlighting the lack of coherence, ethical standards or expertise at the pre- or proto-professional stage. In any event, the Whiggish nature of the interpretative framework inevitably discounts that phase by presenting it as a mere prologue to professionalisation.

The overall dominance of the Carr-Saunders and Wilson paradigm is perhaps one reason why until very recently early modern historians have paid little detailed attention to the professions. Of the few historians writing before the present decade who make something more than a passing allusion to the role of the professions in early modern English society since *The professions* was published, including (in roughly chronological order) David Mathew, Bernice Hamilton, Edward Hughes, Robert Robson, F. J. Fisher, Lawrence Stone, Kenneth Charlton and Christopher Hill, only Hughes refers directly to Carr-Saunders and Wilson, specifically in order to dissent from their emphasis on the qualifying association, since 'most professions . . . had a long history before ever they were organised in professional associations'.[10] Unfortunately Hughes never gathered together the perceptive but scattered pieces in which he demonstrated, largely on the basis of research in early eighteenth-century north-country sources, the fallacy of the notion that the professions became a significant social presence only with the onset of the classical phase of industrialisation.[11] So it was not until 1982 that Geoffrey Holmes, in his monograph *Augustan England: professions, state and society, 1680–1730*, mounted the first sustained challenge to this entrenched orthodoxy.

An eminent authority on later Stuart government and politics, Holmes modestly disclaimed any 'extravagant pretensions' for this venture into social history. Yet the singular achievement of his *Augustan England* is to supersede its author's prefatory apologia: no longer can students

be forgiven for assuming, on the strength of what is available in print, that only a heavily urbanised and industrialised society can support a vigorous growth and diversification of professional services and produce a significant professional element in the social structure.

Holmes surveys at length and in some detail the whole range of (to use his terms) established and nascent professional occupations in later Stuart and early Hanoverian England, including architects, landscape gardeners, surveyors, estate stewards, men of letters, dons and schoolteachers, servants of the state and followers of the profession of arms, as well as the various branches of the three central and traditional professions. In the course of introducing us to this large and fascinating cast of characters, Holmes amply substantiates his claim that during 'a period which saw a striking growth in England's influence, self-confidence and material well-being, there was one group of Englishmen, the members of the professions, whose range of activities permeated almost all walks of life — public, private and corporate'.[12]

Continuities and contrasts

Holmes's *Augustan England* is among the more important
manifestations of a general quickening of scholarly interest in
the history of the professions over the last decade or so, on both
sides of the Atlantic — and, indeed, Pacific.[13] Sheer intellectual
curiosity and dissatisfaction with the available literature,
extension of interest from the history of particular disciplines
to the social context in which they were practised, concern with
the social dimensions of educational change, and suspicion
that neither historians nor social theorists have as yet
adequately explained the rise of the professions to their
present eminence have all served to stimulate this development. It may even be that some historians are sufficiently
conscious of their own relatively recent professionalisation to
feel a special, quasi-autobiographical attraction to the subject!

However diverse in motivation, a common theme underlying this work is the desire to investigate and understand the
professions within a far broader frame of reference than
hitherto. The aim in short is to write the history of the professions as social history at least, if not total history. It might be
objected that the proper subject of social history is the everyday
life of ordinary people in the past, not the powerful and
propertied minority. But there seems no compelling reason
why social historians must necessarily restrict their attention to
certified peasants and proletarians, although (as we shall
shortly see) the professions in early modern England were by
no means wholly identified with the ruling elite rather than the
ruled masses. In any case the structural complexities of society
generally and early modern society in particular can hardly be
adequately represented by a simple dichotomy between rulers
and ruled, or masses and elites. The early modern professions
actually straddled several social strata, while their clients
covered an even wider spectrum; the task of reconstructing
these various milieux and the interactions of their inhabitants
is no less challenging or relevant to an understanding of how
this society functioned than that of the historian whose
primary concern is with village smallholders or urban artisans.

So the new history — or social history — of the professions
seeks both a systematic understanding of its subjects and
attempts to avoid treating them in artificial isolation from the
society in which they worked. These aspirations imply various

methodological desiderata. First, a conscious effort to pay as much attention to the lower status and less prominent or successful practitioners as to the leading lights and eminent worthies, whose backgrounds and careers, although probably better documented, may well be untypical of the majority of their colleagues. Second, that both the social identity and the nature of the work carried out by members of the occupation or occupations in question need to be investigated and (so far as possible) related to each other. Analysis of the parentage, geographical origins, education, earnings and career patterns of, say, lawyers or clergymen which takes no account of how their work moulded their lives is no less inadequate than the traditional discipline-based history which ignores the social context in which the discipline was practised. The effort to understand this interrelationship may be assisted by drawing upon comparative and theoretical perspectives, although sociological writing on the professions cannot provide easy answers to historians' questions, even if it may prompt questions and suggest possible ways of answering them. After a long and not very fruitful preoccupation with large-scale general theories of the professions, some sociologists are now redefining their mission in more modest terms, as a search for 'better means of understanding and interpreting what is conceived of as a concrete, changing, historical and national phenomenon'; this welcome lowering of sights may lead to more productive interdisciplinary co-operation in the future.[14] Finally, the professions are not to be understood solely in material or social-structural terms, but also as cultural and intellectual artefacts; attitudes and beliefs held by and about members of the professions, the changing meanings attached to the term 'profession' itself, and the impact of professions upon the definition of particular areas of knowledge all form an integral part of their history.

The proof of methodological puddings (or recipes) lies in the eating. Not all those historians who have recently been concerning themselves with the professions would necessarily endorse all of these precepts, and some might well want to add additions of their own. Nevertheless work carried out along these broad lines over the last decade or so has opened up a great deal of new territory, and in the process effectively demolished the myth that the industrial revolution constituted the single crucial turning point in the history of the professions

7

in England. It is now abundantly clear that both the numbers and socio-economic impact of what may reasonably be called professional occupations and those who followed them in England before the mid-eighteenth century have been drastically underestimated. This is the main message of Holmes's *Augustan England,* and the same point has been made for earlier periods by the work of a growing number of historians. As a result, we can now see not only that the professions of the fourteenth to the eighteenth centuries have been somewhat overlooked, but that once they are investigated the *qualitative* differences distinguishing professions before and after 1750 or 1800 seem far less clear-cut and straightforward than has hitherto been assumed.

The received elaboration of the original Carr-Saunders and Wilson thesis supposes that before 'industrialisation', 'modernisation' or 'great transformation', the professions largely served and were recruited from the gentry and nobility; hence their members lacked any distinctive occupational identity or set of values (merely aping those of the upper landed classes), while even the word 'profession' had yet to acquire the specific and elevated connotations which it bears today. This picture is of course derived from little more than *a priori* inference and superficial impressions; it could not be based on the findings of detailed and systematic research, for that work had not been done when Carr-Saunders and Wilson wrote, indeed is only beginning now. What there is of it, however, hardly substantiates the orthodox view.

Let us begin with the supposed elitist origins of members of the most prestigious cohorts of the classical learned professions, or at least the law and physic, since no one seems to have claimed that even the upper ranks of the clergy were monopolised by the sons of the landed elite. William Birken has discovered that of 67 physicians admitted between 1603 and 1643 as fellows of the London College (later Royal College) of Physicians, by far the most exclusive and pretentious contemporary body of medical practitioners, 'only sixteen could have made any claim at all to gentle blood', while no fewer than 41 were of 'non-gentle, plebeian or clerical origin'. Among the 814 provincial physicians listed in John Raach's *Directory* covering the same period, those who had studied at Oxford or Cambridge seem to display a broadly similar pattern, which, Holmes's findings suggest, evidently still applied in the early eighteenth century.[15] Turning to the common law, the work of Daniel Duman, David Lemmings and the present writer shows that the proportion of barristers with landed gentry backgrounds declined steadily from an outside maximum of 50 per cent at the very most in the half-century before 1640 to around a quarter by the later eighteenth century; it should also be noted that the gentry in question were often very small parochial fry indeed, like the Cuffe family of Creech St Michael, Somerset, or the Sandells of Saham Tooney, near King's Lynn. As for the civil lawyers, fewer than half of the elite group of advocates admitted to practise in the Court of the Arches between 1600 and 1749 were the sons of peers, baronets, knights, esquires or gentlemen, the balance being mainly from clerical, legal, office-holding or mercantile backgrounds.[16] So while learned physicians, counsellors and advocates at law may have claimed the right to bear a coat of arms and the courtesy rank of esquire by virtue of their calling, the majority certainly would not have been entitled to such marks of status on hereditary grounds alone. Similar conclusions apply even to the profession of arms, where, it is true, the exceptional career mobility enjoyed by buff-coated captains during the Civil War and interregnum contracted sharply after Charles II's restoration, when commissions in the home regiments became the preserve of the well born; but at the same time, as Ian Roy points out below, the opportunities for relatively poor men's sons in garrison service abroad and the royal navy were beginning to expand in a spectacular fashion. Finally, it is worth noting that even the social gulf separating recruits to the upper and lower branches of the legal profession appears to have been narrower than usually supposed. In their careful, regionally-based studies, Christopher Brooks and Michael Miles both draw attention to the substantial representation of the lesser and parochial gentry among young men apprenticed as attorneys in the seventeenth and eighteenth centuries respectively.[17]

It might be argued that even if the early modern professional classes (or at least their upper branches) were not in fact mostly recruited from the younger sons of the nobility and gentry, their members were nevertheless economically and socially dependent upon the patronage of this elite stratum. However, the notion that something like a mass market for professional services came into existence only with the advent of industrial society is very far from the truth. In her chapter below Margaret Pelling emphasises the huge volume of medical care consumed in the early modern period and the socially disparate character of those who received it; her joint investigation with Charles Webster of medical practice in sixteenth-century London and East Anglia indicates that although 'university-educated medical practitioners came . . . to dominate medical practice at the level of the social elite', these practitioners were themselves 'an extremely heterogeneous group . . . who represent only a small fraction of those dispensing medical care in rural communities'. This is not to overlook the existence of fashionable London physicians who made fortunes by charging high fees to anyone who could afford their services (as their successors still do today); nevertheless, a great deal of work on fee books and other records of medical practice remains to be done before we can pronounce with confidence on the relationship between categories of practitioners and the socio-economic backgrounds of their patients throughout early modern England. Our present state of knowledge does not indicate, however, that Victorian medical practice depended on a wider cross-section of the community than had been the case under the Tudors and Stuarts.[18]

It is possible to speak with rather more confidence about the market for legal advice and representation, at least during the eighty years or so before the Long Parliament, when the per capita incidence of civil litigation in England was almost certainly at an all-time high, and with it the effective demand for all kinds of legal services, not just among the upper landed classes, but also the middling sort, urban and rural. Barristers (although becoming somewhat more self-conscious of their status as a distinct professional elite) helped meet this demand, catering for quite a socially mixed clientele, of 'hobnailed boors and sheepskin country clowns' as well as urban craftsmen and merchants like those for whom the young Lincoln's Inn barrister Henry Sherfield acted at the Salisbury assizes during the first decade of the seventeenth century. The clientele served by the bar *may* have become more exclusive after the middle of the seventeenth century, when barristers' fees skyrocketed and attorneys increasingly took over most routine counselling work; but, once again, that plausible hypothesis has as yet to be borne out by detailed research.[19]

If the aristocratic origins of early modern professional persons and those who employed their services both appear to have been overstated, so too has the lack of specific occupational autonomy and identity within the professions. While the Church of England was in constitutional and jurisdictional terms much more clearly subordinated to the temporal power after the Henrician Reformation than before it, Rosemary O'Day argues below that the key element in the transformation of the clergy of the post-Reformation established church from an estate to a profession was their acceptance of a new-found pastoral role and responsibility as ministers of the Word. Hence the Elizabethan and early Stuart clergyman's *raison d'être* came to be based essentially on his relationship with a lay congregation, rather than (as for his medieval predecessor) a special standing with God. As David Cressy also shows us in his chapter, at least some grammar school masters sought to raise their personal status and that of their calling by simply improving standards of teaching. In the legal and medical worlds such vocational commitment was both intense and widespread:

> Full twenty years have I a Servant been,
> To this *Profession*, I live by and in

wrote the poet Alexander Brome (1620–66), when he sought to step down from his attorneyship in the Court of King's Bench:

> . . . and in all this space,
> Have nothing done that mis-became my place;
> Nor have my *actions* been Derogatory,
> Unto my Clients' profit, or the glory
> Of this renowned Court . . .[20]

Christopher Brooks has delineated a developing sense of corporate identity among common law attorneys in the later sixteenth century, encouraged and manifested by both institutional and informal 'sources of unity': oaths of admission which laid down minimum standards of ethical behaviour, judicial rules of practice, the impanelling of expert professional juries to investigate and present malpractices, intra-professional ties of friendship and marriage, not to mention shared possession

11

of esoteric knowledge. Early modern English barristers displayed perhaps an even more pronounced identification with their calling, and were by no means content to rely upon mere ascribed social status, as Chief Justice Sir John Fortescue appears to have done in his late-fifteenth-century treatise in praise of the laws of England. Their spokesmen rather claimed that the inherent worthiness of the lawyer's calling honoured those who followed it; hence the barrister's high social status stemmed not so much from his aristocratic associations as the exercise of his profession, in which (it was argued during the interregnum) 'the professor hath a propriety . . . as he hath in his goods'. While physicians may have made much of their genteel breeding and academic learning, surgeons and apothecaries were also anxious to stress the social utility of their activities, in a similar fashion to merchants and tradesmen of various kinds.[21]

Finally, the concept of a profession in early modern England, although not as fully articulated or self-conscious as it became in the nineteenth century, had already acquired a convenient breadth and ambiguity. In the sixteenth, seventeenth and eighteenth centuries the term 'profession' was most commonly used as a synonym for 'calling, vocation, known employment' (to follow the definition in Dr Johnson's dictionary, first published in 1755), or, as we would say, 'job' — exactly as the word is still very commonly used today. Thus it was possible to speak of the profession of plumber, or shepherd, and in 1633 the recorder of King's Lynn complained to the mayor that 'You have some that are idle because they have no calling or profession, making themselves a profession of idleness.' However, there was also a narrower usage, which contrasted professions as particularly dignified, worthy or (as we might put it) high-status occupations with mere 'mechanical' trades or manual labour. 'Profession' in this sense might embody a reference to the three traditional learned professions, as in the rider which first appeared in the fourth edition of Johnson's *Dictionary* (1773), 'particularly used of divinity, physic and law'.[22] (The specific connection of the word 'profession' with these occupations probably came in the first instance via the higher faculties of the medieval universities, whose degrees served as licences both to teach and to practise, or profess, the disciplines of theology, physic and law.) It is this narrower sense of the word which underlies a

mildly facetious passage from the Jacobean pamphleteer
Barnabe Rich, writing in 1616:

> Now I cannot tell what I should call the study of law,
> whether I should term it to be a profession, a science, or
> an art; a trade, I cannot call it, yet there be some that do
> think it to be a craft . . . But I think it may rather be called
> an occupation.[23]

Where the word 'trade' was applied to the lawyer's calling, the
connotation was invariably derogatory, as in Edward Savage's
account of the dismissal of Sir Robert Heath from the chief
justiceship of King's Bench in 1634: 'his majesty . . . hath upon
Heath's humble petition given him leave to use his trade again,
and it is expected that this great judge will plead without the
bar'. On the other hand, before the nineteenth century people
do not seem to have debated the meaning of the term 'profession', or what distinguished professions from other, less
esteemed occupations; nor is there any evidence that
particular prestige attached to occupations which claimed the
status of professions. The crucial distinction seems rather to
have been that between 'liberal' and 'mechanical' or 'servile'
arts. This Aristotelian dichotomy was in serious disarray by the
mid-seventeenth century, however, when Serenus Cressy
noted that although all arts exercised by the body should be
deemed mechanical and servile, some 'which do make a
greater store of dignity than ordinary are ceased to be called
servile arts in the common manner of speaking'; these
included 'the arts military and naval', surgery, 'the art of
apothecaries and barbers' and, interestingly enough, what he
described as 'merchandise'. The 'title of servile and mechanical
arts is left only to those of an inferior note . . . weavers, tailors,
tanners &c.'[24] An urgent priority on the research agenda now
is to trace the changing taxonomy and etymology of occupations and work throughout the early modern period and
beyond.

The extent of continuity between professions before and
after the industrial revolution must seem a good deal more
impressive once it becomes apparent that the membership and
clienteles of the early modern professions were by no means so
socially restricted as has been supposed, and that the term
'profession' was employed in a specific as well as a general sense

as early as the sixteenth century. Nevertheless, some important differences plainly separate the early modern professions which are the subject of this book and professions as we commonly think of them today. The most obvious contrast is organisational. If what distinguishes a profession from any other occupation is the ability of its membership to determine, directly or indirectly, who may pursue that particular vocation, then there were either very few or very many professions in early modern England. Few, if we are thinking of recognisable prototypes of modern professions, whether legal, medical or other; many, if we include all the craft guilds and trading companies whose members sought to maintain a monopoly on the practice of numerous callings and trades in particular localities. The historical puzzle is to explain, if possible without embroiling ourselves in unprofitable debate about the attributes or definition of a true profession, why the national occupational monopoly form (represented by the professions) has expanded and flourished down to the present day, while the local occupational monopoly form (represented by the guilds) shrank and withered on the vine. No doubt part of the problem facing the guilds was precisely an inability to expand their regulatory powers beyond the walls of particular cities and towns; but then why were lawyers and physicians able to withstand the various economic and ideological pressures which eroded the monopoly privileges of most of the great London-based overseas trading companies? The reasons may well have been not only economic and political in nature, but cultural and social too, including the pervasive influence of the humanists' distinction between learned arts and mechanical trades, and the slightly higher proportions of gentlemen's sons apprenticed as attorneys and apothecaries than, say, chandlers or carpenters.[25]

The main point for our purposes is that before the nineteenth century most occupations which today are widely thought of as professions in a narrow sense (meaning, roughly speaking, middle-class or relatively high-status employments which seek to monopolise the provision of certain services based on the presumed mastery of a body of esoteric knowledge) lacked any kind of formal institutional structure. The two leading examples considered in the present volume are the estate steward and the teacher; others would include (just to begin with the letter 'a') accountants, actuaries and architects. During the early modern period many or most of the present functions of these occupations were performed by persons who had no standardised training or formal 'paper' qualifications and were not linked by common membership of an occupational organisation — a situation which continued within living memory in the case of accountancy and architecture. It would be excessively pedantic to exclude them from a survey of early modern professions on the grounds that they do not conform to twentieth-century notions of what constitutes a profession, especially since that term and concept have in fact no single agreed contemporary definition.

If the provision of professional services was not very highly institutionalised in early modern England, neither did the professions necessarily demand from their practitioners a full-time working commitment. The clergy were perhaps the most versatile and (thanks to their puritan critics) certainly the most notorious moonlighters. During the sixteenth century, when inflation and lay depredations slashed clerical living standards to the bone, many ministers were forced to find additional sources of income as farmers, fishermen, livestock breeders and dealers, money-lenders, teachers, attorneys, surveyors and medical practitioners. Some of these by-employments were obviously more compatible than others with the high standards increasingly demanded of a reformed ministry, not least by the more zealous ministers themselves. Dispensing medical advice and remedies to parishioners, writing their wills and attempting to arbitrate their disputes were generally well-approved avocations, if not simply extensions of the pastoral function, while working their own glebelands was a traditional necessity for clerical smallholders. Many other professional persons combined their primary calling with agricultural pursuits of one kind or another, as might well be expected in a society where land was still the chief source of wealth and status. Conversely, in the industrial West Riding of Yorkshire eighteenth-century attorneys not uncommonly acted as cloth dealers and money-lenders.[26] Yet it would be a mistake to conclude that all those who spread their time and energies beyond the bounds of a single calling were necessarily less conscientious or committed than their modern, supposedly more single-minded, counterparts, many of whom do in fact wear several occupational hats at once. Patrick Collinson points out that the 'professional dedication' of the mid-seventeenth-century Essex puritan minister Ralph Josselin seems to have been unaffected by the fact that perhaps half his income came from farming and teaching, while the relative brevity of the law terms and the judicious use of bailiffs, stewards and spouses to oversee the workings of their estates enabled many barristers to combine a notorious diligence in their work with an active interest in matters agricultural. It is also worth noting that while early modern professional commitments could often be met on a part-time basis, they were typically life-long and concluded not with customary or statutory retirement at a fixed age, but with bodily incapacity or death.[27]

A final distinctive aspect of professional practice in the early modern period may be that those who used professional services often took a more active and demanding role in the relationship than would be normal today. Thus Margaret Pelling draws attention to the prevalence of the conditional contract, whereby on agreeing to treat a specific illness the medical practitioner received an initial down payment, the balance of the fee becoming due only when the cure was successfully completed. Tom Barnes has observed that the typical private litigant in the early Stuart Star Chamber retained and instructed counsel directly, restricting the latter's role to advocate rather than adviser. Even estate stewards, invariably men of considerable experience and maturity, who (as D. R. Hainsworth points out below) increasingly served absentee landlords, showed great reluctance to act on quite routine and trivial matters without first obtaining their masters' assent.[28] Lay assertiveness no doubt often merely reflected the pre-eminent status claimed by (and usually accorded to) members of the landed elite. Conversely, the 'pride and arrogance of our lord-like doctors', the 'height of pride' from which 'great lawyers' dealt with poorer clients sharpened the sweeping attacks on professional pretensions launched by a wide diversity of radical critics in the 1640s and 1650s.[29] The other crucial factor determining the balance of authority in professional–client relations was, presumably, the extent to which professional expertise and standing depended upon mastery of a body of knowledge and skills which lay outside the familiar acquaintance of the uninitiated laity. Hence the post-1660 waning of the fashion for young gentlemen to round off their education with a year or so as a non-professional student at the inns of court, together with the continued growth of specialised branches of common law, must have tended to enhance the authority of the professed common lawyer in his dealings with clients. On the other hand, the clergy of the Church of England never fully regained their pre-Reformation standing as uniquely privileged mediators between God and man, for the individualistic implications of the doctrine of the priesthood of all believers inevitably frustrated their efforts to establish an alternative, non-sacramental monopoly, as exponents and preachers of the word of God.[30]

Some tentative conclusions and further questions

In the absence of a single, universally agreed definition of 'profession', and indeed of widespread self-consciousness or concern about professional status before the nineteenth century, what is the proper and distinctive subject matter of the history of the professions? A possible working convention might include, besides the traditional trinity of church, law and medicine, all other non-mercantile occupations followed by persons claiming gentility. Part of the rationale for this rather simplistic criterion is that the one and only characteristic which seems common to all professional persons, past and present, is their ranking within a broad middle class, situated above the 'fourth sort of men which do not rule', the workers, whether peasant or proletarian, but below the elite whose livelihood is in no way dependent upon their personal exertions. The other justification is that it serves to shift attention away from abstract ideal-type models of what a profession should be to the complex realities of what professions actually were. This does not mean that we should forthwith abandon all recourse to the sociology of the professions; even if sociologists themselves have largely ceased compiling checklists of traits associated with professionalism, it can be quite useful to bear in mind that, for example, monopoly rights of practice, formalised training and certification, and a corporate ideology have all been identified at various times as key elements in the process of professional formation. However, we cannot expect to be handed ready-made theories which will satisfactorily explain the course of development followed by particular professional occupations from their first origins down to the present day. It may be helpful to think of the growth of the professions in general terms as part of a process of occupational differentiation and specialisation; but this broad concept will not enable us to understand the disappearance of canon lawyers and civil lawyers in the sixteenth and nineteenth centuries respectively, let alone why female midwives were largely ousted by their male rivals in the course of the eighteenth century.[31]

These particular instances go to make a further point, that the history of the professions, whether before or after *c*. 1800, should not be conceived of simply as a constant linear progress to 'professionalisation'. Indeed it could be argued that in some respects Professor Holmes's Augustan era was actually a period of relative stagnation, if not recession, for the professional sector as a whole, at least by comparison with the rapid expansion, diversification and consolidation which marked the century before 1660. The numerical growth rate of both branches of the legal profession was certainly lower in the half-century 1680–1730 than the half-century 1590–1640, which must to some extent offset the rapid expansion of the armed forces and civil administration in the later period. Even more significant, perhaps, was a certain retreat from vocational commitment and identification, exemplified in the Hanoverian 'squarson' portrayed by Roy Porter, whose lifestyle was virtually indistinguishable from that of his landed gentry neighbours. The late seventeenth and eighteenth centuries saw the decisive decline of urban craft guilds and trading companies, which (as Christopher Brooks has suggested) might perhaps be regarded as a kind of 'deprofessionalisation'.[32] Even more speculatively, it has been argued that the mushroom growth of the professions (especially law) during 'Tawney's century' (*c*. 1540–1640) siphoned off resources, human and material, which could have been put to more productive use elsewhere in the economy, as mercantilist pamphleteers continued to complain until the end of the seventeenth century. Thereafter we seem to hear less criticism of the excessive numbers of clergy, lawyers and physicians, which may reflect a real swing in career choices following the enhanced opportunities offered by England's booming foreign and domestic commerce.[33]

Yet generalisation across the professions at large is a tricky business. The influence, numbers and wealth of clergy and common lawyers hardly moved in the same direction and at the same pace during the early modern centuries; indeed the rise of the latter was in a real sense at the expense of the former. Whereas the bar contracted in the later seventeenth and eighteenth centuries, the 'lower branch' of attorneys and solicitors was still expanding, as also (it would seem) were the various types of medical practitioner. In other words, and unsurprisingly, different professional occupations responded in diverse ways to the same historical circumstances. But in any case the historian of the professions need and should not be preoccupied exclusively with the teleology of 'professionalisation'; what the professions *were* at given points in time is at least as interesting and important as what they were becoming.

What the professions were includes the sum total of their social relations and roles — their impact upon society as well as the reverse. This is the aspect which is likely to be of most general interest. It embraces the dealings of professional persons (largely, although not exclusively, male until very recent times) with clients, other professional groups and the state, as (among other things) brokers or mediators transmitting metropolitan attitudes and institutional services to the localities, roles recently explored by Peter Clark and Clive Holmes in their studies of early modern Kent and seventeenth-century Lincolnshire.[34] Another large and important area of interest concerns the ways in which the professions ordered knowledge within their particular fields of expertise, no doubt often to their own material advantage. Particular attention has also been given of late to the part which the professions played as channels of upwards mobility in early modern England. Here, according to Geoffrey Holmes, they provided opportunities of advancement for ambitious and talented young men which contributed significantly to the establishment of a prosperous and stable social equilibrium in Georgian England. On the other hand, Keith Wrightson and others have argued that while the enlargement of the professional sector may have enhanced the scope for individual self-betterment, it simultaneously exacerbated the structural divisions — cultural, economic and social — which were increasingly distancing both the elite and the middling sort from the mass of their inferiors.[35]

The extent and significance of upwards mobility via the professions have also been questioned. According to Jeanne and Lawrence Stone, in their recent massive study of the owners of large country houses between 1540 and 1880, this elite was open only to successful professional men and politicians, rather than businessmen or industrialists. However, the professions, in their view, were by no means part of a broad middle class embracing the parochial gentry, merchants, prosperous tradesmen and yeomen, but a distinct genteel stratum intimately allied with the landed elite itself in origins, status and values. For the Stones it is the symbiotic relationship of the great landowners with the professions which is the cardinal fact of English social history — in this respect essentially identical to that of Continental Europe.[36]

This view of the social geography of the professions is remarkably reminiscent of the Carr-Saunders and Wilson paradigm, or at least its first, pre-industrial-revolution component. Yet it does not appear to be based upon any further systematic accumulation of evidence about the role of the professions as avenues for social ascent (or descent) in early modern England. Until that work is done it may be a little premature to conclude that the elite, however defined, was firmly shut to ambitious and talented outsiders rising by way of a successful professional career. Such persons would naturally seek to adopt the lifestyle and mores of the landed classes, in so far as it was practicable for them to do so, if perhaps more wholeheartedly in the eighteenth century than the preceding two hundred years. But their claims to be 'a race of gentry' (as Sir Heneage Finch characterised his barrister colleagues in 1663) were not universally accepted. Thus a Kentish gentleman complained in the 1620s that 'hireling, mercenary barristers, that are but apprentices for some years and after that journeymen to plead and many times prate and wrangle for a penny' were falsely appropriating the title of esquire, while in 1659 another gentleman maintained that a wealthy physician was an unsuitable match for a knight's daughter: 'And great is the discourse at this very time about a Norfolk baronet's matching with a doctor of divinity's daughter in Cambridge, and yet we know divinity is the highest, as physic the lowest of the professions.'[37] Such snobbery was not necessarily typical; many professional men enjoyed close and cordial relations with individual peers and squires. Yet they also often came from urban backgrounds, married merchants' daughters, and lived in the towns where they found lucrative employment. At all events, not the least reason for pressing on with the history of the professions in early modern England is that we may thereby hope to arrive at a much clearer picture of the social structure as a whole, and especially of the middling sort, that class now largely submerged and virtually forgotten by historians.

Notes

1. Cf. W. R. Munk, *The roll of the Royal College of Physicians of London . . . 1518–1825*, 2nd edn (3 vols, 1878); J. F. South, *Memorials of the craft of surgery in England*, ed. D'Arcy Powers (1886); C. R. B. Barrett, *History of the Society of Apothecaries* (1905); E. B. V. Christian, *A short history of solicitors* (1896); A. Pulling, *The order of the coif* (1884); E. Freshfield (ed.), *The records of the Society of Gentlemen Practisers* (1897). Published records of the inns of court and chancery, which began to appear in the 1890s, are listed in D. S. Bland (ed.), *A bibliography of the inns of court and chancery* (Selden Society, Supp. Ser. no. 3, 1965).

2. It is noticeable that the considerable attention devoted at this time by economic historians to the history of guilds and trading companies was not extended to professional occupations: cf. G. Unwin, *Industrial organization in the sixteenth and seventeenth centuries* (Oxford, 1904).

3. A. M. Carr-Saunders and P. A. Wilson, *The professions* (Oxford, 1933), pp. 2, 7–287, 289–318.

4. Ibid., p. 2.

5. P. Elliott, *Sociology of the professions: the recruitment of professional elites* (1972), pp. 14–15, 32 and Ch. 2, *passim*; J. Gerstl and G. Jacobs, *Professions for the people* (Cambridge, Mass., 1976), pp. 2–3.

6. M. S. Larson, *The rise of professionalism: a sociological analysis* (Berkeley, 1977), pp. xvi, 2–7, 254.

7. Ibid., p. 2, and Ch. 1, *passim*.

8. Ibid., pp. 252–5; cf. H. Perkin, *Professionalism, property and English society since 1880* (Reading, 1981), pp. 6–12.

9. J. L. Carey, *The rise of the accounting profession* (New York, 1969); F. M. L. Thompson, *Chartered surveyors: the growth of a profession* (1968); B. Kaye, *The development of the architectural profession in Britain* (1969); P. H. Gosden, *The evolution of a profession: a study of the contribution of teachers' associations to the development of school teaching as a professional occupation* (Oxford, 1972).

10. D. Mathew, *The social structure in Caroline England* (Oxford, 1948), Ch. 5; E. Hughes, 'The professions in the eighteenth century', *Durham University Journal*, vol. 44 (1952), pp. 46–55; R. Robson, *The attorney in eighteenth-century England* (Cambridge, 1959), pp. 168–71; F. J. Fisher, 'Tawney's century' in F. J. Fisher (ed.), *Essays in the economic and social history of Tudor and Stuart England* (Cambridge, 1961), pp. 10–12; L. Stone, 'Social mobility in England, 1500–1700', *P & P*, no. 33 (1966), pp. 24, 27–8, 34; K. Charlton, 'The professions

in sixteenth-century England', *University of Birmingham Historical Journal*, vol. 12 (1969–70), pp. 20–41; C. Hill, *Change and continuity in seventeenth-century England* (1974), Ch. 7. For some Continental comparisons, cf. C. M. Cipolla, 'The professions. The long view', *Journal of European Economic History*, vol. 2 (1973), pp. 37–52.

11. Hughes, 'Professions in the eighteenth century'; E. Hughes, 'The eighteenth-century estate steward' in H. A. Cronne, T. W. Moody and D. B. Quinn (eds), *Essays in British and Irish history* (1949), pp. 185–99; E. Hughes, *North Country life in the eighteenth century: the North East 1700–1750* (Oxford, 1952), Ch. 3.

12. G. Holmes, *Augustan England: professions, state and society, 1680– 1730* (1982), pp. ix–xi and *passim*; see also Holmes's 1979 Ralegh lecture, 'The professions and social change in England, 1680–1730', *Proceedings of the British Academy*, vol. 65, pp. 313–54.

13. See M. Ramsay, 'History of a profession, *Annales* style: the work of Jacques Leonard', *Journal of Social History*, vol. 17 (1983), pp. 319– 38; also my 'Why the history of the professions is not written' in G. R. Rubin and D. Sugarman (eds), *Law, economy and society 1750–1914: essays in the history of English law* (Abingdon, 1984), pp. 300–2 and n. 1.

14. E. Freidson, 'The theory of the professions: state of the art' in R. Dingwall and P. Lewis (eds), *The sociology of the professions* (1983), p. 32; cf. the observation that 'To advance a theory of the professions . . . requires study of the concept as an historical construction in a limited number of societies . . . its development, use and consequences in those societies without attempting more than the most modest generalisations' (ibid., p. 20).

15. W. J. Birken, 'The fellows of the Royal College of Physicians of London, 1603–1643: a social study', unpublished PhD thesis, University of North Carolina at Chapel Hill, 1977, pp. 19–21, 354–7, 375–6; Holmes, *Augustan England*, pp. 206–8.

16. D. Duman, 'The Georgian bar', in W. Prest (ed.), *Lawyers in early modern Europe* (1981), pp. 90–5; D. Lemmings, 'The inns of court and the English bar, 1680–1730', unpublished D Phil thesis, University of Oxford, 1985, pp. 247–53; W. R. Prest, *The rise of the barristers: a social history of the English bar 1590–1640* (Oxford, 1986), pp. 87–95; B. P. Levack, 'The English civilians, 1500–1750' in Prest (ed.), *Lawyers*, pp. 117–19.

17. C. W. Brooks, *Pettyfoggers and vipers of the Commonwealth: the 'lower branch' of the legal profession in early modern England* (Cambridge, 1986), pp. 243, 245–6; M. W. Miles, '"Eminent attorneys": some aspects of West Riding attorneyship c. 1750–1800', unpublished PhD thesis, University of Birmingham, 1982, pp. 50–6.

18. M. Pelling and C. Webster, 'Medical practitioners' in C. Webster (ed.), *Health, medicine and mortality in the sixteenth century* (Cambridge, 1979), pp. 205, 232; cf. Holmes, *Augustan England*, pp. 224–6.

19. Prest, *Rise of the barristers*, pp. 20–5, 31–3.

20. On the remarkable cohesion and influence of the Protestant clergy in early modern Scotland, see R. Mitchison, 'The social impact of the clergy of the Reformed Kirk of Scotland', *Scotia*, vol. 6 (1982),

pp. 1–13. A. Brome, *Songs and other poems* (1661), p. 199.

21. Brooks, *Pettyfoggers and vipers*, pp. 119–20, 264–5; Prest, *Rise of the barristers*, pp. 312–22; Anon., *Reasons against the Bill entituled an Act for County Registers* (1653), p. 24; Holmes, *Augustan England*, pp. 184–205 and Ch. 7, *passim*.

22. Prest, 'Why the history of the professions is not written', pp. 306–8.

23. Norfolk RO, Francis Parlett's Notebook, fo. 48; B. Rich, *My ladies looking glasse* (1616), p. 67.

24. Ellesmere MS 6514, Henry E. Huntington Library; S. Cressy, 'Arbor virtutem', Clifford Papers, Australian National Library, Canberra.

25. I am most grateful to Christopher Brooks for allowing me to read his unpublished paper on 'Guilds, professions and the middling sort of people in England, 1550–1700', to which this paragraph is heavily indebted.

26. Cf. P. Collinson, *The religion of Protestants* (Oxford, 1982), pp. 101–2; for other examples cf. C. Holmes, *Seventeenth-century Lincolnshire* (Lincoln, 1980), p. 56; Miles, '"Eminent Attorneys"', pp. 41–2.

27. Collinson, *Religion of Protestants*, p. 102; Prest, *Rise of the barristers*, pp. 170–3; K. V. Thomas, 'Age and authority in early modern England', *Proceedings of the British Academy*, vol. 72 (1976), p. 242. See also below, pp. 102–5.

28. Cf. Pelling and Webster, 'Medical practitioners', pp. 214, 218; T. G. Barnes, 'Star Chamber litigants and their counsel, 1596–1641' in J. H. Baker (ed.), *Legal records and the historian* (1978), p. 23; see also below, pp. 84, 106–8.

29. Hill, 'The medical profession and its radical critics', p. 158; Anon., *Some advertisements for the new election of burgesses for the House of Commons* (1645), p. 2.

30. See below, pp. 33–4 and 56–8.

31. Cf. J. Donnison, *Midwives and medical men: a history of inter-professional rivalries and women's rights* (1977), Chs. 1–2.

32. R. S. Porter, *English society in the eighteenth century* (Harmondsworth, 1982), pp. 83–90.

33. Fisher, 'Tawney's century', pp. 10–12.

34. On women and the professions generally, cf. A. Clark, *The working life of women in the seventeenth century* (1919; reprinted 1982), Ch. 6; O. Hufton, 'Women in history', *P & P*, no. 101 (1983), p. 134. Holmes, *Lincolnshire*, Ch. 5; P. Clark, *English provincial society from the Reformation to the Revolution: religion, politics and society in Kent 1500–1640* (1977), pp. 287–8.

35. K. Wrightson, *English society 1580–1680* (1983), pp. 140, 188–90. Cf. the reviews by M. Goldie in *History*, vol. 68 (1983), pp. 520–1, and myself in the *Journal of Legal History*, vol. 6 (1985), pp. 123–5.

36. L. and J. E. F. Stone, *An open elite? England 1540–1880* (Oxford, 1984), pp. 225–8. Cf. the review by D. Spring and L. Stone's reply in *Albion*, vol. 17 (1985), pp. 153–6, 167–70.

37. D. E. C. Yale (ed.), *Lord Nottingham's chancery cases, Vol. II* (Selden Society, vol. 79, 1961), p. 950; G. D. Scull, *Dorothea Scott*

(Oxford, 1883), p. 171; M. M. Verney, *Memoirs of the Verney family during the Commonwealth 1650 to 1660* (1894), pp. 199–200.

2

The Anatomy of a Profession:
the Clergy of the Church of England

Rosemary O'Day

Historians have blanched visibly at the very thought of writing a history of the professions in society before the nineteenth century. Why? Historians and sociologists have defined professions as nineteenth- and twentieth-century phenomena. They have extracted those traits which the modern professions have in common and, by implication, have suggested that a true profession will share these. Early modernists see themselves trapped in a horrible bind: Whig history or unthoughtful history. If they accept the definitions provided by sociologists and modern historians, they are liable to concentrate on 'how the present situation came about', to look back into the past for the origins of the present, to neglect the past itself. If, on the other hand, they avoid this trap by ignoring theory, ignoring developments, ignoring the modern meaning of terms like 'profession', 'professional-isation' and 'professionalism', they fall into yet another — that of complete refusal to discuss the concepts involved. The word 'profession' as it was employed in the early modern period implies an ideology, the history of which has been inadequately charted. The phenomenon raises a large number of tantalising and as yet unanswered questions about the nature of social relations and of work in the transitional period between pre-industrial and industrial England. Clearly scholars should continue to avoid anachronistic applications of nineteenth- and twentieth-century definitions to sixteenth- and seventeenth-century professions, but they would be well advised to find definitions appropriate to the early modern period. No historian should judgementally measure the past against the present but, equally, the historian will find the comparative method useful in defining the nature of past societies.

Sociologists of the professions have subjected the modern professions to a form of comparative analysis. They have indicated those features or traits which the professions have in common and have suggested that a profession's 'profession-ness' can be measured according to how few or how many of these traits are displayed. The concept of the continuum has been applied to professional development. This method is useful as far as it goes. But for the historian it does not go anything like far enough. For it divorces the groupings under discussion from their historically specific context — baldly extracting common features and ignoring differences. If the sociologist is happy to study structures and neglect meaning, the historian finds such an exercise most unrewarding. When the historian compares, he or she must also contrast. The historian finds *similarities* intriguing but is fascinated even more by *differences*. Institutions, social groupings, occupations — all must be studied in their immediate historical context, for it is this which gives these features meaning.

In order to study the professions in the past, the historian can learn much from the sociologist. Trait analysis has grave limitations, but it does provide the historian with a crude yardstick against which the early modern professions can be measured. Contrast will help to reveal in what ways the early professions differed from their modern counterparts. The historian will then explore further the function which early modern professions played in their society, the forms which they took and the ideologies which shaped them. Employment of the comparative method (which involves comparing *and* contrasting) will not lead the vigilant historian into crude Whiggery but will intensify his/her awareness of the impor-tance of context in importing meaning to historical develop-ments.

The historian of the professions, then, should not accept the sociological definition of the professions but will sensibly accept that some of the tools provided by the sociologist and the work of sociologists in this area can provide a jumping-off point for a much more sophisticated examination of the early modern professions in society.

There are many ways of accomplishing such an examina-tion. In this essay the emphasis is overwhelmingly upon the internal affairs of the English clergy and upon changes in their organisation during the Reformation. Structural change occurred which was more or less completed by 1662. But it remains important not to concentrate upon structural change at the expense of meaning. Hindsight might tell us that a process of professionalisation was taking place, but contemporaries were unaware of this. How did they conceive of the professions' role? One cannot discuss the internal history of the clergy without reference to the place of this 'profession' within the wider society. That specific groups organised along given lines and justified these developments in similar ways and that this type of 'professionalisation' occurred coincidentally with (or perhaps consequently upon) the advent of capitalism but prior to the development of industrialism should certainly make us speculate on the relationship between the learned professions of the seventeenth century and the emergent middle classes of the eighteenth and nineteenth centuries. There is, however, a real danger that historians will concentrate upon the social relations of professionals, their lifestyles and status symbols, while neglecting the institutional framework and organisation of the professions themselves and the functions which they performed in a given society. A clergyman without the church was nothing; a lawyer without the bar was as naught. Teaching did not become a profession until education became institutionalised; country doctors came to form a profession with the advent of acknowledged specialisms, hospitals and surgeries, training schemes and claims to monopoly. Each of these professions flourished when society as a whole acknowledged — sometimes at knifepoint — that they performed a valuable function (which non-specialists could not or were not permitted to perform) and provided the conditions under which they could operate. As will become evident in this essay, the profession was nurtured by society once its value was recognised, but this very nurturing process restricted the autonomy of the profession concerned. In truth, profession and professionals should be studied in tandem and equal attention accorded the functions which they are both claiming and being acknowledged to fulfil. Unless we attend to these matters, we shall never be able to identify the precise place of 'professions' or 'professionals' in the physiognomy of a changing English society nor to pinpoint the very real difference between 'clergymen', 'lawyers' and 'doctors' in the middle ages and their descendants in the seventeenth century and beyond.

Estate to profession

There had been a clergy in England throughout the middle ages. The medieval clergy professed a devotion to God and, as an estate, they possessed a certain *esprit de corps*. It would, however, be difficult to establish that the medieval clergy possessed *in combination* the features of a recognisably professional structure: hierarchical organisation; emphasis upon service; internal control of recruitment, training and placement; internal enforcement of standards and discipline; stress upon the possession of specific expertise, both practical and theoretical; a developed career structure; and a tremendous *esprit de corps*. Many of these features had their origins in the past — the medieval Catholic Church, for example, was certainly hierarchic in structure and it did claim autonomy. What we have to grapple with is a problem of metamorphosis: the medieval clergy are, if you wish, the caterpillar which eventually metamorphosed into the butterfly of the Jacobean clergy. The highly coloured creature which emerged from the chrysalis is the same as the caterpillar and yet, undeniably, different. The object of this essay is to indicate how, why and when this metamorphosis took place and to describe the butterfly.

Who were the clergy? The answer to this question will vary according to whether we speak of the pre- or post-Reformation period. Before the Reformation the clergy formed one of the three vertical estates of the realm (the others being the aristocracy and the remainder of lay society); after the Reformation the clergy formed a profession — a hierarchically organised but occupational group which claimed status in society on the basis of the expert services which it offered the commonwealth.

Unlike the other estates of the realm, the medieval clerical estate was a creation not of birth but of election. Young boys were taken from the lay estate into which they had been born and were placed in the clerical estate, for which they were educated. When a boy was first tonsured he took the initial step towards full membership of the clergy, but there were many such steps along the way. There were no fewer than eight stages in the progression from lay to priestly status: first, tonsure (which was not an order, but separated the clerk from the layman because it expressed the pious intention to become a priest); *ostiarius*; lector; exorcist; acolyte; and the three major or holy orders of subdeacon, deacon and priest. The boy could not become a full member of the clerical estate (except by dispensation) until he reached the age of 24 years.[1]

There were many casualties along the route to full clergy status. Entrants to minor orders were recruited normally from among youths of the bishops' households or the congregations who showed enthusiasm and ability, but the enthusiasm of adolescence often wore off. Many youths were content to reap the rewards of benefit of clergy without further committing themselves to full orders, membership of the clerical estate and, thereby, celibacy. The grim reaper also harvested large numbers of clerical recruits.

Only when the young man entered the subdiaconate — by which time he must have attained the age of 18 — did he fully commit himself to the clerical estate and to celibacy. At any one time, therefore, there were large numbers of youths and young men who had one foot in the lay world and one outside it. But the clerical estate was differentiated sharply from the lay estates by distinctive uniform and style of life. There were often complaints that clergymen attempted to hide their status by donning lay attire and living lay lives: both lay and ecclesiastical authorities sought to check this tendency.

It is important to grasp the fact that membership of the clerical estate, either in full or in part, did not inevitably imply a career in the *pastoral ministry* of the church. Lay and church administrators, clerks and lawyers (who had to be latinate as well as literate), teachers, scholars and members of the religious orders were all members of the clerical estate and yet they did not share the same occupation as the bishop, rector, vicar or assistant curate. Even where the man was a priest, he was not necessarily a minister. Much confusion has been caused in the minds of scholars by the fact that in the medieval church there were two separate, linked, but by no means synonymous, hierarchies — those of orders (subdeacon, deacon, priest, bishop) and of occupation. In fact, prior to the Reformation there were several hierarchies of occupation among the clergy — the hierarchy of the religious order, that of the pastoral ministry, that of the civil government, that of

29

the ecclesiastical law courts and so on. This remained true to some small extent after the Reformation but it was triply true of the earlier period when clerical status coincided much less with the pastoral occupation. This distinction is pointed by the fact that the Reformers preferred to call the priesthood the ministry, whereas there was no such feeling prior to the Reformation.

How big was the sprawling medieval clerical estate? It is difficult to produce any hard and fast statistics, but the following figures may provide some guidance:

- *c.* 10,000 ecclesiastical benefices (of which 15–25 per cent were served by pluralists);
- at least 10,000 employed but unbeneficed assistants — in major orders;
- *c.* 12,048 religious (including monks, nuns, canons and friars);
- fluctuating numbers of recruits to minor and major orders without employment;
- unspecified numbers of clerks, administrators, teachers, scholars and lawyers in orders.

The number of clergy fluctuated throughout the medieval centuries and the rate of recruitment into the clergy actually increased from 1460 to 1500 and fell thereafter. By any standards, the clerical estate — as conceived of in the early 1500s — accounted for a substantial proportion of the total population of England and Wales. An estimate of 35,000 seems plausible in a total population for England and Wales of 2.5 million.[2]

After the Reformation, clerical numbers fell quite dramatically. The dissolution of the monasteries and houses of canons and friars immediately cut the number of employed clergy by one-third.[3] The definition of clergy also changed and many men who had previously been accepted as members of a separate clerical estate, despite no obvious religious vocation, were now gradually reclaimed into the world of laymen — teachers, clerks and administrators, lawyers, doctors and scholars.[4] The state provided fewer opportunities for clerics to rise to prominence. The church itself now needed far fewer men. The minor orders and one of the major orders disappeared with scarcely a trace. There was no longer any need for priests to serve in the chantries. The number of clergymen was probably reduced to a total of 15,000 in a rising population (1545: 3.5 million; 1603: 4.1 million; 1650: 5.5 million) and the church had to fill only about 300 vacancies through death or retirement 'in the ranks' each year. After 1540, therefore, clergy were much less numerically conspicuous in the English and Welsh landscape than had been the case.[5]

The clergy now ceased to be a vertical estate and became instead a group of men involved in a common occupation — that of the Ministry of the Word. This change did not come about at the drop of a hat, however, or even at the fall of the monasteries. It was a gradual and complicated process, made more complex by the differing views of the crown and various schools of churchmen about the exact nature of the ministry and its relationship to the pre-Reformation priesthood. Indeed, it is this very complexity that makes the story of the professionalisation of the English clergy so interesting and absorbing.

In pre-Reformation England clergy abounded. The 'estate' included many different types of clerk. The regular clergy (monks, nuns, friars, etc.) and the secular clergy (rectors, vicars, curates) form the two most obvious divisions, but there were others which made the word *clergy* all-embracing of men and women with little in common in terms of lifestyle, life purpose, interests or origin, and militated against there ever being a 'profession of the clergy' in any modern sense. That very factor which helped the Catholic clergy to separate themselves from lay society (the different relationship with God) would have proved a positive hindrance to the formulation of any occupational, functional definition of clergy had they remained unmodified within the Reformation Church. Let there be no mistake. One is not saying that the late medieval clergy were corrupt, vocationless and ill educated. The point is that it would be difficult to find an *occupational* bond among the varied groupings within the medieval church, despite the fact that all clergy belonged to one spiritual estate.

It is true, of course, that the medieval church itself acknowledged a pastoral function which was exercised at parish level by the curate or the assistant curate, at diocesan level by the bishop and along the way by other church officials through the courts Christian. But this was just part of the church's work and not the whole. Perhaps we can grasp the situation best if we say that the cleric's role was not defined in terms of his relationship with his flock but in terms of his relationship with God. It was entirely conceivable that a priest should have no flock, whereas it was inconceivable that he should have no mass. The pastoral function is but one, albeit an important one, of the responsibilities of the church, and not all of the clergy are committed to it; the sacrifice of the mass is central to the concept of the priesthood and its relationship with God.

If this were true of the secular clergy, it was all the more true of the religious. By no means all religions were involved in the purely contemplative life — the friars provide a good example of the active character of many of the orders. Religions offered services to the laity — alms, hospitality, sermons and teaching — but their chief role was inward looking. In their life of contemplation they may have had some relationship with the laity but, if so, this was essentially representative. They reflected, they prayed, they mortified themselves on behalf of the laity.

In summary, then, the secular clergy could not be defined in terms of occupation. They comprehended but were not confined by the commitment to the cure of souls. Similarly, the regular clergy performed a number of services to the laity but their function within the church was defined not in terms of their relationship with man but with God. One is left with a concept of the clergy that is extremely diluted when compared to the later protestant or post-Tridentine Catholic definitions. The medieval clergy were far too broadly based to professionalise in a modern sense — they formed, in truth, a spiritual estate and not an occupational profession.

The dissolution of the monasteries (and eventually the chantries) assumes, therefore, great importance in the redefinition of clergy in occupational as opposed to status terms. It represented a sharp blow to the idea of a double standard of Christan life and access to salvation; to ascetic traditions within the church; and to the idea of a purely contemplative and representative practice of religion. If Henry VIII and Cromwell dissolved the monasteries for non-spiritual reasons, Protestantism could not help but rejoice at this rejection of the ideal of monasticism. Many saw monks as idle, corrupt individuals, living off the fat of the land, and for what? For Protestants it was the tossed-off comment, 'For what?' that mattered most of all. Monks had no more access to salvation than had the ordinary layman; salvation could not be achieved by good works, still less could it be achieved by the pursuit of pietistic or ascetic rituals. The dissolution of the chantries, in its turn, attacked the mediating role of the priesthood and also its representative role. The politically motivated dissolution of the monasteries and chantries, therefore, paved the way for the erasure of the distinction between cleric and layman as they stood before God and also for the redefinition of the clerical role in terms of specific activity and service. The Church of England, while not Protestant, became committed to a pastoral definition of the ministerial function. The clergy would no longer act on behalf of the laity or mediate for them with God; instead, the clergy would teach and prepare the laity to receive salvation. The church had to justify anew the continued existence of a clergy to an anti-clerical laity on the basis of an essential service offered to the people.[6]

The place of a clergy within the reformed Church of England

But was there room for a clergy at all within Protestantism? For the Catholic the priest was an essential intermediary between the individual and God; for the Protestant each man was his own priest. At core, Protestantism was democratising and levelling in its tendencies. One might have anticipated that its advent would spell the end of a clerical profession. In practice, however, Protestant churches, both in England and abroad, did not evolve in a vacuum. A variety of political, religious, social and economic considerations dictated the form of the new churches, their personnel and organisation. Protestantism was a creed which called for a return to the primitive condition of the church as described in the New Testament and which strove to ignore subsequent social, economic and political developments in western Europe. Unfortunately for its revivalist message, Protestantism's leaders were as much caught up in the sixteenth-century world as were the church and churchmen they attacked. The resulting tension between revivalist and institutionalised faith is most important for our discussion of professionalising tendencies within the post-Reformation English church.

The leaders of the English Reformation never broke loose

for more than a moment from the context of a state church. The moment — gone in the twinkling of an eye — was the Marian exile. The state was determined to retain the divide between clergy and laity. Its conception of the church in England remained that of an institutionalised church, led by expert ecclesiastics, which would serve as a bulwark of order in the state. The ecclesiastics themselves assumed that it was they who should reform the church. After all, they were the experts, were they not? They were the ones who were conversant with the doctrinal and legal bases for reform. If each man was his own priest, each man was not his own teacher and pastor. Predictably, the clergy were disinclined to attack their own *raison d'être*.

Despite this implicit entanglement with the idea of a special fitness for their task and of the need for a clergy, the founding fathers of English Protestantism were not clericalists in the Roman sense and had no intention of stressing the power and authority of a clerical estate within the church's communion. When Cranmer and others produced a new ordinal in English they interpreted the ministry in an essentially Protestant fashion.[7] The ministers are called by both God and man to preach the word of God and to administer the sacraments; there is no hint of priestly caste or a sacrificial intention; the function of the ministry is explicitly pastoral. Men are not ministers if they have no pastoral responsibility: the emphasis is upon the encouragement of a caring, responsible ministry by insisting on residence, commitment to the service of one congregation, ethical behaviour, exemplary action and exposition of the Word, and is never upon a clerically ruled church.

The English ordinal assumed the truth of the doctrine of ministerial order that was emerging on the Continent. While it predicated a distinction between the specific Christian vocations of ministry and laity, it denied any suggestion of a separate status before God or of different standards of expected behaviour. The ordinal was based not upon a translation of a medieval ordinal (in the way that Cranmer's Prayer Book used the Catholic Service book), which would have involved a good deal of unacceptable sacrificial language and an interpretation of the priesthood in the context of the sacrifice of the mass, but upon the rite produced by Martin Bucer. Minor orders were neglected. Cranmer provided for the ordination and consecration of deacons, priests and bishops, but he does not appear to have believed, strictly speaking, in a threefold order of the ministry. Rather, bishops were priests who were given pastoral oversight: the episcopate was not a necessary or separate order of the ministry. Neither does the ordinal present the diaconate and priesthood as similar and consecutive orders. The diaconate is a distinct order with a different function from that of the priesthood; this conception of the order of deacons probably owed much to Cranmer's reading of their role in the primitive church. Nevertheless, Cranmer was clearly unable to dissociate himself entirely from the traditions of the Catholic Church — there are points in the ordinal when it is assumed that most deacons will proceed to the priesthood and that one of their chief functions will remain that of assisting the priest in the cure of souls and administration of the sacraments.[8]

Some Protestant leaders, notably John Hooper, were more able to shake themselves free of the shackles of the Catholic conception of priesthood. Hooper was a radical and a primitivist who resisted the compromising tendencies displayed by Cranmer and others. He felt that any compromise which threatened to reverse the acceptance of the doctrine of the priesthood of all believers should be regarded with suspicion and loathing. The minister had no special access to God. The only earthly qualification needed by a minister was an intimate knowledge of the Scriptures — for preaching the word of God with God's mouth was his prime function.[9] As a bishop, Hooper tried to train his parochial clergy as evangelists, as missionaries. Clergy were needed to awaken the people to the Scriptures.[10] The ideal was not expansionism on the part of the clergy but the withering away of the need for a clergy.

Accommodation: the changing function and meaning of clergy in Elizabethan and early Stuart England

If the leaders of the Reformed Church in England conceived of a ministry rather than a priesthood, their views were not shared by the Tudor monarchs. Elizabeth insisted upon the retention of episcopacy and was adamant that the diocesan structure should remain.[11] She saw the diaconate as part of the ministry proper, a first or even a second step towards ordination as priest. She clung to the idea of a celibate clergy, made distinct from the laity by their ceremonial and everyday garb and by their sole right to administer sacraments. In her church these sacraments were the means of grace. The cleric was more than 'God's mouthpiece' or 'ambassador' in the pulpit: he was the keeper of the 'keys of the kingdom'.

This, then, was the problem before the fledgling Church of England — the need to reconcile traditions of semi-autonomy with the reality of the royal supremacy and the clamour of a vocal minority for new forms of church government and discipline. It was a problem which did not grow smaller upon further acquaintance. For as long as the crown maintained a political interest in controlling the pulpit, the autonomy of the clergy as a profession would be limited. For as long as the church sought to be comprehensive of a variety of theological, doctrinal and disciplinary views, the structure and function of the profession for which the clergy themselves were working would be, of necessity, muddled.

Two of the abiding problems before the clerical profession were signalled early in Elizabeth's reign: the extent to which the clergy were to be distinguished from the laity; the form of government of the church and of the profession. The former is a story familiar to students of Elizabethan church history. There were those who saw the emergent Elizabethan settlement as conducive to a new separation between ministers and people: a view of the functions of the ministry and ordering of the church's life which smacked all too strongly for some of the Catholic pattern, albeit with an emphasis upon pastoral responsibility. The controversy concerning vestments brought the issue into focus. By the mid-1560s the primitivists — Laurence Humphrey and Thomas Sampson — were seeking advice from both Zurich and Geneva regarding the Queen's insistence that clerical attire be worn to distinguish clergy from laity:

> whether laws respecting habits may properly be prescribed to churchmen, so as to distinguish them from the laity in shape, colour etc.? ... whether the distinguishing apparel of the priesthood is to be worn on all occasions, like a common dress? Whether this does not savour of monkery, popery and judaism?[12]

They were shocked by the guarded response of Peter Martyr and Heinrich Bullinger. For the English Protestant primitivists this 'indifferent' matter summed up the difference between the Catholic priesthood and the Protestant ministry:

> As ceremonies and sacerdotal habits are signs of religion and marks of profession, they are not of a civil character; and being borrowed from our adversaries, as all allow them to be, they cannot be convenient; and being marked with the divine anathema, and detested by all godly persons, and had in honour by the wicked and the weak, who think that without them we can neither be ministers, nor that the sacraments can be rightly administered, they cannot nor ought to be reckoned among things indiffe-
> rent.[13]

Whatever their objections, the English primitivists lost their fight against the preservation of a clerical uniform. The clergy remained visibly distinct from the laity.

Historians have been rather more lax in attending to the second problem — that of the form of church government — within the context of the professionalisation of the clergy. True, attention has been drawn to proposals for the reorganisation of church administration in Elizabeth's reign — for the introduction of superintendents, for example. And objections to episcopacy (as practised in the Elizabethan and Jacobean church), because they loomed so large in 'puritan' thought and action, have formed the focus of several important studies of the religious life of the period. But no one has drawn out the full implications of the arguments concerning church government for the development of the profession. The issue is important for two reasons: firstly, the status of the church as a community within a community, with the power to legislate, of itself, for itself — through convocation — was in doubt from the Reformation Parliament onwards; secondly, the question of who should control the church and its personnel in its executive, legislative and administrative aspects was a very real one. There is room here only to summarise these basic issues, but their importance should not be underestimated.[14]

During the Reformation Parliament there were outspoken objections to the claims of the church to legislate for itself. The Submission of the Clergy and the Act in Restraint of Appeals gave parliamentary authority to the earlier agreement of the clergy that convocation 'always shall be assembled by authority of the king's writ'. The legislation of the Reformation Parliament had tremendous implications for the range of the church's independent activities. In the convocation of 1536, for instance, Thomas Cromwell sat as vicar-general of the King, although he did not supplant the Archbishop as president of convocation. When he sat again in May 1539, Cromwell presented a schedule of questions for consideration by the assembly. The supreme head of the church, represented by his vicar-general (substitute), evidently intended to act as an ecclesiastical person, guiding the direction of convocation's deliberations and legislation. New canons had to receive royal assent and there was no suggestion that they should be submitted to Parliament for approval; nevertheless, the Act of 1534 did insist that canons of the church must in future accord with 'the customs, laws or statutes of this realm'. Quite commonly Parliament enacted opinions expressed in convocation: for example, the Act of Six Articles gave authority to convocation's views on the eucharist, clerical celibacy, religious vows and confession.

Such developments seemed to spell the demise of the church as a separate community within the state, legislating for itself. But Elizabeth preferred to preserve the *status quo* as established in 1534. She strove consistently to prevent Parliament carrying through legislation which affected the church and to allow convocation to enact its own measures. The crown would remain as initiator of clerical policies.

Monarchs from Elizabeth to Charles I wanted to work through convocation. It was important that convocation be malleable. The trend in church government and administration was definitely towards centralisation in the hands of the bishops and the crown. This was a development which the crown both favoured and fostered: the clergy outside the hierarchy was difficult to handle, relations with the bishops even were often fraught with tension — in this situation the crown preferred to deal directly with a small coterie of bishops and to rule the church with and through them.

There were many complaints during Elizabeth's reign that convocation had ceased to be a representative body of the clergy of the realm. Convocation had played an important part in defining the Elizabethan settlement but the lower house was already given a wholly advisory significance. As the reign progressed, many clergymen who were excluded from the government of the church alleged that the lower house of convocation had ceased even to represent their opinions because the machinery for the election of clerical proctors to convocation had fallen into disuse: deans and archdeacons, already members of the upper house, were acting as deputies of the parochial clergy. In 1597 a rule was introduced which forbade this practice, but it is not known whether or not it was observed.

Certainly, those clergymen who believed that the interests of the church as an institution were being served at the expense of the interests of individual congregations had reason to complain. The activities of convocation were guided by Whitgift and Bancroft to centralise the administration of the church and to quash nonconformity. At the beginning of the new reign, puritan ministers had hopes that the system might be reformed. What they wanted was not presbytery, but increased participation by the lower clergy in the life of the church and a reversal of the programme of centralisation. At the Hampton Court Conference Reynolds spelt out a programme for clerical discipline and for increased activity by the parochial clergy in church government at local level. Some bishops were sympathetic; others preferred to see the lower clergy who argued this case as schismatics. Concessions were made, but the balance of power within the church was not significantly altered, perhaps because James I lost interest and allowed Bancroft to interpret the report of the conference. Bancroft's canons demanded conformity. They confirmed the oligarchical tendency of church government. They asserted that convocation was the church representative and that its canons bound the church. Local conferences could not and must not act unilaterally.[15]

As a result of these developments, the role of the lower clergy both in the decision-making process and in church administration and discipline was limited. Individual bishops still attempted to utilise ministers in the work of the dioceses, but there was less room in the Jacobean and Caroline church for experiment than there had been in that of Elizabeth.

At the beginning of Elizabeth's reign the hierarchy was faced with the unenviable task of recruiting and organising clergymen who would be acceptable to the crown and who would yet approximate the vision of the ideal minister as conceived by most Protestants. From what we have said already of the development of church government and of the crown's very real determination to command the church militant in battle, it will be clear that this was no easy task. In an ideal world the ecclesiastical hierarchy would have been king of its own castle. In the real world, this king was the vassal of another more powerful than he, who interfered to varying degrees with the processes of recruitment, training and maintenance and who was far from consistent in his protection of the vassal — demanding continual homage but often withholding largesse. When, therefore, we speak of the professionalisation of the clergy, we must be continually aware that the clergy had not achieved complete autonomy and had to work within the constraints which crown and society placed upon it.

The first problem to be tackled by the Elizabethan episcopate was the undoubted shortage of clergy. The decline in the overall number of clerical recruits may be dated to the 1530s. Possibly this was owing to the higher standards of admission supposedly being imposed, but it is more probable that the unsettled state of the church and the financial insecurity of the ministry deterred many would-be clerics. As a result of the dissolution there were even fewer opportunities for advancement.[16] And despite a demand for better qualified clergy, the financial remuneration of most parish clergy remained pitiful and uncertain. As late as 1585 Archbishop Whitgift was to complain that there were scarcely 600 livings (out of 9,000–10,000) capable of supporting a learned minister. Of course, Whitgift drew upon the outdated Valor Ecclesiasticus for his precise figures — and these must be disregarded.[17] Nevertheless, although clerical incomes for the beneficed kept pace with or exceeded inflation after 1535, clerical poverty remained a problem both in real terms and relative to the prospects offered by other careers such as the law.[18]

As a profession the clergy did not solve the problem of inadequate and uncertain clerical incomes during the early modern period. Beneficed clergymen — rectors and vicars — drew their incomes from tithes upon the labour and produce of parishioners, from fees for services performed, from offerings, and from their own glebe farms, which they either worked themselves or leased out. The value of benefices varied enormously: when Jeremy Collier analysed the Valor Ecclesiasticus returns for 8,803 livings he found that 4,503 rectories and vicarages were assessed as worth less than £10 (and of these 1,000 were valued at below £2 and a further 1,978 at below £5), while the remainder spanned a range of £10 to £30, with a mere 392 exceeding £30 in value.[19] In the period down to 1660 most livings rose in money value and kept pace with inflation but, if anything, the inequality of incomes became more acute, not less. Rectories, for example, improved in value much more than did vicarages. Moreover, livings with extensive glebe were more secure than those with little landed endowment, especially when they were farmed by the incumbent and his family. Clergymen who depended entirely upon tithe found that they prospered when their parishioners prospered and suffered when their parishioners suffered poor harvests. Glebe farmers, on the other hand, had some hedge against both inflation and undue dependence upon successful collection of tithes.

Prior to the Reformation, when the plight of multitudinous non-beneficed clergy had been severe, it had been common for clergy to supplement their official incomes by engagement in secular or semi-secular occupations and by undertaking incidental religious duties, such as singing intercessary masses, assisting beneficed clergymen on the major feast days and witnessing wills and other legal documents. After the Reformation the number of opportunities for supplementary income were reduced: masses were no longer said or sung (although, to some extent, the fashion for funeral sermons provided a substitute), and reduced ceremonial called for fewer assistant clergy. Even more important, although poor clergymen persisted in taking secular jobs, the hierarchy did everything it could to restrict this practice. In 1599 the pluralist vicar of Marston and Doveridge, Derbyshire, was hauled before the consistory court for 'as a layman' purchasing land, buying leases, lending money at interest, 'hunting, fishing and breeding beasts . . . and selling them your own self at fairs and markets wherein you do daily exercise yourself still nothing regarding your charge and calling'.[20] The church authorities felt that clerics should not indulge in secular occupations. In an age when wage labour was not the norm and when even city dwellers, craftsmen and tradesmen still engaged in subsistence farming, it must have been difficult to maintain the distinction between 'professional' and 'unprofessional' activities on the part of the clergy. Nevertheless, the hierarchy did insist that clergymen stuck to their calling, while never succeeding in making the income from that calling sufficiently rewarding or regular to attract enough able recruits. In such a climate of opinion, the church did not seem to be a very happy choice of hunting ground for the ambitious or merely hungry young. Indeed there has always been a marked imbalance between the 'status' claimed by the church as a profession and the economic position of the clergy.

How did the Elizabethan hierarchy attract recruits of quality and overcome the short-term implications of a shortage of manpower in the parishes? In 1558 between 10 and 15 per cent of livings were vacant. The position was even worse in the populous south-east — a third of livings were vacant in the archdeaconries of London and Canterbury. There was also an acute shortage of assistant curates. Deprivations and resignations accounted for some of these vacancies, but an unusually high death rate from 1556 to 1560 was even more important.[21]

The new bishops seem to have used mass ordinations to solve the problem — accepting into the ministry almost anyone who was willing to come forward. In the first eight months of his episcopate Archbishop Parker ordained 233 men in the diocese of Canterbury,[22] and 167 deacons were ordained at London between 28 December 1559 and 24 March 1561.[23] Recruits were rushed into the parishes by the expedient of ordaining to both orders simultaneously or on consecutive days. Despite some attempts to control the quality of recruits, these ordinations were largely indiscriminate: any pastor was better than no pastor at all.

Archbishop Parker viewed mass ordinations as a temporary expedient. He quickly became aware of their unwelcome long-term implications. In August 1560 he advised the bishops of the southern province to raise and monitor standards of admission and to refuse to ordain recruits with a history of non-clerical background or base (i.e. secular) occupation. It was time to curb the flow of uneducated recruits: for, once possessed of benefices, it would be nigh on impossible to oust such men from the profession.[24]

Parker evidently tried to introduce a stop-gap measure to provide adequate pastoral care by laymen until well-educated clergy could be recruited and trained. His scheme involved an elaborate system of circuits. A circuit of parishes would be supervised by a single rector or vicar; each parish would be served by a lay lector empowered to read the prayerbook services but not to administer the sacraments. Between December 1559 and 1562, no fewer than 71 lectors served in Canterbury diocese alone. Lectors, of course, could be easily removed once suitable ministers became available. The experiment was abortive, however: unfortunately the bishops had no power, other than in exceptional circumstances, to refuse institution to the livings in question; to make such an experiment work the bishops required the active support of patrons of livings, which was presumably unforthcoming.[25]

The bishops did try to respond to Parker's directive regarding ordinations. At Ely, which was an ordination centre for the whole country and not simply involved in ordaining men to serve in Ely diocese, examiners were careful to enquire into the age and background of candidates. Those middle-aged and older were referred to the bishop for further examination. Of 32 candidates who presented themselves for ordination on 21 March 1561, five were rejected outright and one bound over for a year. The rejection rate increased during the decade. Lack of knowledge of the Scriptures was the chief reason for turning away candidates for orders; in December 1568 six of the seven denied admission were turned away on these grounds. Nicholas Wallys found that neither his BA nor a personal recommendation from the Dean overruled the decision of his examiners that he was 'in the Scriptures ignorant', and therefore not to be ordained, when he was examined in April 1568. It was now accepted that the cleric's expertise lay in knowledge of the Scriptures: without this learning he was unfit for his pastoral duties.

It was important also that new recruits had been 'brought up in learning'. Middle-aged and uneducated recruits were regarded with suspicion. The chances of the older recruit having lived a secular life and besmirched his character were higher and great emphasis was laid upon the need for the older recruit to have immaculate and impressive references. In the long run, the bishops hoped to rely upon a system of recruitment which began in the grammar schools and universities and excluded older candidates from the profession.[26]

Despite all the efforts of the bishops and their examiners the educational qualifications and the vocational aptitude of parochial clergy remained deplorable during the sixteenth century. In 1584 only 14 per cent of clergy in Coventry and Lichfield diocese were graduates: the percentage had risen to a mere 24 per cent by 1603. In part this reflected the fact that improved recruitment took time to show itself at parochial level, because of low rates of mobility and the barriers raised by the patronage system. But this is only a partial explanation. Initial recruitment itself, outside the university ordination centres and London, showed only gradual improvement. Only 1 of 282 ordinands at Chester between 1560 and 1570 was a graduate; recruitment in that diocese was far from entirely graduate in the 1590s. As these ordinands were fed almost exclusively into livings within that diocese, it followed that Chester ministers remained poorly qualified until well into the seventeenth century. Unfortunately for the profession's reforming spirits, the clerical career was one marked by exceptional longevity.[27]

The hierarchy's approach to the reformation of the ministry was marked by two linked interests. First was the concern that the ministry become a graduate profession. This involved the encouragement of recruitment via the universities and the provision of adequate financial and career incentives. Secondly, there was a movement to ensure the vocational suitability of ministers, associated with a demand for more effective clerical supervision of the exercise of ecclesiastical patronage. Eventually it might be possible to flood the market with well-trained ordinands, but until that time the hierarchy had to find ways of influencing patrons in their choice of clergymen. For he who controlled patronage, controlled the church.[28]

The Elizabethan and Jacobean bishops undoubtedly tried to encourage future ordinands to attend university. Preferments within the Elizabethan church automatically went to university men. In 1560 Elizabeth instructed her Lord Keeper to make prebends worth less than £20 available to theology students. Under James I the crown became involved in an ambitious but abortive project for the reclamation of tithes in the hands of the universities to augment parish livings. Jacobean and Caroline bishops effected piecemeal improvements by founding scholarships from grammar schools to colleges at the universities, designed to provide subsidised education for able young recruits.[29]

There were also many attempts to achieve the placement of

well-educated ministers in the available livings and to train the less well qualified who were already *in situ*.[30] Attempts to control placement all worked within the existing patronage system. At best the bishops could hope to control the type of man eligible for patronage and to prevent flagrant disregard for the rules. Only very occasionally could a bishop successfully reject an unsuitable presentee.[31]

The efforts of the bishops were best helped when patrons themselves conscientiously examined candidates for livings. The crown, the single largest advowson holder in the kingdom, was in the best position to do this. The Lord Chancellor presented to around 100 livings per annun; the crown presented to an additional number of wealthier livings. In theory the Lord Chancellor's office could have organised its exercise of patronage to ensure that only well-suited men were presented. It employed examining chaplains to this end and had the bureaucratic machinery necessary to make such a policy workable. In practice, however, the Lord Chancellors were inconsistent in their pursuit of this goal. Some were more interested in the personal exercise of their patronage than others. Lord Keeper Egerton, for example, was sufficiently concerned to eradicate pluralism and to ensure a preaching ministry that he denied livings to pluralists (preferring in Camden's words to see that 'some might have single coats, that wanted them, before others had doublets') and made some clergy enter into bonds to deliver sermons before he would agree to present them. But even Egerton's interest was patchy. Others, notably Puckering and Bacon, delegated the business of selection to their registrars and lesser officials, thus opening the way to loss of control and corruption. The problem was that the Lord Keeper saw his church patronage as part of the wider web of patronage in society as a whole and not solely as an instrument for reforming the church's ministry. He saw in ecclesiastical patronage a convenient way of rewarding particular groups or individual petitioners. Nicholas Bacon, Elizabeth's first Lord Keeper, allowed the bishops considerable say in the exercise of his patronage. After this, however, the bishops lost their control when noble courtiers began to petition the keepers on behalf of their own protégés. Any hopes that the profession's hierarchy may have had of controlling crown patronage were thus lost.[32]

If the episcopate did not find the crown consistently helpful, other patrons were even less reliable. 'Puritan patrons' might present troublesome clerics, but at least they were concerned to prefer well-educated and conscientious candidates. Yet puritan patrons were markedly active in certain areas only. Most lay patrons of advowsons were not puritan and there is evidence to suggest that many had little interest in using their patronage to further any religious programme whatsoever. They regarded the possession of an advowson as a useful form of property ownership — the advowson might be sold directly to the agent of a job-hungry clergyman or the right to present for one or more times might be sold. Men who wished to place their relatives and friends bought such grants of presentation to suitably valued and located livings. Especially during the reign of Elizabeth there was much trading in these *hac vice* presentations. This fragmentation of patronage hindered the attempts of both hierarchy and puritan laity to install a worthy ministry.[33]

At every turn the efforts of the hierarchy to control recruitment into the profession and the placement of recruits were stymied by the structure of patronage. In order to defeat the system, the choice of clients before patrons would have to be limited to educated, worthy ordinands. This dream was realised in the early seventeenth century when the expansion of university numbers begun in the 1560s was well established. Between the beginning of 1600 and the end of 1606, 82 candidates for deacons' orders in London diocese (out of a total of 109) were graduate and 12 were students. By the 1620s recruitment throughout London diocese was wholly graduate. Even more remarkable was the position in more backward dioceses: of the 87 ordained deacon at Gloucester between June 1609 and May 1621, 52 were graduates; 43 of the 60 ordained priest were graduate. Four-fifths of the candidates at Lichfield between 1614 and 1632 were university products. And all this is to leave out of account the staggering impression of total university recruitment which is obtained from reading the ordination lists of the centres at Oxford, Peterborough, Ely and Lincoln, traditionally fed by their local universities.[34].

This situation was not brought about entirely by the efforts of the hierarchy to encourage potential ordinands to attend university. Recruits and their parents learned by example: they noticed that graduates not only gained place in the church but also preferment. This, combined with the enlarged provision of educational facilities within the provinces, made progression to the university appear an attractive route for the intending cleric. The universities and colleges themselves maintained efficient and extensive communications with the schools in the provinces, making certain that able boys were advised of the desirability of further education. Parents, godparents, teachers and clergy added their voices to the clamour.[35]

Once it was accepted that preferment was within the grasp only of the well educated, the re-routing of ordinands via the universities was self-generating. Richard Baxter was almost deterred from entering the ministry because his 'want of acedemical honours and degrees was like to make me contemptible with the most, and consequently hinder the success of my endeavours'.[36] In fact, there is little evidence to indicate that on the lower echelons of the clerical ladder educational qualifications cut more ice with patrons than did connection, but clerical recruits believed that they constituted the key to preferment. By the late 1620s and 1630s, a bachelor's degree was held by so many recruits that it could not in itself prove a positive advantage. Higher and higher qualifications were demanded if the cleric in question coveted a place of distinction within the church. The MA became the most popular degree among clergymen.[37] The ambitious were encouraged to study theology. Even obtaining a benefice was more difficult for the graduate than it had once been. The more scrupulous of the bishops, faced with a large pool of graduate ordination candidates, tended now to question the vocational value of the BA degree — they bewailed the poor quality of the recruits. And even when they were ordained, supply of graduates so exceeded demand that some inevitably had to kick their heels for a while before finding 'tenured' placement.[38] The patronage system, of course, meant that it was not always the able who found positions quickly and the less able who had to wait.

By the 1630s the clergy had become a graduate profession. But the profession did not, strictly speaking, control the means of education and training. Although the colleges of the universities continued to be staffed by clerics and although certain colleges in particular took their role as seminaries seriously, the universities did little to adapt their formal curriculum to the needs of a church which set great store by preaching and pastoral care. It was a strictly academic regimen which produced classical scholars and theologians, not pastors. It was only outside the universities, through *ad hoc* schemes of in-service training, that the bishops could tackle the problem of providing more vocational expertise. Unfortunately, such schemes became thin on the ground after the reign of Elizabeth. It was as if the bishops took refuge behind the outward success of the drive to produce a graduate profession. And, of course, both hierarchy and crown were then less anxious to encourage independent preaching and more insistent upon the value of the printed homilies as vehicles for the instruction of the laity.[39]

The lack of vocational training designed to help the cleric to communicate with his congregation had an undoubted impact upon clerical–lay relations during the seventeenth century, for it led some laymen to question the value of the clergyman's expertise. The church had replaced the mystery of the mass with yet another — the clergy seemed determined to hide the secrets of the Scriptures from the people behind obscure language and incomprehensible scholarly techniques in order to justify their own monopoly of religious teaching in the state. A claim to theoretical expertise formed the foundation of the clergy's monopoly. The polarisation of the positions of laity and clergy became most evident during the ordination controversy of the 1640s and 1650s when the sectaries contested the claim of the clergy that human learning and a call from men was essential to the cleric. But the problem was not a new one. It may be that clergy–laity relations would not have reached this impasse had the in-service training schemes of the sixteenth century been continued and had the hierarchy remained committed to a preaching ministry.[40]

There can be little doubt that the Elizabethan and Stuart clergy developed a sense of corporate identity. The growth of clerical family dynasties, of professional meetings, of informal friendships, of common educational background, of similar lifestyles all served to strengthen the cleric's sense of belonging to a profession. Many of these developments received no direct hierarchical encouragement and some were actively discouraged, but there can be no question that the institutional apparatus of the church, largely untouched by the Reformation, facilitated their occurrence. The growth of a community of the clergy is immensely important for an understanding of the social significance of the professions in early modern England. A profession was much more than an occupational grouping; it was, equally, much more than a status grouping. The strength of a profession depended upon the organised expression of common occupational, social and economic interests. A profession was more than just a union, concerned to protect entry to the occupational group and control conditions of work, pay and preferment. We must beware of concentrating upon these aspects of a profession's work at the expense of defining professional lifestyles and relationships both with members of the profession and with others.[41]

Indeed, the study of the clerical profession demands that we consider the implication of professionalisation for social relationships. Unfortunately, the consolidation of professional feeling appears to have taken place at the expense of further alienation from the members of lay society. Antagonistic relationships with the laity seem to have fed clerical unity. The clergy, often themselves from relatively humble backgrounds, were more than keen to emphasise the status of their calling and their acquired social position. This did not increase their popularity with their congregations. Gentle patrons despised them; humble farmers and traders resented them. Their standing as officers of courts of morality did not make them appear lovable in the eyes of defensive parishioners. The policemen of today search the body; those of yesteryear stripped the conscience bare. The archdeacon may have been 'oculus episcopi', but it was the eyes of the vicar, peering round the curtains of both marital and extra-marital beds, that the hapless parishioner wished to evade. And the economic hold which the clergy had upon their parishioners — as collectors of tithes and fees and rents, as lenders of money and writers of references — did not endear them to laymen. Of course, we must not exaggerate the tension between clergy and laity: the clergy had lay friends and individual clergymen maintained excellent relations with their congregations. Nevertheless, the tendency was towards polarisation of interest and towards a questioning of the value of the professional services offered by the clergy of the Church of England.[42]

Characteristics of the profession of the clergy by the mid-seventeenth century

By the Civil War the clergy of the Church of England were more recognisably a profession in the modern sense of that term than their medieval predecessors had been. But if this butterfly was in the process of emerging from the chrysalis, it had not yet fully metamorphosed. The sixteenth- and seventeenth-century professions were not the same as those of the industrial period. While modifications in role had occurred since the Reformation, this role differed from that of professions in the modern world and the professions themselves exhibited many different characteristics. It is helpful to imagine the process of professionalisation as a continuum and to attempt to place the early modern clergy upon this.

By the mid-seventeenth century the clergy had many features of a modern professional structure listed above. Yet on closer inspection it becomes apparent that the seventeenth-century professions possessed other important characteristics. And the years following the civil wars spelt further change in some important areas.

Control of its own means of recruitment, training and placement was not total. Contemporary churchmen found this irksome. Crown, universities and laity all intervened to prevent the church recruiting whom it wished, training them in the way that it wanted and placing them where they were most needed. This was inevitable, given the retention of old forms of patronage, the role of the church in the state, and the monopoly of higher education held by the ancient universities. But the truly autonomous profession is in fact a myth. It is unrealistic to expect that any profession — which by definition offers essential and specialist services to its clients — can be or will be entirely freed from outside constraints. It is arguable that it was only when the service offered by the clergy ceased to be prized above all others that the hierarchy gained more control over recruitment, training and preferment. Full autonomy of organisation would imply that the church's services no longer seemed relevant to society. Of considerable interest to the historian, then, is the extent and character of outside intervention in the recruitment procedures of the Church of England.

Because the Church of England retained the bureaucratic

administrative and pastoral machinery of the pre-Reformation diocesan, parochial and court structure, it maintained the internal enforcement of standards and discipline, despite protest from some quarters. This is not to say that there was not considerable objection (among the common lawyers, for instance) to the idea of the clergy standing outside the law of the land and to the claim that the clergy could evade punishment if they disobeyed the law. It is to say that the church courts disciplined recalcitrant clergy and sought to impose conformity to the church's own rules. They fulfilled this role after the restoration as before. Even so, influential patrons could always protect erring clergymen. It was the 'masterless men' who suffered most as a result of disciplinary procedure.

If a reformed ministry was its goal, the Church of England had not developed an appropriate career structure. There were, in reality, two clergies: a clerical elite drawn from among high-flyers at the universities and protégés of the well connected; and the rank and file, increasingly well educated but possessing little hope of preferment outside the work of the parishes. There was no single career ladder in the Church of England, reaching from assistant curate to bishop, which was accessible to all recruits. This brought into question the criteria which were being adopted for leadership and fuelled the arguments of Protestant critics who believed that the church was but halfly-reformed. The division between elite and rank and file signalled potential tension which sometimes surfaced in relations between church office holders and groups of venturesome preachers and in arguments about control of the church's institutional apparatus. The old argument about whether the church should adopt a monarchical/autocratic government or a mixed constitution was ever present.[43]

There is some debate concerning the effects of career structure upon the clergy themselves. Mark Curtis, over twenty years ago, believed that the pressure of an increasingly well-educated (and, as we now suspect, an increasingly well-born) clergy upon too few benefices and elite posts alienated many able clergy during Charles I's reign and drove a significant number into opposition politics during the mid-century crisis. More recently scholars have cast considerable doubt upon this thesis. Over-production of graduate clergy in the long term has been exaggerated. The recruitment pattern of clergy was subject to fluctuations, so that there were brief periods of fierce competition for available livings as well as of shortage of new recruits. Short-term over-compensation was the characteristic response, in either case, but, in fact, recruitment patterns appear to have adjusted remarkably well to changes in demand. As a result, qualified ordinands generally found permanent employment in the church, although the acceptable period of apprenticeship (in a curacy, lector's post, lectureship or school) was considerably longer for clergy entering the profession in the seventeenth century than in the later sixteenth. There is little sign that either beneficed or unbeneficed were alienated by their experiences. Indeed, as Ian Green has observed, the clergy were trained not to question but to conform. While the alienated may stand out from the crowd, the historian must remember that it was the crowd to which the majority belonged. There is no reason to doubt that this majority accepted the reality of the church's existing career structure and sought to fulfil their vocation within it. Equally, there are strong indications that the beneficed clergy approved much of Laud's programme which bolstered the church's strong points — its stability, its distinctiveness and its comprehensiveness. A rift between the crown's hierarchical leadership and the rank-and-file majority is not apparent. It may well be that a radical minority found the church's career structure and the policies of its leadership incompatible with 'reformed' status but this position could have more to do with ideological conviction than material concerns.[44]

While the structure of the profession had serious repercussions for the nature of the church's leadership and certainly curbed the ambitions of parish clergy, the parson's loss may well have been the people's gain. Parish clergy had long careers. A third of London ordinands, 1600–18, held livings for between 15 and 30 years and over a third had even longer clerical careers, of between 31 and 50 years' duration. Rather over half the entrants to first benefices were between the ages of 26 and 30 and slightly less than half were between the ages of 30 and 35. Once ensconced in benefices, the clergy tended to stay put. There was nowhere to go. There were occasional imbalances between the supply of recruits and the demand for parochial clergy, but in general supply exceeded demand. The clergy had effective tenure. With the exception of ejections at times of crisis (the reign of Mary, the beginning of Elizabeth's reign, the interregnum, the restoration), deprivations were rare. Even temporal suspensions were relatively uncommon. The parson more often than not put down roots in his parish which were 'deep and widespread', offering pastoral care based upon personal knowledge of parishioners and their circumstances. Continuity of service was apparently in direct relation to the wealth or poverty of the living concerned. For example, John Pruett discovered that it was the tiny minority of Leicestershire clergy in the period after the restoration who held livings worth less than £50 per annum who searched for further moves; almost half obtained better livings. But the great majority of clergy in Leicestershire held wealthier livings and were immobile.[45]

All this pointed to the importance of providing all beneficed parish clergy with appropriate financial support. Sixteenth-century churchmen related the lack of preaching ministers to the poverty of many livings — the argument ran that graduates of good background would be attracted by the superior status and financial rewards of alternative callings, especially the law. By the later seventeenth century the view that only an economically independent clergy could chastise the parishioners into righteousness and exercise a moral authority over all members of the flock, whatever their social standing, joined the older arguments that good recruits were deterred by poor prospects and that poverty inevitably led to the twin evils of pluralism and non-residence. An appropriate income would guarantee gentility in the clergy — a feature as important as learning.

Did the early modern church provide its clergy with the income with which to maintain their status and their function in society? Until recently it has been difficult to chart with any degree of confidence the movement in clerical incomes between 1535 and 1714. John Pruett's work has made the task much easier. He demonstrates that, in the long term, the trend in clerical incomes was definitely upwards. Improved agricultural productivity meant rising incomes for clergy with glebe to farm and tithes in kind. Differential inflation increased this effect. In some cases the clergy did not reap the benefit of these rises themselves because of leasing of glebe and tithes to laymen, but Pruett contests Christopher Hill's view that this was normal. The years of the interregnum represented severe ecclesiastical dislocation and accompanying falls in clerical receipts. It has been usual to claim that clerical finances stagnated after the restoration, but Pruett argues that they continued to improve, although unevenly. By 1707 the real values of Leicestershire rectories had risen by 81 per cent; of vicarages by 45 per cent. There were wide regional variations: the respective figures for Hertfordshire, Buckinghamshire and Huntingdonshire were 105 and 26 per cent. The rise in the real value of livings seems to have meant a marked improvement in the standard of living of the parochial clergy between 1535 and 1666, setting them apart from the majority of their parishioners. Increased taxation of the clergy after 1690 made serious inroads into these gains.[46]

If we accept that the financial lot of the English clergy improved in the century and a half after the Reformation, it remains true that the church did not provide the clergy with a coherent pay structure. The differential between the income of rectors and vicars was enormous. There were noticeable regional variations. Contemporaries were, as we have suggested, aware of the repercussions of this situation for the performance of the clergy as pastors. Schemes for the overhaul of clerical pay arrangements abounded. On the one hand there were private, voluntary augmentations of poor livings. On the other there were more grandiose 'public' schemes, sometimes involving the purchase and reallocation of impropriations. The most notable of these was the attempt to reform parochial finance under the Commonwealth and Protectorate. Under this scheme a high proportion of the very poorest livings (valued at below £10) and of the large, populous parishes were augmented, using local revenues. The absence of a centralised, efficient bureaucracy made a nation-wide overhaul of clerical finance impossible.[47]

By common consent, it was the introduction of Queen Anne's Bounty which 'marked the decisive first step' in the elimination of clerical poverty by perfecting a 'workable and enduring system of relief'.[48] No accurate information was available concerning the nature of clerical poverty until the Governors conducted their surveys between 1705 and 1719. In 1736 a report prepared for Parliament presented a detailed list of poor livings. This seems to have painted an unduly pessimistic picture of clerical poverty by its inaccuracies. During the eighteenth century the Bounty Commissioners raised over £2,450,000 and made over 6,400 grants to poor livings in England and Wales. By 1810 the number of livings valued at less than £50 stood at 1,000, compared to 5,600 in the early eighteenth century.

P. N. Virgin's more detailed work on the economic position of the clergy has suggested phenomenal improvements, particularly in the incomes of the poorer clergy. Between 1700 and 1830 perpetual curacies rose in value by 659 per cent; the poorer rectories and vicarages by 466 per cent and the richer incumbencies by 325 per cent. These economic advances were relatively untouched by general inflation — which stood at about 100 per cent over the same period — or by the higher expenses to which the clergy were subject. He posits a rise of 200 per cent in the real incomes of the parochial clergy between 1700 and 1830. 'The beneficed clergy enjoyed a much higher standard of living in the 1830s than they had done a century and a quarter before'.[49]

All this seems to suggest that the clergy improved their economic status in society over the period as a whole, with the earlier period (1535–1700) seeing an uneven rise in real incomes of between 20 and 45 per cent for vicarages and 80–106 per cent for rectories and the later (1700–1830) an overall rise in real income of at least 200 per cent, from which the poorer livings benefited most of all. Talking in percentages can take us just so far and no further. Did the clergy have an income adequate to support their pastoral activities and their necessary status in society? Virgin demonstrates that by the end of the eighteenth century, when the cleric's economic and social position was at an all-time peak, the median income for a clergyman (£275 in England and £172 in Wales) was not considered sufficiently high. A figure of £400 was suggested as adequate. In other words, contemporaries believed that the beneficed clergy needed the income of one of the upper middle classes or above to do their work properly. In fact almost a quarter of clergy had incomes in excess of £500, which put them with the lesser gentry in economic terms. The remainder normally had an income well in excess of that of the majority of their parishioners. The contemporary lower-middle-class income stood in the range £60–200 p.a. One-tenth of the beneficed clergy earned less than £100 p.a. but even they were in a higher economic bracket than their parishioners. Both Virgin and Pruett argue that this improvement in the economic position of the clergy was matched by a rise in the social origins of the parish clergy and in their social status as clergymen. In theory at least the clergy of the Church of England were now better equipped to offer spiritual and moral leadership to all ranks of men and to concentrate upon their supreme pastoral function. This, however, was an eighteenth-century development — we are left with the impression that at least a large minority of sixteenth- and seventeenth-century clergymen were unable to sustain their professional obligations adequately even though their real income was often improving considerably.[50]

Initially the status of the Reformation clergy had rested upon their claim to offer a unique service. One of the salient features of a modern profession is the claim to exercise a monopoly of a particular service to the community, for altruistic reasons, based upon a specific theoretical expertise. This feature was possessed already by the seventeenth-century clergy to the nth degree. The clergy of the established church claimed to be uniquely qualified to bring people to Christ by opening up to them the mysteries of the Scriptures. No other 'ministers' were recognised. The penalty for nonconformity to the church's rules was severe: the offender was forbidden from practising his profession. Clergymen did not perform this service for monetary gain — they were called to the profession by both God and man and their motives were alleged to be altruistic in the extreme. They received for their services no salary but rather fees and offerings and the means of subsistence provided by the charitable who had endowed their livings with glebe and tithe.

The manner in which the clergy exercised their monopoly differed markedly from that prevailing in other early professions. Clients could select their own doctor or lawyer or teacher within a reasonably free market; consumer choice within the church was specifically forbidden. Not only were nonconformist practitioners banned (as was the case in other professions), but the client was bound to the services of one or two clergymen by the parochial structure — attending any other than one's own parish church was frowned upon and punishable in the courts. And the services of a minister, unlike those of a doctor or lawyer, were made obligatory by the state and were often intrusive in character. Occasionally it has been argued that this monopoly was destroyed at the end of the seventeenth century. The Toleration legislation of 1689 has been seen as damaging the Anglican clergy's professional status. This is a moot point. The Anglican clergy remained the state clergy. Their social status was much higher than that of the dissenting minister. Moreover, toleration was granted to a minority (however sizeable) who wished to opt out of the state church. All other citizens, lukewarm or enthusiastic, by defin-ition were members of the Church of England. The parochial incumbent was at the service of any Englishman who did not choose to declare his dissenting status. Moreover, laymen were still forbidden to perform clerical functions within the estab-lished church. The rights and functions of the clergy within the Church of England remained inviolate. Laymen had no more role within it than before. It might be possible to argue that by reducing the comprehensiveness of the established church, the crown protected its clergy against inevitable onslaughts from lay enthusiasts.

By the end of Charles I's reign the clergy possessed a sense of community as a profession. This community served the laity, yet often stood ranged against the very people whom it served. For the clergy's function as agents of control, imposed upon them by the civil authorities, meant that, unlike the client's doctor or lawyer who acted at the behest of the individual, the clergy sometimes seemed to act in the state's rather than the individual's interest. They could look remarkably like spiritual policemen and singularly little like spiritual doctors. Added to this was the fact that the clergy claimed a status which was not acknowledged by all.

For the clergy, while in some sense remaining a paradigm for the other learned and ancient professions, cannot in another sense be compared with them. The medical profession had its *raison d'être* in the service of mankind; the legal profession justified its existence likewise; the military profession served society. If they served another God it was Mammon. The clerical profession was different: it served both God and man. The pre-Reformation clergy had placed the service of God uppermost — we see the clergy adoring God, offering to him the sacrifice of the mass, mediating his wishes to the people. After the Reformation, this function was retained, although modified, but the clergy were given another role — that of serving the spiritual needs of the laity. They were shepherds tending their sheep. It is instructive to regard the development of the post-Reformation clergy as characterised by the tension between these two clerical functions — serving God and man. Contemporaries differed considerably about which element of the cleric's role they considered paramount. There were those who esteemed the pastoral role above all. The pastor was there to serve his congregation; he was their servant, they employed him, they could demand particular behaviour of him and dismiss him if he failed to please. Others had no doubt but that the clergyman served God according to his conscience. He should be in a sufficiently independent position to do so. The church should recruit and appoint ministers and discipline them in a manner consistent with God's will. But there were many intermediate positions. The monarchs, in particular, were ambivalent in their attitudes to the functions of the clergy. Elizabeth, for example, placed the adorative role of the clergy high and seemed determined to preserve its marks of separation from the laity (celibacy, dress, clerical function in worship). Yet she also appeared keen to use the cleric's relationship with his earthly client (the individual parishioner) to reinforce behaviour acceptable to the government. She was sure of one thing: the laity should not be allowed to make the clergyman their servant — he was a teacher, a shepherd.

Conclusion

The historian can usefully employ the concepts of professions and professionalisation provided by modern sociologists when studying the early modern clerical profession. By using the measure of the modern professions, the historian is able to highlight the similarities and differences between early modern and modern professions. The historian, however, must not stop here. The sociologist is interested in static snapshots of social structure: the historian, on the other hand, is concerned with movement, with change, with those factors which gave rise to a given structure. The sociologist compares professions. Trait analysis involves extracting those traits which professions at a given point in time have in common. The features which divide professions are largely ignored, regarded as aberrations from a norm, or seen as features indicating different stages of development. The historian is as interested in the contrasts between professions as in the points of direct comparison. The clergy in the early modern period were not the clerical profession of the nineteenth and twentieth centuries. Neither were they the same as the medieval clergy. The structure of the clergy was changing — although it changed relatively little after the restoration — and its meaning and function in society were in a continual state of flux. What was the clergy's function and who was going to decide what it was? Any study of the clergy as a profession must needs concentrate upon the relationship between this profession and the state, for the civil authorities were striving to define the clergy's social function. Moreover, much attention must be accorded the peculiar relationship which the clergy shared with their clients — individual souls. While there are points of similarity between the services which a cleric offers his parishioners and those which a doctor or a lawyer accords his clients, there are also very marked distinctions. Some of these arise from the nature of the service offered — intangible spiritual benefits are difficult to measure against tangible physical or legal gains. Some stem from differences in the internal structure of the profession itself, its historical origins, the extent to which contemporaries considered it important, the extent to which it was autonomous of outside concerns. Medicine, for example, was not institutionalised; the clergy and the lawyers existed within an institutional framework — independent activity was curtailed as a result. The clergy and the lawyers had a long history as institutionalised, learned professions — when change was called for there were traditions to overthrow, legacies of earlier times to displace, compromises to be made. Some distinctions derive from the relationship of the particular profession with the state. In the case of the early modern clergy, those in positions of national leadership were convinced that the church was of great importance in national life. Conformity in religion spelt loyalty to the state. The clergy were agents of public order. A properly ordered church underpinned the social fabric of the kingdom. Judges were similarly important. Doctors and lawyers had a more personal relationship with their clients.

Sociology is a simple science. Historians know only too well the complexity of human society — laboratory experiments are redundant. The historian of the clerical profession must make plain the complexity of its development and the web-like intricacies of its relationship with the changing society which it served and of which it was a part.

Notes

1. P. Heath, *English parish clergy on the eve of the Reformation* (1969), pp. 3–15.

2. Estimates taken from: M. Zell, 'Economic problems of the parochial clergy' in R. O'Day and F. Heal (eds), *Princes and paupers in the English church, 1500–1800* (Leicester, 1981), pp. 21–2; D. Knowles and R. N. Hadcock, *Medieval religious houses* (1981), p. 364. For a comment on the fluctuating rates of recruitment see J. A. Hoeppner Moran, 'Clerical recruitment in the diocese of York, 1340–1530', *Journal of Ecclesiastical History*, vol. 34 (1983), pp. 19–54.

3. Knowles and Hadcock, *Religious houses*, p. 364.

4. The gradual nature of this change is emphasised in R. O'Day, *Education and society 1500–1800* (1982), pp. 170–6.

5. Population estimates from E. A. Wrigley and R. S. Schofield, *The population history of England, 1541–1871: a reconstruction* (1981), pp. 208–9.

6. See C. Haigh, 'Anticlericalism and the English Reformation', *History*, vol. 66 (1983), pp. 391–407, for an interesting if unconvincing comment on anti-clericalism before the seventeenth century.

7. J. Ketley (ed.), *The two liturgies* (Parker Society, Cambridge, 1844), pp. 159–86, 329–54.

8. J. L. Ainslie, *The doctrines of the ministerial order in the reformed churches of the sixteenth and seventeenth centuries* (Edinburgh, 1940), *passim*; the issue pertaining to the number of orders is discussed in W. K. Firminger, 'The ordinal' in W. K. Lowther Clarke (ed.), *Liturgy and worship* (1932), p. 661 and *passim*. The question of Cranmer's reliance upon Bucer's rite is also discussed in Lowther Clarke, *Liturgy and worship*, pp. 670–2. For a succinct account of the Protestant character of the ordinal see A. G. Dickens, *The English Reformation* (1964), pp. 240–1.

9. See especially John Hooper, *A declaration of Christ and of His office* (Zurich, 1547).

10. F. D. Price, 'Gloucester diocese under Bishop Hooper', *Transactions of the Bristol and Gloucester Archaeological Society*, vol. 60 (1931), pp. 51–151.

11. P. Collinson, 'Episcopacy and reform in England in the later sixteenth century' in G. C. Cuming (ed.), *Studies in church history*, vol. 3 (Leiden, 1966), pp. 91–125, describes the reforms which the first generation of Elizabethan bishops favoured, and Elizabeth's opposition to them.

12. 'Laurence Humphrey to Heinrich Bullinger, 9 February 1566' in W. Hastings Robinson (ed.), *Zurich letters* (Parker Society, Cambridge, 1842), Letter lxviii, pp. 151–2; see P. Collinson, *The*

Elizabethan puritan movement (1967), pp. 71–84.

13. 'Laurence Humphrey and James Sampson to Heinrich Bullinger, July 1566' in Robinson, *Zurich letters*, Letter lxxi, p. 160.

14. For convocation, see E. Cardwell (ed.), *Synodalia* (Oxford, 1842); Elizabeth's use of convocation is treated in M. C. Cross, *The royal supremacy in the Elizabethan church* (1969), pp. 86, 92–5. The attitude of the crown to forms of church government is discussed in W. P. Haugaard, *Elizabeth and the English Reformation* (Cambridge, 1968), *passim*; M. C. Cross, *Church and people 1450–1660* (Glasgow, 1976), pp. 124–52.

15. M. H. Curtis, 'The Hampton Court Conference and its aftermath', *History*, vol. 46 (1961), pp. 1–16; Collinson, *Puritan movement*, *passim*; see K. C. Fincham, 'Ramifications of the Hampton Court Conference in the dioceses, 1603–1609', *Journal of Ecclesiastical History*, vol. 36 (1985), pp. 208–27, which suggests that a transitory vitality was imparted to diocesan government, in some dioceses at least, as a direct result of Hampton Court.

16. M. Bowker, 'The Henrician Reformation and the parish clergy, *Bulletin of the Institute of Historical Research*, vol. 50 (1977), pp. 30–47; R. O'Day, *The English clergy* (Leicester, 1979), pp. 29–30.

17. J. Strype, *Life and acts of John Whitgift* (3 vols, Oxford, 1822), vol. 1, p. 536.

18. A benefice is a tenured ecclesiastical office for which revenues are received: rectories and vicarages are commonly described as benefices, although other ecclesiastical offices such as archdeaconries, while not parochial cures, also fit into this category. See O'Day, *English clergy*, pp. 172–89.

19. J. Collier, *An ecclesiastical history of Great Britain* (9 vols., 1852), vol. 9, pp. 362–3.

20. Lichfield Joint RO, B/C/5/1598/9: case of Henry Trickett.

21. D. M. Barratt, 'Conditions of the parish clergy from the Reformation to 1660', unpublished D Phil thesis, University of Oxford, 1950; F. J. Fisher, 'Influenza and inflation in Tudor England', *Econ. Hist. Rev.*, vol. 18 (1965), pp. 120–9; O'Day, *English clergy*, p. 8.

22. J. I. Daeley, 'The episcopal administration of Matthew Parker, Archbishop of Canterbury, 1559–1575', unpublished PhD thesis, University of London, 1967, p. 178.

23. Guildhall London MS 9535/1.

24. J. Bruce (ed.), *Correspondence of Matthew Parker* (Parker Society, Cambridge, 1853), pp. 120–1.

25. O'Day, *English clergy*, pp. 130–1.

26. Ibid., pp. 49–54, 58–65, 131–2.

27. Lichfield Joint RO, B/V/1/15; Lambeth Palace Library, CMXIII; Lichfield Dean and Chapter Muniments, MS A.A.11; Cheshire RO, EDA1/3; for clerical longevity and studies of mobility see Zell in O'Day and Heal, *Princes and paupers*; O'Day, *English clergy*, pp. 1–32.

28. For a general study of patronage and its implications see R. O'Day, 'Ecclesiastical patronage: who controlled the church?' in F. Heal and R. O'Day (eds), *Church and society in England, Henry VIII to*

James I (1977), pp. 137–55.

29. *Calendar of state papers domestic, Addenda, Elizabeth I, 1547–65*, pp. 505–6; Inner Temple Library, Petyt MS 538–38, fo. 137.

30. For examples see O'Day, *English clergy*, pp. 46–7, 66–74; P. Collinson, *The religion of Protestants* (Oxford, 1982), pp. 92–140 and *passim*; P. Collinson, 'Lectures by combination: structures and characteristics of church life in seventeenth-century England', *Bulletin of the Institute of Historical Research*, vol. 48 (1975), pp. 182–213.

31. For the law of patronage see O'Day, *English clergy*, pp. 75–85.

32. See R. O'Day, 'The ecclesiastical patronage of the Lord Keeper, 1558–1642', *Trans. Roy. Hist. Soc.*, 5th ser., vol. 23 (1973), pp. 89–109.

33. O'Day, *English clergy*, pp. 86–112.

34. Guildhall Library, MS 9535/2; Gloucester City Library, GDR Bishops' Act Books; Lichfield Joint RO, B/A/4A/17 & 18; Oxfordshire RO, Oxford Diocesan Papers, C264, vol. 11, e9, e12, e13; Northamptonshire RO, Ordination Papers of the Diocese of Peterborough, 1570–1642.

35. For college recruitment see R. O'Day, *Education and society*, pp. 77–105; R. O'Day, 'Room at the top', *History Today*, vol. 34 (1984), pp. 31–8; R. Tyler, 'Children of disobedience', unpublished PhD thesis, University of California at Berkeley, 1976, pp. 91–2 and *passim*.

36. R. Baxter, *Reliquiae Baxterianae* (1696), p. 12; for Adam Martindale see O'Day, *Education and society*, p. 174. The advantages of being 'on the spot' are discussed in O'Day, *English clergy*, pp. 14, 135–9, and the problems facing the graduate ordinand are treated in *English clergy*, pp. 21–3.

37. For example, Bodleian Library, Tanner MS 179: of 1,380 presentees to benefices by the Lord Keeper between 1627 and 1640, 825 had MAs, 301 had higher degrees, 97 had BAs and only 157 had no degree at all.

38. O'Day, *English clergy*, pp. 55–8; W. Laud, *Works of William Laud*, ed. W. Scott and J. Bliss (7 vols, Oxford, 1847–60), vol. 5, pp. 363, 330.

39. O'Day, *Education and society*, pp. 132–50 and *passim*; for use of printed homilies see H. Davies, *Worship and theology in England, from Cranmer to Hooker, 1534–1603* (Princeton, 1970), pp. 227–54.

40. O'Day, *English clergy*, pp. 207–30; O'Day, *Education and society*, pp. 142–6; R. L. Greaves, 'The ordination controversy and the spirit of reform in puritan England', *Journal of Ecclesiastical History*, vol. 21 (1970), pp. 225–41; J. F. Maclear, 'Popular anticlericalism in the Puritan Revolution', *Journal of the History of Ideas*, vol. 17 (1956), pp. 443–70.

41. O'Day, *English clergy*, Chs 12–15.

42. Ibid.

43. Ibid., pp. 144–58.

44. M. H. Curtis, 'The alienated intellectuals of early Stuart England', *P & P*, no. 23 (1962), pp. 25–43; O'Day, *English clergy*, pp. 1–23; I. Green, 'Career prospects and clerical conformity in the early Stuart church', *P & P*, no. 90 (1981), pp. 70–115.

45. J. Pruett, *The parish clergy under the later Stuarts* (Urbana, Ill.,

1978), pp. 74–5; O'Day, *English clergy*, pp. 19–20, 21.

46. Pruett, *Parish clergy*, pp. 100–10.

47. R. O'Day and A. Hughes, 'Augmentation and amalgamation: was there a systematic approach to the reform of parochial finance, 1640–1660?' in O'Day and Heal (eds), *Princes and paupers*, pp. 169–93.

48. I. Green, 'The first five years of Queen Anne's Bounty' in O'Day and Heal (eds), *Princes and paupers*, pp. 231–54; P. N. Virgin, 'Church and society in late Georgian England, 1800–1840', unpublished PhD thesis, University of Cambridge, 1979, pp. 67–80.

49. Virgin, 'Church and society', pp. 87–90.

50. Ibid., pp. 112–32.

3

Lawyers

Wilfrid Prest

Following the Reformation dethronement of the priesthood and before the nineteenth-century elevation of the medical practitioner, the engineer and the man of science, lawyers plainly constituted the pre-eminent English profession. Historians have long recognised their central importance in the constitutional conflicts and political culture of the seventeenth century. Yet despite the recent upsurge of a new-style socio-legal history[1] we still know surprisingly little about the men who made part or all of their livings from providing their fellows with legal advice and representation. Recent research, much of it still in progress or unpublished, has supplied some broad outlines, but the remaining gaps in our knowledge are still so numerous that any general survey of the kind attempted here must be in large part a catalogue of admitted ignorance and tentative speculation. This chapter will describe the various categories of lawyers active in England at the beginning of the sixteenth century, and then trace their divergent fortunes over the next 250 years. By the mid-eighteenth century the legal profession had acquired many of its modern institutional characteristics, most notably a rigid division into two quite separate 'branches', of barristers on the one hand and solicitors (or attorneys) on the other. How and why that distinction arose is discussed in the final section of the chapter.

Definitions and structures

It is straining language to speak of an early modern English

64

legal *system*. There was little thought out or coherent about that fragmented chaos of overlapping (and frequently conflicting) jurisdictions — national, regional and local courts, ecclesiastical and secular courts, courts occasional and permanent, courts dispensing English common law, Roman civil law, canon law and a bewildering variety of local customary law, courts of considerable antiquity and courts newly erected or asserted, courts swamped with business and courts moribund for lack of suitors. Not surprisingly, English lawyers were hardly less diverse than the courts whose workings provided their ultimate *raison d'être*. Over the whole period *c*. 1500 – *c*. 1750, those known as common lawyers constituted the largest and most flourishing body of legal practitioners. By 1500 the common law had established a formidable institutional and intellectual base in the three great royal courts of Common Pleas, King's Bench and Exchequer sitting at Westminster Hall, the twice-yearly assize circuits which brought both civil and criminal justice to subjects throughout the realm, and the inns of court and chancery in Holborn, where common lawyers lived and worked during the four legal terms and where would-be lawyers came to learn from established masters of the craft.[2] These practitioners were already wont to follow the Lancastrian Chief Justice Sir John Fortescue in tracing the common law's origins to a misty and largely mythical pre-Roman Britain, a pedigree which helped bolster their self-esteem *vis-à-vis* the civil law and lawyers, whose ancestry went back even beyond the *Corpus iuris civilis*, a codification of Roman law prepared for the Emperor Justinian in the sixth century AD.[3] Yet neither classical antecedents nor academic respectability equipped the university-trained civilians to mount a successful challenge to the power, prestige and wealth of the much better-entrenched and more numerous common lawyers. In an increasingly nationalistic era, civil lawyers were suspect as agents of malign alien influence, whether political (Continental-style absolute monarchy), religious (popery), or both. A still more fundamental weakness was their confined and, as it turned out in the long term, steadily contracting sphere of practice in the church courts, which they took over from the canon lawyers after Henry VIII's Reformation. Although still monopolising the business provided by the hearing of mercantile disputes in the Court of Admiralty, as well as enjoying opportunities for office-holding in the courts of Chancery and Requests, by the beginning of the seventeenth century civil lawyers generally perceived themselves to be an embattled and dwindling tribe: 'it is almost a discredit for any man to be a civilian in this state', claimed the eminent Sir Thomas Ridley LLD in 1607, 'and the profession thereof doth scarce keep beggary from the gate'.[4] Of course such exagg-erated laments conveniently ignored the flourishing state of certain prominent individual civilians whose practices brought them substantial honours and riches, men like Sir Julius Caesar, Master of the Rolls under James I and Charles I, Sir Leoline Jenkins, who became a Secretary of State to Charles II, and indeed Ridley himself. Yet these striking exemplars of personal success qualify rather than contradict a general picture of shrinking opportunities and overall decline for civil lawyers, especially after the end of the sixteenth century.[5]

Like contemporaries, historians have tended to highlight the differences in organisation and interests which distinguished civil from common lawyers. Yet there were also some notable parallels and similarities. Both professions were headed by relatively small bands of fairly high-status practitioners (the civilian advocates, the common law apprentices, utter-barristers and serjeants at law), who specialised in advising clients and pleading their cases in court. Those university-trained doctors of civil law (common law was not taught at Oxford and Cambridge until the nineteenth century) who enjoyed the exclusive right to plead before the highest ecclesiastical jurisidiction, the Court of the Arches, were matched on the common law side by the serjeants, who monopolised pleading before the Court of Common Pleas, traditionally the realm's busiest and most lucrative venue for civil litigation. Moreover this select band of civilians had their own collegiate society in Doctors' Commons, a body set up in the late fifteenth century perhaps in conscious emulation of the longer-established inns of court and chancery at Holborn, although without any comparable educational function.[6] Again, the attempt to exclude proctors (for whom see below) from Doctors' Commons after 1570 followed closely upon the first efforts to banish attorneys and other so-called mechanical practitioners from the inns of court.

Proctors, attorneys and solicitors stood in roughly the same relation to the elite civil and common lawyers as did apothecaries and barber surgeons to the learned (i.e. academically qualified) physician. Their primary vocational responsibilities, for managing the day-to-day conduct of litigation, could be plausibly represented as demanding skills gained through practical experience rather than from book learning. Their main mode of training was by some form of apprenticeship; hence proctors, unlike advocates, did not require a university degree, while attorneys were not necessarily members of an inn of chancery (although these bodies had in any case largely abandoned their former educational functions by the early seventeenth century). Above all, there was a considerable and widening gulf in social origins and status between the learned elite and the 'mechanical' lawyers, both civil and common. By and large, civilian advocates and common-law barristers claimed and were accorded the courtesy title of esquire, whereas the attorney, proctor or solicitor was at best a mere 'gent'.[7]

The ancestral resemblance of the practitioners discussed so far to the modern barrister and solicitor seems fairly clear. But in early modern England legal practice was by no means restricted to those who held some recognised professional qualification. Nor was there complete agreement as to which practitioners were embraced by the term 'lawyer'. When in the 1630s Sir John Oglander recalled that 'heretofore there was no lawyer nor attorney' resident on the Isle of Wight, he was clearly using the word in the exclusive sense favoured by barristers and judges when distinguishing their own learned order from other, subordinate practitioners. But the more respectable or ambitious of these lesser breeds were quite prepared to adopt the same strategy; thus the anonymous author of a mid-seventeenth-century handbook for solicitors complains that 'simple sots' who lack either learning or skill and yet practise as solicitors have thereby been 'allowed to usurp . . . the worthy name of lawyer'.[8] In point of fact the term 'lawyer' is most commonly met with in a general or collective sense, at least during the first half of our period. Individual practitioners are more usually described or describe themselves by an 'addition' denoting their rank or degree (typically 'esquire' or 'gent.'), sometimes with a reference to their inn of court or chancery, or an office which they held; the use of more specific occupational designations, such as apprentice, attorney, barrister, counsellor or serjeant (with or without the suffix 'at law') was relatively less common, at least before the mid-seventeenth century, although by no means unknown, especially in memorial inscriptions.[9] If some solicitors evidently did lay claim to the title 'lawyer' by the mid-seventeenth century, it does not appear that the term was normally extended much wider in contemporary usage. Mere knowledge of the law, or its occasional application by way of advice to others, did not suffice to make a lawyer, although in the last analysis the distinction must have been one of degree rather than kind. Thus part-time provincial practitioners, like John Furse the elder of Moreshead, Devon, whose 'exercise was making of writings and keeping of courts' do not seem simply to have been lumped in with those men who regularly accepted fees for advising and representing clients.[10] The latter would often, but by no means always, belong to one of the corporate legal societies in London, or have been formally admitted as attorneys or proctors in a court of law, whether local or national, or both.

So while historians find it convenient to use institutional affiliation as the main test of an individual's identity as a lawyer, simply because the surviving records of the institutions concerned provide us with invaluable lists of names, this convention does have some warrant in contemporary usage. On the other hand, it is likely that the most common and straightforward way of identifying lawyers in early modern England was by their appearance and dress. Thus when John Smyth (1567–1641), barrister of the Middle Temple and steward to the Berkeleys of Gloucestershire, sought in his chronicle of that family to disparage Anthony Huntley, one of his unlearned predecessors, he mentioned that Huntley was accustomed to preside over his master's manorial courts wearing 'a white feather in his hat'. Such a sartorial lapse was evidently conclusive proof of Huntley's amateur status and low standing, 'a man fitter for fairs and markets of cattle . . . than to grapple in the combats of Littleton'.[11] Lawyers (except judges and serjeants) wore black or dark colours; in the late sixteenth and early seventeenth centuries they were notorious for affecting ruffs and well-trimmed beards, 'cut as close as a stubble field' and might carry a pen case at the waist, but not a sword. So it was easy enough for a waggoner to make a joke against lawyers out of a question put to him by a person 'not knowing whom he was otherwise than he judged him a lawyer by his habit'.[12]

The early modern legal profession may therefore be envisaged as a fairly solid core of institutionally affiliated lawyers, surrounded by a very broad fringe of more or less marginal practitioners. These 'empirics of the law' (as they were called by Serjeant William Sheppard, adapting the derogatory label applied by the College of Physicians to medical practitioners who lacked formal academic qualifications) undoubtedly provided a substantial (if quite unquantifiable) share of the legal services available to the general public throughout our period. Despite the claims of Sheppard and his colleagues that 'great mischief' was caused to consumers by 'the unskilfulness of these workmen', the conveyancing of land (to take one notable instance) did not become a monopoly of attorneys and solicitors until the beginning of the nineteenth century. Precisely because they usually operated in a more or less free-floating and informal fashion, it is not at all easy to discover who these men were, how they acquired whatever skills they possessed and the extent of their vocational commitment to the law. But recent research suggests that there was hardly less activity and diversity on the fringe than in the mainstream, while the boundaries between the two were both flexible and permeable.[13]

Throughout our period yeomen farmers, tradesmen and small merchants evidently found occasional employment as attorneys and scriveners, drafting bonds and deeds for a localised clientele. Many such part-timers gained their initial experience of the law from a period of service as clerk to a local lawyer or justice of the peace. Clerkship in one form or another seems to have been the usual route by which men of relatively humble means entered the legal world, although established attorneys could charge substantial premiums for accepting a young lad into their service as an apprentice clerk. Clerkship might constitute a career in itself (lawyers' clerks seem usually to have operated as individual entrepreneurs, rather than employees, being paid not by their masters but directly by his clients). Alternatively, it could be a stepping stone to other things: practice as an attorney in a London or provincial court, a position in the petty bureaucracy which serviced the judicial machinery of every county and incorporated borough, or the much larger infrastructure attached to the Westminster courts, perhaps even membership of an inn of court and call to the bar.[14]

An alternative way to acquire at least an acquaintanceship with the law was by service in the household of a great nobleman and landholder. It is in this milieu that we typically encounter the legal 'man of business', like Thomas Grice, 'learned steward and auditor' to Thomas Lord Darcy from 1492 until the 1530s, who collected rents, kept manorial courts, organised meetings with counsel, acted as arbitrator, advised on drawing a will, was indeed 'solicitor, bailiff, land agent, accountant and confidant, all in one'.[15] As D. R. Hainsworth points out below, stewards responsible for the management of large landed estates could hardly avoid involvement in legal business on their masters' behalf. Thus the journal of David Evans, steward to the first Earl of Bridgewater in the 1620s and 1630s, is little more than a record of dealings in London with lawyers and the courts in furtherance of Bridgewater's multifarious lawsuits.[16]

Yet another variety of legal practice followed by men who often lacked any formal or institutional connection with the legal world was that of the notary or scrivener. Both engaged in drafting and 'engrossing' (that is, writing up on parchment) legal instruments of all kinds, including bonds for debt, contracts, indentures, mortgages and conveyances of land, besides playing a substantial role as investment and loan brokers. Notarial authentication of documents was required in some of the procedures of the church courts and more generally in the Court of Admiralty's dealings with international trading disputes. Most cities and larger towns probably generated enough work to support several scriveners by the middle of the seventeenth century. The Company of Scriveners, incorporated in 1617 as successor to the guild of Writers of the Court Letter of the City of London, held a theoretical monopoly of conveyancing work in the City and suburbs until their defeat in a mid-eighteenth-century power struggle with the attorneys and their newly founded Society of Gentlemen Practisers, a forerunner of the modern solicitors' Law Society. In a handbook of careers advice published in 1747, the 'money scrivener' and 'conveyancer' are characterised as 'another species of attorney; they are generally bred such', whereas the 'notary-public' is distinguished as following 'a branch of the law . . . only conversant with the law of merchants', for which the training was entirely practical and unbookish.[17]

Whatever their other differences, all the various fringe, semi-professional or para-legal practitioners mentioned so far operated on an individual basis, providing their services directly to clients, although sworn attorneys, for instance, were theoretically officers of the courts in which they practised. The main body of such officials, however, was composed of those responsible for administering the written processes of the central and provincial courts. A few of the most important legal bureaucrats, such as the custos brevium and prothonotaries of Common Pleas, or the clerk of the crown and chief clerk in King's Bench, were usually members of one of the inns of court (typically that where their office was physically located), and associated *ex officio* to its governing body of benchers, while officers of lesser status frequently occupied a similar position in an inn of chancery. The legal scholarship and publications of a few exceptional officials, such as Richard Brownlow, chief prothonotary of Common Pleas from 1590 until his death in 1638, or his successors Sir Thomas Robinson and Sir George Cooke, ensured that the medieval tradition of learned clerkship did not altogether perish during our period. Yet it was very largely eroded, partly on account of procedural changes which tended to devalue the importance of the written records of the courts in the process of litigation, partly by the reform of 1739 which put an end to the use of Latin and stylised court hands in those records, but above all because of the proliferation within the legal bureaucracy of lay sinecurists lacking any pretensions to legal knowledge.[18]

Officers derived a good part or all of their incomes from the fees which litigants paid them directly for the documents and processes necessary at each stage of a law suit. In addition they sometimes either practised as attorneys in their own court or were assigned (like the Six Clerks in Chancery) to handle the business of particular clients. Yet the collective interests of the legal bureaucrats could diverge significantly from those of individual legal practitioners, who were wont to blame the burdensome delays and expense of litigation on the high fees and dubious practices of the officers of the courts.[19] So it makes good sense in this instance to follow Gregory King in regarding the latter, together with their under-clerks, deputies and menial servants, as 'persons in the law', part of that large and amorphous legal establishment which facilitated, recorded and drew material sustenance from the business of the courts.[20] It is true that they all performed legal functions of some kind, and needed some knowledge of the law, as indeed did gaolers and hangmen, serjeants of the mace, tipstaves, bailiffs, undersheriffs, JPs, informers, pursuivants, apparitors and registrars, town clerks, commissaries, vice-chancellors and manorial stewards. But these functionaries were not held to be lawyers merely because they occupied such posts, even though some of these offices were frequently found to be in the hands of professed lawyers. While certainly ragged around the edges, the early modern legal profession was not totally inchoate.

Numbers

We cannot establish precisely how many men were practising as lawyers at any time during our period. Apart from the difficulty of deciding exactly who qualifies for the title 'lawyer', there is only the most scanty and haphazard evidence about those who were not affiliated to the major central professional institutions, as sworn attorneys or members of the inns of court and chancery. While there were a great many contemporary complaints about an excess of lawyers, these usually relied on generalised hyperbole and uncorroborated anecdote to make their point. When figures were invoked their polemical purpose is generally apparent, as with the claim of the disgruntled civil lawyer Thomas Wilson that 'about 2,000' counsellors-at-law or barristers were active in 1600, when the true total could hardly have been more than a quarter as many.[21] In 1707 an anonymous attorney, urging Parliament to adopt various *Proposals . . . for remedying the great charge and delay of suits at law, and in equity*, asserted that there were at least 'twenty thousand attorneys, solicitors and clerks of court in England'. In 1750 another would-be reformer put the numbers of 'lawyers, their clerks and assistants, or officers in and dependants upon, the courts of justice in Westminster Hall, the Duchy of Lancaster, the Great Sessions of Wales, or in other courts and places of South Britain' as 'at least sixty, some say one hundred thousand persons', although he actually adopted the figure of twenty thousand as a conservative minimum.[22] Both of these are plainly notional estimates, based on a very broad concept of the national legal establishment. Hence they may be directly comparable with the figure produced in 1659 by the radical pamphleteer William Cole, who claimed that he had:

> often both in City and country, made as near an inquiry as possibly I could in a general way, what numbers of lawyers there might be in England and Wales, in all offices, as judges, masters of chancery, serjeants at law, counsellors, attorneys, solicitors with the rest of the rabble; and I cannot find by calculation, but that there be great and small, masters and servants, by the best account I can make, above thirty thousand.

It is hard to see how Cole could possibly have arrived at such a total without taking any account of clerks, both those attached to court offices and individual practitioners, although he gives no explicit indication that he has done so. Yet there is no reason to suppose that the entire legal establishment shrank by as much as a third between the mid-seventeenth century and 1707 or 1750, as a comparison between this figure and the estimates quoted above would suggest, even if some slight contraction did indeed occur under the later Stuarts; so we must conclude that Cole's estimate was considerably inflated by his evident animus against the men of law.[23]

Very much smaller totals than any of these were suggested by the political arithmetician Gregory King (1648–1712) and his mid-eighteenth-century disciple Joseph Massie, who respectively put the numbers of 'persons in the law' at 10,000 in 1688 and 12,000 in 1759. While King's figure evidently does not include barristers, whom he seemingly grouped in the general category of esquires, the numbers involved were not very large. Of course it would be a very different matter if he had similarly categorised attorneys, solicitors and other lesser practitioners under the heading 'gentlemen'. More likely King was simply unwilling or unable to recognise the size and socio-economic importance which the legal establishment had assumed by the end of the seventeenth century; a conviction that the professions contributed little or nothing to the national wealth inclined him to understate both the incomes and numbers of 'persons in the law'. This suggestion is strengthened when we consider another estimate compiled by King in the course of producing his consolidated tables of national income and expenditure. Here 'cursitors, philazers, attorneys, solicitors, clerks in Chancery, or Exchequer or other courts in law or equity, scriveners, chancellors, commissaries, advocates, proctors, public notaries and other officers' are put at 'about' 2,000 persons, which is plainly far too low when compared with other contemporary estimates and lists. Sixty years later King's follower Massie was prepared to recognise a 20 per cent increase in the numbers of 'persons in the law'; this is particularly interesting given that Massie, unlike those responsible for the other estimates discussed so far, had an explicitly comparative purpose in mind.[24]

To demand high standards of objectivity and precision from these heroic pioneers would be unfair as well as unrealistic; even today considerable difficulties are encountered in gathering accurate occupational statistics. Fortunately their estimates can be supplemented with calculations of the numbers of practitioners active in the central courts during our period, derived from the surviving records generated by litigation, although these sources provide little assistance towards establishing the size of the marginal fringe. Nevertheless the available data does establish beyond reasonable doubt that a massive expansion in the numbers of lawyers at large occurred during our period, notably between the accession of Elizabeth and the meeting of the Long Parliament.

The most striking and incontrovertible evidence concerns attorneys officially enrolled in the courts of Common Pleas and King's Bench, who appear to have multiplied no less than fivefold, from some 200 to over 1,000 individuals, between the early sixteenth and early seventeenth centuries. Most of this increase took place in Elizabeth's reign, continuing at a slightly slower pace under her early Stuart successors; in 1633 the judges informed the privy council that as many as 1,725 attorneys were enrolled in Common Pleas and King's Bench, a figure which ties in closely with Christopher Brooks's estimate of *c.* 1,750 Westminster Hall practitioners by 1640.[25] These six or seven decades of breakneck expansion were followed by a long pause, perhaps even a slight decline; returns to parliamentary committees of inquiry in 1672 and 1698 suggest that there may actually have been fewer attorneys attached to the central courts in the later seventeenth century than during the 1630s. True, the 1698 data was provided by the two chief justices to a House of Lords committee which was contemplating quite drastic law reform measures and so may well have been intended to demonstrate that the numbers of attorneys in the courts under their charge had not risen excessively. Conversely, the four attorneys who monopolised the arcane mysteries of practice in the Court of Exchequer informed the same committee that they believed no fewer than 4,000 attorneys were practising in Common Pleas alone![26] This last claim was certainly exaggerated, considering that no more than 4,252 individuals appear to have registered as enrolled attorneys or solicitors of the central and certain provincial courts in accordance with the 1729 Act for the Better Regulation of Attornies and Solicitors. It seems likely that one effect of this measure was to flush out marginal and unaffiliated practitioners who had previously practised under the names of others, or worked largely in the country, or found occasional employment as conveyancers, scriveners and so forth, and wished to gain the privileges of attorneys without necessarily wishing to practise as attorneys. If so, the apparent doubling of attorneys' numbers, from under 2,000 in the late 1690s to around 4,000 by 1731, must be somewhat discounted. Unfortunately it is impossible to put a figure on those who thus come into the historian's view for the first time, let alone the remainder still out in the half-light beyond both official contemporary and later historical recognition. If the anonymous 1707 estimate referred to earlier of 20,000 'attorneys, solicitors and clerks of court' is to be credited, the unofficial fringe was at least twice as large as the core of sworn practitioners. But then we have absolutely no way of checking the accuracy of that 1707 figure.[27]

It is possible to be a little more definite about the size and growth rate of the common law bar. Estimates of the numbers of pleaders before the King's judges in Westminster Hall during the first half of the sixteenth century and a little later range between around 80 to perhaps 150 individuals; however, at least 400 and probably closer to 450 barristers were practising before the major central courts in Easter term 1638. The rate of expansion suggested by these figures cannot be corroborated directly from the records of calls to the bar at the four inns of court, due to gaps and omissions. Nevertheless, the threefold scale of growth between the 1570s and 1630s indicated by the surviving bar call statistics fits in well with the rate given by upper estimates of the bar's size *c*. 1550–70.[28] Of course any such correlation is complicated by the fact that not all those called to the bar necessarily took to pleading in the central courts; nor is it entirely clear how the judges had determined who might appear before them as pleaders before the degree of utter-barrister was accepted as the standard minimum qualification for counsel towards the end of the sixteenth century. To complicate matters still further, we cannot be sure that the proportion of practising barristers remained constant over the centuries. Indeed recent research suggests that the ratio of practisers among those called may have declined significantly during the later seventeenth and early eighteenth centuries, as the inns became accustomed to call 'of grace' members who had neither fulfilled the formal requirements for call nor had any intention of practising at the bar.[29] Having stated these caveats, it must be added that the long-term pattern revealed by the bar call figures corresponds closely with other evidence; after a more or less continuous upwards movement from the 1560s, calls peaked in the 1660s and thereafter dropped slowly back to reach a trough in the 1720s and 1730s well below the level achieved a century before, while the numbers of counsel pleading in the central courts shrank by nearly a quarter between 1680 and 1720, returning the practising bar to something like its Jacobean level of around 300 active practitioners.[30]

There is no obvious way of comparing the changing numerical fortunes of the common lawyers with those of their civilian counterparts, although the elite body of advocates admitted to practise in the Court of the Arches appears to have shrunk by nearly two-thirds between the second half of the sixteenth and the first half of the eighteenth century.[31] Yet even the very incomplete and often shaky data surveyed so far does point to some general conclusions. For 'official' common lawyers practising in the central courts, as well as civilian advocates, Elizabeth's reign was evidently an era of massive expansion. However, growth slowed in the early years of the seventeenth century, and then halted altogether, or even went into reverse, with perhaps a limited recovery for the official lower branch in the first decades of the eighteenth century.

The sequence of rapid expansion (*c.* 1560–1600), slower growth (*c.* 1600–60), no growth or decline (*c.* 1660–1700) and partial recovery (*c.* 1700–50) plainly follows a roughly parallel course to the broad national demographic contours recently mapped by Wrigley and Schofield. At the same time, the initial growth spurt in the numbers of barristers and attorneys was a good deal more intense than that of the population at large, which does not appear even to have doubled in size over the two hundred years 1550–1750, let alone during the first century 1550–1650.[32] So while part of the explanation for the proliferation of lawyers in early modern England must be found in the fact of overall demographic increase (and likewise the lag or decline thereafter), this is plainly not the whole story. Indeed we can hardly avoid the conclusion that for a century after 1560 demand for lawyers' services was rising considerably faster than the national population. Litigation is the lawyer's ultimate justification, and what has been termed 'a temporary explosion of civil litigation' coincides very noticeably with the Elizabethan boom in the numbers of attorneys and barristers.[33] Between 1490 and 1560 caseloads handled by the courts of Common Pleas and King's Bench more than doubled, from just over 2,000 to some 5,278 a year. During the next half-century the total rose again by a factor of four. By 1640 the two chief common law courts were together handling nearly 30,000 cases a year, although the fastest rate of increase occurred before 1606. Chancery business also rose sharply in Elizabeth's later years, falling off somewhat between the second and fourth decades of the seventeenth century.[34] We do not know how widely the boom spread beyond Westminster Hall. It is theoretically conceivable that the undoubted expansion of litigation at the centre merely reflected a massive redirection of business from church and local courts throughout the realm. Yet while there can be little doubt that most manorial and some borough jurisdictions were losing popularity with litigants, who showed an increasing preference for the London-based courts throughout this period, all the literary evidence and some key socio-economic trends, especially price inflation and a booming land market, point to a net overall rise in litigation.[35] The position after 1660 is at present less clear. Most evidence brought forward to date suggests some decline in the popularity of the central courts during the later seventeenth and early eighteenth centuries, but the dimensions and timing of this contraction have yet to be plotted with any precision.[36]

Be that as it may, although the Elizabethan–early Stuart litigation boom goes a long way towards accounting for the overall increase in lawyers' numbers during the century before 1650, a probable Westminster Hall recession in the following century did not prevent the numbers of attorneys rising substantially between the late 1690s and *c.* 1730 (even if this increase was in part a paper phenomenon resulting from the formal registration of practitioners who had had no previous affiliation with the central courts). Population decline or stagnation might partially explain the shrinkage of the later Stuart bar recently monitored by David Lemmings, who also found that the amount of business handled by barristers during this same period in virtually every major jurisdiction either dropped, sometimes quite precipitously, or else remained virtually static.[37] However, a further factor which cannot be ignored if we are to understand why some 10 per cent fewer men were being called and some 20 per cent fewer actually practised at the bar in the 1720s than the 1630s is the changing vocational balance between attorneys and barristers.

Once again, the precise timing and scale of this development are conjectural. But in the autobiography which he compiled towards the end of his life the barrister Roger North (1653–1734) noted as a 'vulgar observation, that the attorneys get ground of the long robe, as it is called, the reason of which is, the gown has derelicted the practice of forms, so that all is now left to them'. North's evident nostalgia for the days of his youth, when barristers routinely handled a good deal of straightforward non-contentious work, especially run-of-the-mill conveyancing and court keeping, was fully shared by his Middle Temple contemporary, the serjeant at law and antiquary Sir Henry Chauncy.[38] By retreating from everyday dealings with clients to the more rarefied sphere of courtroom advocacy, barristers were actually encouraging a decline in demand for their services. Why they should have followed this seemingly irrational course of action will be considered further below.

Among other factors which served to reduce the attractiveness of a career at the post-restoration bar were the steeply rising costs of qualifying for call, the proliferation of enticing career alternatives, especially in overseas trade, the burgeoning civil service and the armed forces, the economic squeeze experienced by many smaller landholders, together with a more realistic appreciation among potential entrants and their parents of the heavy odds against success in the lottery of the law.[39] Most of these disincentives would have had less deterrent effect on those contemplating the lower branch, where training was acquired mainly by apprenticeship and practical experience, and recruits were traditionally drawn in the main from a marginally lower social stratum than members of the bar.

Lawyers and the laity: division, differentiation and professionalisation

Despite its overwhelming importance in shaping the distinctive configuration of the modern English legal profession, the process by which a largely undifferentiated mass of common lawyers was transformed by the mid-eighteenth century into two clearly distinct 'branches', of barristers on the one hand and attorneys and solicitors on the other, has been surprisingly little studied. This may reflect an assumption that the division between upper and lower branches has existed more or less since legal practice first began in England. Yet while the offices or functions of common law attorney and advocate were indeed quite distinct by the end of the fifteenth century, no hard-and-fast institutional or social barrier then separated the persons who discharged them. The respective roles of serjeant and sworn attorney in the Court of Common Pleas were not interchangeable, but elsewhere both could and did advise clients, draft various categories of legal documents and plead at the bar (in the case of attorneys, at the side bars of the central courts and in lesser provincial jurisdictions). While the serjeants constituted a small exclusive elite, whereas the attorneys were much more numerous and on the whole less distinguished in terms of social origins or wealth, both classes of practitioner claimed to be 'learned in the law'; moreover attorneys, although clustered most thickly at the inns of chancery, were also to be found as members and even treasurers of the inns of court. The blurring of functions and status was still more pronounced between attorneys and apprentices at law, those advocates below the rank of serjeant who frequently practised as attorneys or solicitors in the early stages of their careers and continued thereafter to undertake a wide variety of general counselling for a heterogeneous clientele of country neighbours and kinsfolk.[40]

So how and why did it all change? The detailed chronology of differentiation at both local and national levels remains remarkably obscure. But from the middle of the sixteenth century the judges, the privy council and (rather less enthusiastically) the self-perpetuating oligarchies of senior lawyers who now governed the inns of court began to proclaim the exclusion of attorneys from these 'honourable societies' (as they were beginning to style themselves). At the same time there was a codification and tightening up of the conditions under which members could be called and practise as utter-barristers, the internal rank of membership now increasingly recognised as the minimum qualification for audience before the common law judges. These measures were accompanied and justified by much rhetorical insistence upon the necessity of maintaining good order and seemly proportion by distinguishing between the elevated functions and status of the counsellor at law, who stood next to the judges and serjeants in dispensing justice, and the 'attorneys and solicitors, which are but ministerial persons and of an inferior nature', in the words of a judge's order promulgated in 1614.[41]

This divisive policy does not seem to have been initiated as part of a conscious plan to better the competitive position of one set of lawyers at the expense of another. It was not, in other words, the first stage of a deliberate project of the kind which some sociologists believe all professions must undertake, in order to win control of their market by excluding any potential rival practitioners. But neither was it (as a still more influential sociological school would maintain) the natural outcome of a process of functional rationalisation, whereby new occupational specialisms proliferated in response to the changing requirements of an ever more complex and diverse society.[42] Although those who framed and sustained the policy of differentiation and segregation have not left behind any discussion of their motives, they appear to have harboured no desire whatever to adjust the existing job boundaries between barristers (or counsellors at law) and other practitioners. Their aim seems rather to have been to emphasise and widen the *status* gap, in line with a general trend throughout early modern England, not least in educational institutions, where it was reinforced by humanist prejudices against most kinds of social mobility and manual or non-bookish skills. Throughout the sixteenth century Sir Thomas Elyot, Thomas Starkey,

Richard Mulcaster and others argued that gentlemen by birth were best suited to practise law, a conviction which underlay James I's notorious edict of 1604 forbidding plebeians (that is, men who could not claim to be of gentle blood and birth) even to enrol at the four inns of court.[43]

So the initial division between that which Sir Edward Coke termed the '*officium ingenii*' (literally, noble-spirited or high-minded employment) of what would come to be known as the upper branch and the '*officium laboris*' of the lower was primarily one of status, not function. It had no obvious immediate effect on the readiness of barristers to undertake a broad range of non-contentious tasks under direct instructions from clients, even those barristers who insisted upon their resemblance to the noble jurists of classical Rome. Not until after 1650 do we find indications of a significant realignment of vocational spheres to match the social and institutional differentiation of attorneys and barristers, as the latter gradually relinquished general counselling and conveyancing to concentrate upon advocacy, taking their briefs from attorneys rather than dealing with clients face to face.

Why did this shift occur? Two main reasons suggest themselves. First, there were many more lawyers and a great many more attorneys available in the provinces by the mid-seventeenth century than had been the case at the beginning of Elizabeth's reign. In the three counties of Devon, Hertfordshire and Warwickshire studied by Christopher Brooks, the numbers of resident attorneys enrolled in Common Pleas and King's Bench virtually doubled in the twenty years after 1560 and doubled again by 1606.[44] Even if the presence of counsellors and other practitioners, especially the more amateur and part-time varieties, did not mushroom to a similar extent, most lawyers and clients were in any case prepared to travel across county boundaries in order to find one another. Lawyers also flourished in cities and market towns, almost certainly more conspicuous to contemporaries than to later historians. But as the attorneys colonised the shires, the barristers increasingly tended to cluster in and around London. Hence, according to Mathew Hale, writing in the 1660s or 1670s, one likely benefit from establishing a system of county courts would be that 'students and professors of the law, which are now generally driven or drawn up to London, so that there are scarce any left in the country, will have some encouragement to reside in the country, and the country not left to the management of attorneys and solicitors'.[45] While Hale perhaps exaggerated the extent of rural depopulation so far as barristers were concerned, the key point is his perception that the lower branch had come to dominate the provision of legal services at the grass roots.[46]

Was it then simply that attorneys increasingly outnumbered and undercut barristers at the local level, hence effectively driving them out of the general counselling and conveyancing business? While an element of market pressure must have been present, there is little indication that barristers generally resented the narrowing of their vocational sphere to advocacy and the provision of opinions on tricky points of law. The main reason for their complaisance, apart from the fact that the transition occurred in a gradual, piecemeal fashion, was almost certainly the huge inflation of fees at the bar from the 1650s onwards. Holmes and Lemmings have shown that the average scale of payment for advocacy rose perhaps fivefold between the late sixteenth century and Charles II's restoration, possibly doubling again between the 1680s and 1720s, a period when the general consumer price level remained virtually stagnant.[47] As the rewards received by the successful advocate rose so breathtakingly, while inflation slowed and the numbers of practising counsel dropped, it is little wonder that barristers tended to concentrate on developing their increasingly specialised Westminster Hall practices rather than attempting to compete with a still growing body of attorneys for the much less substantial sums received from drafting bonds, indentures, leases, wills and so forth. Their resolution may well have been strengthened by the contrasting images of barrister and attorney current from mid-Tudor times, which by emphasising the elevated, intellectual and even non-mercenary character of the barrister's calling made it possible to regard certain routine, 'mechanical' legal activities as incompatible with that high status. But it seems most unlikely that such cultural considerations would have prevailed alone without the changing market situation outlined above.

Most attorneys, for their part, accepted without demur or protest the relatively lowly role and status to which their social and vocational superiors now confined them. A few sought to demonstrate personal qualities of learning and respectability which would distinguish them from their less worthy colleagues, an urge which became more pronounced in the early eighteenth century and lay behind the foundation of the Society of Gentlemen Practisers, a precursor of the Victorian 'qualifying associations' which eventually came to control most professional and would-be professional occupations.[48] Their acquiescence must have been encouraged by the material benefits which accrued in the medium to long term; in any case, relations between bar and 'lower' branch were of necessity closer and more cordial on a private, informal, day-to-day basis than much public rhetoric might lead us to expect. Attorneys and solicitors were not finally excluded from membership of the inns of court until the nineteenth century; kinship ties as well as business dealings (especially the barristers' increasing dependence on briefs brought to them by the London-based attorneys who conducted litigation for country firms of attorneys and solicitors on an agency basis), and, perhaps, changing patterns of recruitment at both ends of the professional scale were powerful emollients.[49] There was also a common interest in squeezing out lay 'empirics', an aim supported with enthusiasm by at least some barristers, as is evident from a very successful handbook for manorial stewards first published by the Gray's Inn bencher John Kytchin in 1580, with a further eight editions over the next sixty years. Addressing the 'students de les measons del Chauncerie' in the learned language of his calling, Kytchin explained that his manual was intended for those of their number who already kept manorial courts very competently, in order to help them acquire 'plus science' and better understanding of 'the authorities in our books concerning matters adjudicable in those courts'. A further motivation, however, was the desirability of excluding landholders' servants and other amateurs from such important offices: 'For how can they dispense law who are ignorant of law?' Kytchin is not able to show how his book would actually help to achieve this end, rather than merely providing a handy source of reference for such 'ignorants persons, serving homes . . . queux ne professe ley, et queux ne sont de ascun meason del court ou chancery'. This may help explain his somewhat implausible closing assertion that courts kept by such persons were liable to forfeiture by writ of quo warranto.[50] Nevertheless, it does seem that in the late Elizabethan–early Stuart period manorial court-keeping was largely taken over by attorneys and barristers.

Despite Kytchin's contemptuous dismissal of lay persons who rashly ventured into the domain of the learned lawyer, early modern men and women seem often to have played a more active and decisive role in the transaction of their legal business than we would usually expect today. This reflected a very widespread acquaintance with the law's workings, which impinged so constantly on the daily life of so many that even the Book of Common Prayer found space to print the dates of the four secular law terms next to the calendar of holy days and church festivals. Moreover, because interactions between the main participants in legal transactions tended to be highly personalised, with relatively little distance separating judges, lawyers and litigants, clients had a strong incentive to involve themselves in both the grand strategy and day-to-day tactics of litigation. So Norfolk yeomen, for example, were said to carry their copies of Littleton's *Tenures* 'at the plough's tail', Star Chamber suits were conducted by the '"learned lay client" who not only retained his counsel directly but instructed him directly', while even an earl might 'apply his abilities much to the knowledge of the law'.[51]

The declining prominence of the 'learned lay client' during the second half of our period may be attributed to the greater availability of specialised, full-time legal practitioners in the provinces and the devaluation of legal knowledge as a fashionable accomplishment — evident in, among other things, a gradual winding down of 'non-professional' admissions to the inns of court and Wycherley's parody of the learned client as the absurd and unnatural Widow Blackacre in *The plain dealer* (1674). If clients were, on the whole, less able to take an assertive role in their dealings with lawyers, lawyers had good reason for increasing self-assurance, with even the lowly solicitor encouraged to regard himself as part of 'so weighty a profession', only to be undertaken by 'such as have sound discerning judgements and know what they are about'.[52] Barristers for their part were more and more sheltered by attorneys from direct dealings with clients, an arrangement which must have reinforced that neo-classical image of the common lawyer as disinterested and honourable counsellor which gained currency with the bar's expansion in wealth, size and influence during the later sixteenth and early seventeenth centuries.[53]

Conclusion

In 1750 no less than 1500, the legal world embraced a bewildering array of codes, courts, institutions and practitioners. But the scene is actually a good deal less complex and confused than it was at the beginning of our period. The canon lawyers had long disappeared altogether as a separate class, and the civilians are now little more than a dying race; the conciliar courts at Ludlow and York, as well as the courts of Requests, Star Chamber and Wards have all disappeared; the jurisdiction of the ecclesiastical courts is much contracted; Chancery has been effectively colonised and expropriated by the common lawyers, who now enjoy a virtual monopoly of profitable litigation in Westminster Hall; the common law itself has even discarded its barbarous medieval law-French.

By 1750 barristers enjoyed large measures of vocational autonomy and social prestige, while attorneys and solicitors were laying the groundwork for similar claims on their own behalf. Nevertheless, legal practice was not yet monopolised by full-time, 'professional' lawyers, and in some respects the professed lawyers of Hanoverian England were actually rather less 'professionalised' than their Tudor and early Stuart predecessors. The lower branch was certainly subject to a more rigorous external regulation, while members of the bar seem generally more conscious of being 'by their profession . . . the first class of gentlemen' than anxious to assert and defend the social importance and worth of their calling.[54] The decline of the corporate life and educational functions of the inns of court and chancery had left a vacuum not yet filled by other forms of professional association and academic provision. It might even be a mistake to attach overmuch importance in this context to the deepening of the division between upper and lower branches during our period. While doubtless an essential requirement for the emergence of the structure of the English legal profession as it exists today, recent pressures on the bar's monopolistic prerogatives suggest that this structural idiosyncracy may not survive indefinitely in its present form, or indeed at all.

Historians and sociologists have tended to assume that the medical, scientific and technological professions represent the norm, at least of 'modern' professions. But from the emergence of professional occupations in medieval times down virtually to the present day it has been the church first, and then the law, which offered the greatest opportunities of acquiring wealth and exercising power. Even today lawyers continue to be disproportionately prominent in public life, and indispensable in many private transactions. Although the foundations were laid well before, it was during the enormous transformations of the economy, government and the social order which marked the sixteenth and seventeenth centuries that the common lawyers first acquired their remarkable dominance, and thereby helped bring a new world into being.

Notes

Acknowledgements

I am most grateful to Christopher Brooks and Christine MacLeod for their incisive comments on an early draft of this essay.

1. For an extensive bibliography and comment, see the editors' introduction in D. Sugarman and G.R. Rubin (eds), *Law, economy and society: essays in the history of English law 1750–1914* (Abingdon, 1984).

2. J. H. Baker, *An introduction to English legal history* (1979), Chs. 2–3, 6–8, 10.

3. S. B. Chrimes (ed.), *De laudibus legum Angliae* (Cambridge, 1943), Ch. 17.

4. T. Ridley, *A view of the civile and ecclesiastical law* . . . (1607), p. 228.

5. B. P. Levack, *The civil lawyers in England 1603–1641* (Oxford, 1973); B. P. Levack, 'The English civilians, 1500–1700' in W.R. Prest (ed.), *Lawyers in early modern Europe and America* (1981), pp. 108–28; C. Kitching, 'The Prerogative Court of Canterbury from Warham to Whitgift' in R. O'Day and F. Heal (eds), *Continuity and change: personnel and administration in the Church of England 1500–1642* (Leicester, 1976), pp. 192, 204.

6. G. D. Squibb, *Doctors' Commons* (Oxford, 1977); W. R. Prest, *The inns of court under Elizabeth I and the early Stuarts, 1590–1640* (1972).

7. C. W. Brooks, *Pettyfoggers and vipers of the commonwealth: the 'lower branch' of the legal profession in early modern England* (Cambridge, 1986); see also below, pp. 91, 95.

8. W. H. Long, *The Oglander memoirs* (1884), p. 22; cf. R. Fenton, 'Tours in Wales', *Archaeologia Cambrensis* (1917), Supplement, p. 299, T. M., *The Sollicitor. Exactly and plainly declaring, both as to knowledge and practice, how such an undertaker ought to be qualified* (1663; first published 1643), p. 22.

9. Because men who undoubtedly did practise as lawyers are not invariably identified as such in tax assessment and other census-type

lists, or even their own wills, historians have consistently tended to underestimate their presence; it may be that the apparent urban invasion mounted by lawyers in post-restoration England reflects a more widespread use of professional occupational labels rather than (or as well as) a significant demographic change.

10. H. J. Carpenter, 'Furse of Moreshead', *Transactions of the Devonshire Association*, vol. 26 (1894), p. 174.

11. J. Smyth, *The lives of the Berkeleys* (Gloucester, 1883–5), vol. 2, pp. 310–12.

12. J. H. Baker, 'History of the gowns worn at the English bar', *Costume*, no. 9 (1975), pp. 15–16. W. Fennor, *The comptor's commonwealth* (1617), p. 44, and cf. T. Middleton, *Father Hubberd's tales* in *The works of Thomas Middleton*, ed. A. H. Bullen (8 vols., 1885–6), vol. 8, p. 85; *The miscellaneous works . . . of Sir Thomas Overbury*, ed. E. F. Rimbault (1856), p. 85; *'Merry passages and jeasts': a manuscript notebook of Sir Nicholas Le Strange 1603–1655*, ed. H. F. Lippincott (Salzburg, 1974), p. 36.

13. W. Sheppard, *The touchstone of common assurances* (1649), quoted in N. L. Matthews, *William Sheppard, Cromwell's law reformer* (Cambridge, 1984), p. 90; B. Abel-Smith and R. Stevens, *Lawyers and the courts* (1967), pp. 23–4. Close investigation of most early modern communities is likely to reveal several small-scale providers of local legal services, often related to each other. Thus in the Cornish parish of Week St Mary, Thomas Clifton was described as 'of Lyon's Inn, Middlesex', an inn of Chancery, in 1612, while his nephew John was clerk to George Evelyn, a Six Clerk in Chancery, and another nephew, Cornelius, drafted wills and conveyances for his neighbours. (I am grateful to my research student Stuart Raymond for this information.)

14. Brooks, *Pettyfoggers and vipers*, pp. 152–6; W. R. Prest, *The rise of the barristers* (Oxford, 1986), pp. 43–4.

15. E. W. Ives, *The common lawyers of pre-reformation England* (Cambridge, 1983), pp. 13–15.

16. Henry E. Huntington Library, Ellesmere MS 6477; see also below, pp. 165–6, 172–3.

17. J. H. Baker, 'The English legal profession, 1450–1550' in Prest, *Lawyers in early modern Europe and America*, p. 27; Brooks, *Pettyfoggers and vipers*, pp. 43, 46–7; R. Campbell, *The London tradesman* (1747), pp. 79, 82.

18. J. H. Baker, 'Sir Thomas Robinson (1618–83), Chief Prothonotary of the Common Pleas', *Bodleian Library Record*, vol. 10 (1978), pp. 27–40. G. E. Aylmer, *The King's servants: the civil service of Charles I, 1625–1642* (1961), pp. 44–57; Baker, 'English legal profession', pp. 21–4; Brooks, *Pettyfoggers and vipers*, pp. 12–16.

19. Brooks, *Pettyfoggers and vipers*, pp. 21–4, 126, 129–31.

20. G. Holmes, *Augustan England: professions, state and society, 1680–1730* (1982), pp. 19–20.

21. T. Wilson, 'The state of England anno dom. 1600', ed. F. J. Fisher, *Camden Miscellany*, vol. 16 (1936), p. 25.

22. [An Attorney], *Proposals humbly offer'd to the Parliament, for*

remedying the great charge and delay of suits at law, and in equity (1707), p. 31; Anon., *Animadversions upon the present laws of England* (1750), p. 25.

23. W. A. Cole, *A rod for the lawyers* (1659), p. 8.

24. G. Holmes, 'Gregory King and the social structure of pre-industrial England', *Trans. Roy. Hist. Soc.*, 5th ser., vol. 27 (1977), pp. 41–68; Holmes, *Augustan England*, pp. 19–21, 154; P. Mathias, 'The social structure in the eighteenth century: a calculation by Joseph Massie', *Econ. Hist. Rev.*, 2nd ser., vol. 10 (1957–8), p. 37; J. Thirsk and J.P. Cooper (eds), *Seventeenth-century economic documents* (Oxford, 1972), p. 769.

25. Public Record Office, SP16/248/53; Brooks, *Pettyfoggers and vipers*, pp. 112–13.

26. HMC, *Ninth report*, pt. II, p. 20, and *House of Lords (new series)*, vol. 3, pp. 81–7. Cf. Anon., *Enchiridion legum* (1673), pp. 130–1.

27. Holmes, *Augustan England*, pp. 150–4.

28. Prest, *Rise of the barristers*, pp. 5–6, 327–8.

29. D. Lemmings, 'The inns of court and the English bar, 1680–1730', unpublished D Phil thesis, Oxford University, 1985, pp. 103, 119–21. I am grateful to Dr Lemmings for allowing me to consult and refer to this important thesis.

30. Ibid., pp. 105, 200.

31. Levack, 'English civilians', pp. 109–10.

32. E.A. Wrigley and R.S. Schofield, *The population history of England, 1541–1871: a reconstruction* (1981), pp. 208–9.

33. L. Stone, 'The history of violence in England: a rejoinder', *P & P*, no. 108 (1985), p. 219.

34. Brooks, *Pettyfoggers and vipers*, pp. 50–2 and Ch. 4, *passim*.

35. Ibid., pp. 96–101. R. Houlbrooke, 'The decline of ecclesiastical jurisdiction under the Tudors', in O'Day and Heal, *Continuity and change*, pp. 245–6, 253–7.

36. Stone, 'History of violence', p. 220; Prest, 'The English bar', p. 77 and sources there cited.

37. Lemmings, 'English bar, 1680–1730', pp. 373–88.

38. *The lives of the Norths*, ed. A. Jessop (3 vols, 1890), vol. 3, p. 139; H. Chauncy, *Historical antiquities of Hertfordshire* (2 vols., 1699), vol. 2, p. 435.

39. Prest, 'English bar', pp. 77–8.

40. J. H. Baker, 'Counsellors and barristers: an historical study', *Cambridge Law Journal*, vol. 27 (1969), pp. 205–29; J. H. Baker, 'The English legal profession, 1450–1550', pp. 17–18, 25–6.

41. A. W. B. Simpson, 'The early constitution of the inns of court', *Cambridge Law Journal*, vol. 28 (1970), pp. 241–56; Prest, *Inns of court*, pp. 12–27, 41–3; W. Dugdale, *Origines juridiciales* (1666), p. 317.

42. Cf. M. S. Larson, *The rise of professionalism: a sociological analysis* (Berkeley, 1977), Chs. 4–5; T. Parsons, 'Professions' in D. Sills (ed.), *International encyclopaedia of the social sciences* (1968), vol. 12, pp. 536–47.

43. P. Lucas, 'Blackstone and the reform of the legal profession', *English Historical Review*, vol. 77 (1962), pp. 467–73. Cf. J. P. Cooper, 'Ideas of gentility in early modern England' in *Land, men and beliefs*,

ed. G. E. Aylmer and J. S. Morrill (1983), pp. 54–66.

44. Brooks, *Pettyfoggers and vipers*, pp. 112–13.

45. M. Hale, 'Considerations touching the amendment or alteration of lawes' in F. Hargrave (ed.), *A collection of tracts relative to the law of England* (1787), p. 284.

46. Cf. Brooks, *Pettyfoggers and vipers*, pp. 112–15.

47. Holmes, *Augustan England*, pp. 126–32; Lemmings, 'English bar', pp. 231–7.

48. M. Miles, '"Eminent attorneys": some aspects of West Riding attorneyship *c.* 1750–1800', unpublished PhD thesis, University of Birmingham (1982), p. 23, notes that attorneys themselves were the most prolific eighteenth-century critics of sharp practices in the lower branch.

49. Cf. Miles, '"Eminent attorneys"', pp. 43–56; D. Duman, 'The English bar in the Georgian era' in W. Prest (ed.), *Lawyers in early modern Europe and America* (1981), pp. 90–5.

50. *Le Court leete & Court Baron collect par John Kitchin de Graies inne un apprentice in ley* (1587; first published 1580), sigs. Aii v–Aiii.

51. *The boke of common prayer* (1559), sig. Bii v ('A brief declaration when every term beginneth and endeth'). R. W. Ketton-Cremer, *Norfolk in the civil war* (1969), pp. 20–1; T. G. Barnes, 'Star Chamber litigants and their counsel, 1596–1641' in J. H. Baker (ed.), *Legal records and the historian* (1978), p. 23; L'Estrange, '*Merry passages and jeasts*', p. 142, Cf. C. Holmes, 'Drainers and fenmen' in A. Fletcher and J. Stevenson (eds), *Order and disorder in early modern England* (Cambridge, 1985), pp. 186–95. The nature and extent of popular legal knowledge would be well worth investigating.

52. T. Clay, *A chorologicall discourse . . .* (1619), p. 4.

53. Baker, 'Counsellors and barristers', pp. 226–9. For literary images and stereotypes of common lawyers, see E. F. G. Tucker, *Intruder into Eden* (Columbus, Md., 1984).

54. R. Campbell, *The London tradesman* (1747), p. 76.

4

Medical Practice in Early Modern England: Trade or Profession?

Margaret Pelling

The success of the medical practitioner in recent times has done much to arouse and inform the professionalisation debate. Medicine's apparently unique combination of cognitive and ethical values has given ample scope for discussion, and it is medicine which provides the most striking contrasts in historiography. Positivist and conspiratorial interpretations of professionalisation alike see the modern medical practitioner as a powerful figure in society, thrown up by changes associated with industrialisation or urbanisation. Both sides have inherited terms of debate from nineteenth-century struggles and discussions, and the nineteenth century is still regarded as the main period of transition. Part of the fascination with medicine lies in the late and dramatic change from comparatively humble origins. The exact point at which scientific knowledge became effective in medicine now tends to be placed at the end of the nineteenth century or later. However, even where growth of knowledge and/or competence is not seen as in itself conferring professional status, attention is given to the cultural or non-technical value of knowledge in achieving social legitimacy and independence for marginal groups within the nascent nineteenth-century profession.[1] More perceptive analysts have raised the possibility that professionalism represents an ideal, rather than reality, in all historical situations, including the present day.[2] In this essay I hope to show that a broader approach to medicine in the early modern period reveals continuities which both enlarge the discussion as a whole and point to areas of neglect which have relevance to more recent periods in which professionalisation can be better defended as a full interpretation of historical events. Definitions of professionalisation are still remarkably exclusive. Their lack of historical value with respect to the whole occupation of medicine is simply more striking for the early modern period; it is not that they are unproblematic with respect to later contexts.

It is not surprising that medicine as a profession in the early modern period has received relatively little attention. A few have been confident: Bullough's reason for terminating his book with the sixteenth century was that 'medicine was recognised as a profession' by that time.[3] Most such claims have been made on the basis of the overriding importance of tiny elites, usually physicians, but occasionally (as in the recent work of Gottfried for the fifteenth century) surgeons.[4] In some cases the numbers involved hardly exceed single figures. Clark's supremely confident justification of the (Royal) College of Physicians was compatible with the view of physicians adopted by Raach, but predicated on an even greater degree of selection.[5] The physicians gained in importance through being seen as the top of a pyramid otherwise composed of (barber-) surgeons and apothecaries; little doubt is felt about their position, while that of the latter two of the 'three orders' of practice is more uncertain. The tripartite division of medicine into physicians, surgeons and apothecaries derives from modes of organisation developed on the Continent. Such a division appears to some to support two related criteria of professionalisation–specialism and the division of labour. That it was effectively observed in England at some time continues to be implied, even though this traditional phase of development becomes increasingly hard to locate chronologically as more detailed studies are made of different periods.[6]

The significance of small groups is increased by reference to their institutional context. Bullough made all professional organisation in European medicine dependent upon the evolution of medical faculties in the universities, even while admitting that the latter were crucial only in Italy, France and England. The College of Physicians of London continues to attract attention as an institution, while Gottfried, writing of the period before its foundation, has made rather less defensible claims for the connections of medical men with fifteenth-century hospitals.[7] This stress on institutions means that discussion has had to be limited to urban centres, but there is no sign of reluctance on this point, in spite of Raach's stress on the presence of qualified medical men in country areas.[8] The existence of local forms of control of medical activity (including civic control) has hardly been admitted by recent writers; only pretensions at the national level, such as those of the College of Physicians, are seen as significant, however unsuccessful. The same selected institutions have also been made to serve the function of providing suitably lengthy training, and of dividing the professional from the layman in terms of knowledge and experience. Apprenticeship is not seen as serving these purposes. Obsolescence is said to be built into this mode of transmission of knowledge, but not into textbook-based instruction.[9]

It is important to stress the degree to which the historiography of medicine — and thus of the professions — has followed, for the early modern period, lines of interpretation established by nineteenth-century apologists and antiquarians.[10] The chosen few memorialised in Munk's *Roll* of the Royal College of Physicians are presented from the first fellow to the last as literary gentlemen. Munk also found it fitting that he could say little of the actual practice of his subjects. He asserted not only a norm of social status, but a legitimacy based on the private transactions between patient and practitioner, which were of necessity hidden from public view. *Public* statements were made through *publications*, literary or scientific. Yet, private transactions may not have been a major part of medicine in the early modern period, although they are assumed to be integral, not only to the forms of authority now enjoyed by the medical profession, but also to the face-to-face, 'patronage' relations said to be characteristic of medicine before 1800.[11]

Other nineteenth-century writers exaggerated the credulity and eccentric behaviour of earlier practitioners in order to distance the educated or scientific medical man from superstitious practices; and perhaps, also, to justify his sometimes notorious lack of religion. Past raffishness was contrasted with present ideals of propriety. Some painted a picture of the lowly barber or apothecary of earlier periods in order to contest the claims of rival groups within the nineteenth-century profession. Whatever the trend towards uniformity in the nineteenth century, the level of internecine warfare was very high. Other writers, who, like the nineteenth-century antiquarians, were aware of how many remnants of the sixteenth and seventeenth centuries their own period had swept away, saw earlier craftsman ancestors more romantically but impossibly far away in the past.[12] By and large later commentators have followed these leads and emphasised the novelty and uniqueness of the nineteenth century with respect to medicine. Thus, we are told, before 1800 or the onset of industrialisation (often kept vague as to exact timing), most of the population depended on a ragbag of lesser and lay expedients. The university-trained physician was learned, but may not have practised much, and then almost exclusively among the elite. He had an immense scarcity value, but at the same time demand for his services was low, and medicine consequently of little importance in economic terms. Professional autonomy was out of reach even of the qualified practitioner, because he was subject to lay and local control within the patronage relationship.[13]

Holmes's recent work set itself to break this mould by boldly shifting the chronology of professional development back as early as 1680, with particular reference to the medical profession.[14] Claims are made not simply for a small elite of medical men but for a substantial and uniform body serving the needs of a large and prosperous proportion of the population. In Holmes's golden age, the links connecting professionalisation with industrialisation, though not with urbanisation, are broken. However, Holmes's interpretation is none the less an extrapolation backwards, locating in the eighteenth century the middle-class intellectual and economic vigour which nineteenth-century writers saw as belonging to their own age. (Similarly, but even more radically, Gottfried makes a claim for medicine as part of the rising middle class more than two centuries earlier.[15]) Holmes's framework is also notable for a reassertion of the distinction between works of brain and hand reminiscent both of Clark's history and of Victorian ambitions for medicine.

The failure until recently to explore medicine in the earlier period on its own terms has had a number of identifiable effects. First, and perhaps most importantly, by far the larger part of medical activity remains undescribed, at least for England. Secondly, there is a disguising of the elements of continuity before and after 1800, so that the modern profession comes to approximate to the 'ideal'. Thirdly, there is persistent understating of the connections between medicine and other economic and social activity. This defect is also carried through until the present day. The 'medical market', for example, is drastically and artificially limited to transactions involving qualified practitioners. Fourthly, in order to provide a contrast with middle-class solidarity and professional uniformity (whether of the nineteenth century or after 1680), medicine in the earlier period is made to look like a series of battlegrounds, largely lacking in standards or centralised control, and yet at the same time over-rigidly stratified into the three parts of practice represented by apothecaries, surgeons and physicians.[16] Those writers for whom professional values exist before professional development can be identified find them then in the guardianship of tiny elites. Other important effects have tended to follow from this depreciation of the earlier period: for example, civic control of medicine has been disregarded; and conflicting accounts have been given of apprenticeship and of specialism. The growth of specialism is seen as a sign of increasing knowledge and professional maturity, but the resistance to this development has until recently received scant attention, and its existence in practice in the earlier period is regarded as an aspect of quackery.

We have already seen that writers on the earlier period lay stress on institutional developments. This reflects the fact that the focus for many points of definition of medicine post-1800 is the institution, and in particular the hospital.[17] Professions are also seen as communities, and doubt has been expressed whether even modern medicine would appear as a community outside the institutional context.[18] In a more whole-hearted return to traditional views Holmes has seen the voluntary hospital movement of the eighteenth century as generating 'intimacy', co-operation and unity among previously divided callings.[19] This interpretation seems open to considerable reservations, as the hospital movement itself had many divisions, and was under lay control until a late date; the hospital has also been the means of consolidating elite privileges within the profession.[20] But the importance of institutions, thrown back on the earlier period, has caused much medical practice, including the relief of the poor, to become invisible, since it took place largely outside them, and even out of sight of the qualified medical practitioner. As already suggested in the context of the 'medical market', it is not clear how historically useful a definition can be which excludes so much relevant activity. The excluded areas involve qualified as well as unqualified practitioners, especially the common round of provincial practice, and the long-standing arrangements whereby some access to qualified practitioners was given to patients in receipt of poor relief. The neglect of the sick after the Reformation likewise has been inferred principally from the loss of provision of bricks and mortar.[21]

As we have already seen, selected institutions of the early modern period and before are made by some authors to carry a considerable burden of interpretation. The reality of the tripartite division of medicine in England depends on the universal significance of certain well-known developments in the institutionalisation of medicine in London: the foundation of the College of Physicians (not 'Royal' until the late seventeenth century) in 1518; the merging of the Barbers' Company with the tiny elite of the Surgeons in 1540; and the splitting off of the Apothecaries from the Grocers' Company in 1617.[22] Older writers, more sympathetic to the guilds, noted the extensive organisation of barber-surgeons' and apothecaries' companies in the provinces, and the numerical strength of the Barbers' Company in London.[23] Later occupational analysis, based largely on formal records such as freeman's rolls, has revealed as a by-product that barbers appear among the twelve leading trades in important towns such as Coventry, Chester and Bristol.[24] The apothecaries, though fewer in number and usually in combinant guilds, were commonly further up the civic hierarchy than barber-surgeons in the early modern period, yet this status is disregarded in accounts of their rise from humble origins to become the 'general practitioners' of the late eighteenth century. Where apothecaries are given higher status for the earlier period, this is by virtue of their connections with medicine and particularly with physicians, rather than because of their equality with goldsmiths and mercers.[25] In a kind of bastard remnant of this situation, apothecaries can be given precedence above surgeons in the medical hierarchy simply because non-manual trade is assumed to be of higher status than any manual craft.

In the nineteenth century, the guilds were idealised primarily in order to prove either that they were or that they were not precursors of trade unions.[26] More recent commentators have stressed the decline of the guilds as an acceptable face of the 'rise of capitalism' hypothesis, and have adopted a similar line in distinguishing the professions as of higher status than the crafts, possessing an ideal of service, and exclusive of occupations purely commercial, agricultural and mechanical. From this point of view, the only organisational institution of importance in the early modern period was the College of Physicians.[27] The guilds are also bypassed by those who have seen the origins of the ethics of professionalism in the post-Reformation work ethic.[28] This view has the advantage of drawing attention to major social and religious changes,and is at least preferable to the interpretation which sees the qualified medical practitioner before 1800 as a mere appendage of the landed elite. The notion of (some) physicians as feudal lackeys has its attractions, but, as well as concentrating on a small minority, it leaves out of account a vast range of social and economic fluctuations, notably the early development of socio-economic independence of towns. By implication it supposes a uniform persistence of an ill-defined 'traditional' form of society up until the major upheavals of eighteenth-century industrialisation.

The views just noted seem to take too little account of the social and ethical traditions of the craft and mercantile guilds. The relevance of the guild tradition even for the physicians is recognised by Clark in a backhanded way in discussing the possible models for the foundation of the College. Clark was concerned to stress that the College, a pre-Reformation body, had a distinctive character which was related to the role of the profession as a 'beneficent and civilising force'. After describing the rules under which physicians were required to renounce personal gain in the public interest, Clark notes that 'up to a point, no doubt they are generally the same as the rules of the fraternities or companies of craftsmen and traders; but, if we consider how much of human good or ill hinged upon them, we see that they stood on an altogether different, a much higher, plane'. The weakness of this is apparent, the more so as the two new bodies which Clark found most similar in England to the College were Doctors' Commons and the College of Arms, neither of which had the high ethical pretensions he ascribed to the College of Physicians.[29]

Clark also underestimates the presence of physicians in urban craft companies, going so far as to say that 'there seems to be no clear case in Tudor England of a boy or youth bound by indentures to a master to serve him and to learn the mystery of physic'.[30] The formal presence of physicians in civic life at this period is certainly minor, as their numbers were small compared with other medical groups, but it is underrepresented in most official sources to a degree for which Clark does not allow. Even on the formal level, physicians were included in medical guilds in Bristol, Norwich, York and Canterbury. At a later date in York it was assumed that outsiders practising physic and surgery in the city would be contributory to the barbers' guild.[31] With respect to apprenticeship, by this time a proportion of many occupations, including the medical crafts, were working without being apprenticed, made free, or ever having an apprentice of their own, so that it is less remarkable to find no such records in the case of physicians. However, one example which could be quoted against Clark's statement is that of John Potell of Leicester, physician and apothecary, whose apprentice was made a free man in 1594. It was relatively common at this period for a craftsman to be indentured to learn more than one craft, so this feature of the Potell instance is not sufficient to disqualify it.[32]

Inconsistent views have been taken of apprenticeship, reflecting its later history of social devaluation. Ironically, in view of Clark's comments, apprenticeship of an increasingly formal kind was to become an important part of medical education in the nineteenth century. In this context as well, it is necessary to break out of the inherited framework of Victorian social distinctions. Clark's view here may be contrasted with that of Holmes, who is otherwise often reminiscent of Clark: Holmes sees apprenticeship as providing in the eighteenth century an inexpensive uniform education without recourse to the universities.[33] It should be noted that in the sixteenth century at Cambridge, as at Oxford in the eighteenth century, students of medicine practised outside the university under the guidance of an experienced physician; the assistants of physicians often set up practice on their own account; and famous practitioners like Richard Napier attracted pupils eager to learn their special skills. In the mid-seventeenth century, Thomas Sydenham, whose systematic practical writings and example did much to revive the reputation of physicians, recommended apprenticeships in physic to the exclusion of any attendance at universities, and acted on this principle in his own career.[34]

Although enormous changes had taken place in the guilds

since the high middle ages, the trades were not further from the guilds in the sixteenth century than the term 'profession' was from its religious context. The guilds showed many of the features thought to be definitive of the professions: for example, they specialised, they were self-regulating, they were recognised by both the public and by authority, and they were the source of criteria of qualification. Two features which the craft companies were careful to take over in the sixteenth century were the requirement of confidentiality about the secrets of the craft and the company's affairs, and the regulation within the company of disputes among members. Company members were usually forbidden to resort to law without first bringing their case before senior officials of the company. This internal regulation covered a very wide range, from personal behaviour to serious disputes, and is an under-estimated factor among the forces in early modern society directed at controlling the behaviour of the male sex in particular.[35]

The guild's sense of responsibility towards the public was expressed in its supervision of standards of production and the signs by which the craftsman declared his qualification to the public: his distinctive dress and accessories, his shop sign and his shop window. These traditional methods of control were those which the College of Physicians sought to impose on the apothecaries of London. The College has been given credit for its pursuit of incompetent practitioners, but this activity was routine in other occupations, and it could also be argued that the College was primarily concerned to eliminate competition.[36] It is important to stress the generality of the guilds' codes of conduct because such standards are often implied to be peculiar to the select institutions of medicine. It could be suggested that the oaths which continued to be taken within the guild or company context have been far more a living part even of medicine in England than the Hippocratic oath, itself a memorial to the compatibility of religious, philosophical and craft principles.[37] Clark's dismissal of the guilds and companies also ignores the extent to which the regulation of crafts and trades, especially but not only the food trades, was concerned with public health as an aspect of the public interest. This regulation was exerted internally as well as by municipal authorities.[38] With respect to health and medicine it is likely to have done more for the protection of the consumer than any university training, however lengthy. The role of guilds and municipal authorities has been diminished by the assumption that effective control of standards can be maintained only within the professional peer group as organised on a national basis independently of all forms of local authority.[39]

As an institution, the London College undoubtedly (although perhaps tautologically) comes closest to the criteria selected by modern commentators as defining a profession. As we have seen, however, it was not uniquely endowed with a sense of moral responsibility about its activities. Other features of the College, which suit modern definitions, actually militated against its success in modern terms. There is nothing to suggest that its members were any more full-time than any other practitioner of the period; but with respect to autonomy the College seemed to achieve a good deal. Its strongest obligations seem to have been to the crown; its relations even with the universities were limited and often negative, and it was not subordinated to the City authorities. On the other hand, this degree of autonomy often worked out in practice as a weakness rather than a strength, and the College certainly failed to achieve the public recognition and control over the practice of physic on which the analysts of the professions insist. The continued viability of the guilds as companies is instanced by the greater degree of integration into civic life of the London Barber-Surgeons as compared with the College.[40]

There are major features of medicine in the early modern period which seem to point to the value of shifting the emphasis away from the conventional definition of a profession as a full-time, autonomous activity, and towards other crafts, trades and occupations. As we have seen, the tendency in the past has been to take the claims of certain minorities at their own valuation. Raach looked beyond London institutions and revealed the high incidence of academically qualified physicians even in small rural centres. This is confirmed by, for example, the finding that more than half of sixteenth-century medical graduates of Cambridge, and a larger proportion of the licentiates and unlicensed practitioners from the university, settled in the provinces.[41] However, it is not clear that this is definitive of professional activity when many such graduates may have practised only sporadically. Much has been gained historically by taking Raach's quantitative approach further, to make an assessment of the occupation of medicine as a whole. This has involved the adoption of a generic category of 'medical practitioner' in place of the conventional tripartite distinctions, and the inclusion in this category of any individuals recognised by their contemporaries as involved in the care of the sick. Behind this approach lies the assumption that 'any balanced view of medicine in the early modern period, or in non-western societies, must take into account all practitioners involved in dispensing medical care'. The inclusive view is also justified on the grounds of the lack of historical justification for most criteria of selection:

> the difficulties involved in framing consistent and historically fruitful criteria for isolating responsible medical practitioners from empirics and quacks have often not been fully appreciated. Terms such as empiric tend to be used without consistency or sound historical justification. Adoption of technical criteria for the isolation of empirics based on the legal code, professional attachments, or educational attainment is practicable, but it tends to generate a trivial and unrealistically narrow conception of legitimate medical practice. Reference to more meaningful criteria related to professional efficiency, reliability and responsibility, or the ideal of service rather than pecuniary gain, is difficult to operate because of lack of evidence, but if applied objectively it is likely to reinforce the use of a broader rather than narrower conception of responsible medical practice.

Even if fairly strict criteria are adopted, a high ratio of practitioners to population emerges. An estimate for London in the late sixteenth century, which is consistent with estimates of later date, leads to a ratio of at least 1:400. This body of *c.* 500 practitioners comprised: 50 fellows, candidates and licentiates of the Physicians' College; 100 members of the Barber-Surgeons' Company, including those prosecuted by the College; 100 apothecaries, some of them also the subject of prosecutions; and 250 practitioners (of all descriptions but excluding midwives and nurses) lying outside the London institutions except for the possession of licences. At the parish level, where occupational realities are often best reflected, a single London parish at the same period contained a barber-surgeon of some repute; a grocer free of the Barber-Surgeons' Company; two unlicensed and one immigrant practitioner; a 'professor of physic and other curious arts', and a poor man who also professed physic; and a woman 'counterfeit' physician and surgeon.[42] A similar quantitative approach applied to Norwich over the period 1550–1640 revealed a group of 150 physicians, barber-surgeons, surgeons, lithotomists and bonesetters, all of whom had some formal connection with the barber-surgeons' company of the city; and an additional group of 120, apparently lacking any such connection, which included physicians, women practitioners, immigrant practitioners, midwives, clerical practitioners, practising schoolmasters, and keepers of poor-houses (male and female) who practised medicine. Even though the apothecaries were excluded, this more exhaustive assessment produced an even higher ratio of practitioners to population. That the present estimates are minimal rather than over-high is indicated by the fact that many of the practitioners have been identified by their being prosecuted for unlicensed practice, by the College or by the ecclesiastical authorities. Other evidence suggests strongly that prosecution by either authority was far from exhaustive. These estimates have led to the conclusion that medicine was a much more significant occupation in the early modern period, both economically and culturally, than previous analysis had suggested.[43]

What was there for so many practitioners to do? There seem to be a number of answers to this question. Perhaps most importantly, all the evidence suggests that the 'patient' in the early modern period was extremely 'active', being critical, sceptical and well informed to a degree not anticipated in analysis of the professions, except in the extremely limited context of the pre-professional patronage relationship. This latter phenomenon is assumed to go with low demand. However, it seems clear that the critical consumer of the early modern period absorbed enormous quantities of medical care, of all kinds, and that this consumption probably increased at crisis periods such as the later sixteenth and early seventeenth centuries, just as the consumption of similar consolations such as alcohol also increased.[44] Poverty did not inhibit the consumption of certain forms of medicine at least; in periods of economic crisis, loss of health or mobility was more threatening than ever. Not only was a scale of payment generally adopted, from pennies and payment in kind, to high fees; there is some evidence to suggest that high fees failed to deter many patients, and that municipalities and parishes regarded medical expenses as being as legitimate an object of charity as losses by fire, or shipwreck.[45] Poverty could also be a justification for practising medicine, and presumably could be depended upon to alleviate it, like the granting of alehouse licences. One example was Adrian Colman, the widow of a practitioner of physic, who was licensed at Whitehall in 1596 to practise on women and children in Norfolk, because she had no other means of support.[46] Clerics also pleaded poverty as an excuse for practising medicine. Poverty could thus increase both supply and demand. At the same time, by 1600 medical care was already an aspect of consumption in towns like Norwich and York, which early became centres for professional and social life.[47] Holmes attributes the 'rise of the doctor' in the early eighteenth century to increased middle-class prosperity, with a generalised tendency for towns to become service centres.[48] This argument has previously been applied to the nineteenth century, with a shift from patronage to commodity relations associated with industrialisation. As already suggested, this argument has not been precisely articulated in historical terms, and tends to be based on minorities. Here it should be stressed that prosperity was not the only engine either of consumption or of the proliferation of medical practice.

This phenomenon of high but fluctuating consumption is complemented by a characteristic which probably applies to a wide range of other occupational groups, and which may not be irrelevant to later periods when the professions seem firmly established. Both formally and informally a great many medical practitioners either practised medicine part-time or combined it with a range of associated activities.[49] This was a feature of urban as well as of rural life. Barber-surgeons traditionally diversified into tallowchandling, knitting, netmaking and wigmaking; in towns dominated by the textile trades they also engaged in these in a minor level. Particularly strong and widespread was their involvement in music, which was one aspect of the social and public context represented by the shops of barbers and barber-surgeons. The latter offered a range of personal services which, in sophisticated urban environments, led to a natural intermingling with other tradesmen concerned with dress and adornment, such as dyers and perfumers. As well as their traditional diversifications medical practitioners showed themselves highly responsive to new economic opportunities. Among these, in the seventeenth century, were the manufacture of small consumer goods relating primarily to dress and accessories, the selling of tobacco, and distilling. An enterprising surgeon of the early seventeenth century was William White of Midhurst, Sussex, a small centre near Chichester. White possessed a wide range of surgical instruments but also barber's gear, distilling equipment, apothecary drugs, a considerable library of books, a stock of wine, and tobacco. The alertness of the apothecaries to new botanical discoveries and the growth in imported drugs is well known.[50] Barber-surgeons and physicians as well as apothecaries were involved in distilling of various kinds. Such flexibility could be formal: a citizen waxchandler around 1660 could accept an apprentice in 'the several arts of chirurgery and distillation'. When distilling reached the level of an industrial process, thus prompting attempts to monopolise it under the sponsorship of the crown, objections were heard from the barber-surgeons as well as the apothecaries and the vintners. Distilling related to the production of new drugs as well as strong liquors.[51] The association of medical practitioners with alcohol took many forms, and involved all kinds of practitioner. For Holmes, on the other hand, convinced of the difference between 'patient' and 'customer', the provision of alcohol by a practitioner after bloodletting around 1730 is simply a quaint relic of the 'curious hybrid' of barbery and surgery.[52]

Practitioners of physic diversified as well as surgeons and barber-surgeons. At one extreme there is the 'professor' of physic of London already mentioned who also practised 'other curious arts'; at the other is the well-known tendency of schoolmasters and clerics also to be physicians. Scriveners and physicians enjoyed close relations, and were sometimes (as with surgeons) combined in one person, possibly because of the congruence of skills and occasions.[53] In the country, John Crophill could be both bailiff and medical man.[54] Also striking as a characteristic of response to economic opportunities is the involvement of practitioners in the Muscovy Company, which was founded in an attempt to dominate trade with Russia in the mid-sixteenth century. Physicians as well as surgeons and even midwives formed part of the diplomatic commerce between

England and Russia, and many of these took the opportunity to engage in trade, one leading example being Arthur Dee, the son of the astrologer John Dee.[55]

Medical practice in early modern England was neither well organised nor firmly controlled; no system of surveillance had more than a partial application. The tripartite structure more strictly adopted on the Continent remained the aim of minority groups. This kind of flexibility is compatible with the occupational flexibility just described, which seems entirely at odds with the full-time, self-sufficient, life-long commitment characteristic of the professional as usually defined. For Bullough, full-time dedication had to be the inevitable consequence of the protracted training in medicine developed by the medieval universities, but neither the training nor its aftermath was necessarily so specific. Where occupational diversity in medicine has been recognised, it has been assumed to signify simply low status, low demand for qualified practice, poverty, and other features outside the professional pale, including too great a degree of integration into local communities.[56] To put it into metaphorical terms, explored in more detail elsewhere: medical historians who have tended to favour what might be called a Linnaean classification of medical practitioners into fixed, clearly defined species, see any merging or mingling as unnatural and something to be resisted.[57] Historians of the professions are perhaps closer to a kind of vulgar Darwinism in seeing the professions as a highly evolved but rare species, extremely successful (according to certain criteria) but peculiar to a specialised environment. Historians of occupations in general have the advantage of being interested in a wider range of organisms but have in some respects a similarly Darwinian point of view. They see different species evolving, dominating, or becoming extinct according to changes in the habitat, whether natural or artificial. The picture of a large but versatile occupational population defined by part-time activity and intimate relations with other social and economic areas suggests instead a more Lamarckian situation in which specific differences may be arbitrary or temporary, and which allows adaptation to environmental pressures, favourable or unfavourable.

We have already seen that early modern medical practitioners were involved in the drink trades at various levels. In selling drink in alehouses and tippling houses they were inevitably also involved in the food trade.[58] In addition, strong drinks were often flavoured with grocery items like dates and raisins, and these and similar food items were also indistinguishably part of an apothecary's goods.[59] Another connection is that both the food and drink trades and medicine were notable as employments of women.[60] Apart from the actual difficulty of telling the difference between food and medicines, there are many parallels on both the material and the spiritual planes, which reflect on the nature of medicine as a transaction.[61] On the more profane side, each can be seen as an item of consumption, a daily necessity which could be bought in the market place and publicly consumed. The range of diversions — food, music, drink, tobacco, games, conversation, news and displays of curiositites — which could be found in the shops of early modern medical practitioners was undoubtedly deployed to attract as well as to divert their clientele. The range of activities which could be encompassed in the shop of a medical practitioner has been obscured by nineteenth-century commentators who were thinking primarily in terms of emancipating the practitioner from the retailing of drugs. Thus the connection has been effectively severed between the shop of the earlier period and the 'surgery' of the modern general practitioner, which, as in the former case, was almost always part of the practitioner's own house.[62]

The range of provision within shops also draws attention to the delivery of medicine at this period as a public rather than private act. Mountebanks and itinerants obviously sold their cures in public places, and in an urban context especially the practitioner's shop could be a place of resort, but even at home the patient and the practitioner were unlikely to be alone together. Many consultations took place by proxy, a reflection of the kind of services offered, but also of the important role played by the patient's friends or relatives. The stress on privacy and confidentiality can be seen as an aspect of later phases of social differentiation, although persistent restrictions on the examination of patient's bodies may owe less to Victorian prudery than the continued presence during the consultation of other people, including friends and servants, overlapping with changes in attitudes to the body. The face-to-face but unequal contact posited as characteristic of the patronage relationship in medicine before 1800 emerges as too limited a description of contact with practitioners on a number of counts.[63]

On the less profane side, medicine, again like food or drink, could be and often was given for nothing, an aspect which became a feature of the voluntary hospitals, survives to the present day, and is relatively unexplored in a historical context.[64] Medicine in the early period thus shows a variety of types of exchange. At one extreme, the mountebank Valentine Raseworme, having cut a woman for the stone, handed the alleged stone to the woman's husband with one hand, and received the large sum of £10 from him with the other.[65] More widespread at different levels of practice was the conditional contract, in which the terms defining the disease and the cure were agreed on, and the practitioner was first paid something on account, and the balance when the cure was completed. The conditional contract seems to have had a long life through the late medieval period to at least the late seventeenth century.[66] The patient could be dominant to the point of hiring the practitioner to cure the form of disease as he or she, the patient, had diagnosed it. With respect to high-risk cures, where things were most likely to go wrong, the terms of the agreement were overseen either by civil authorities or by senior members of the craft under civil authority.[67] Given the nature of these contracts, it is not surprising that when they did not go according to plan, patients first sought to get their money back, and only secondarily went into the difficult area of damages. The case of Susanna Levine, brought to the London Lord Mayor's Court in 1687, is one in point. Susanna's witnesses, medical and otherwise, described not so much her injury and its treatment as the details of the financial agreements between the patient and her practitioner. Susanna was trying to avoid paying her bill by claiming that the practitioner had neglected her over the two years of her cure. She further claimed that during this period she, as the owner of a painting business, had painted one of the practitioner's houses. Cases of this sort tend to be labelled malpractice suits simply because they relate to medicine, rather than because this is an accurate description of proceedings which could occur in other circumstances.[68] Again the effect is to sever the connection between medicine and other areas of economic life.

A cure at this period could thus be more or less material, but it was still in many respects bought as an item. This contrasts with a definition of the 1830s, which stated confidently — or perhaps aggressively — that the professions dealt with 'men as men', and trades with 'external wants or occasions of men'.[69] It also casts doubt on the idea that 'commodity relations' in medicine began only in the nineteenth century with the increased market said to be created by industrialisation.[70] With respect to hospitals and the medical treatment of the poor, the practitioner of the earlier period could be paid for unspecified cures on unspecified patients as an extension of the system of paying certain sums yearly to retainers of households. This retaining system proved very enduring, and became increasingly rather than less competitive. The conditional contract was of course in its very essence competitive. Failure to recognise the effects of competition, for example in the use of a practitioner from a more distant centre or the desire of a town authority to obtain the services of a highly qualified practitioner or specialist by compounding for a lump sum, has been one factor behind the assumption that practitioners were not numerous in the early modern period. Compounding for a lump sum also occurred with respect to specific individuals, where the practitioner gambled on effecting a permanent cure of his or her patient's condition. This particular kind of arrangement bears some relation to the 'maintenance' agreements of the later medieval period, and may have faded out in the course of the seventeenth century.[71] The retainer system, on the other hand, which consisted of a kind of contractual bulk buying, with a similar calculation on either side of the balance of probabilities, is familiar in the poor law context in the eighteenth century, and also occurs later in factories, schools, collieries, sick clubs and other institutions. However, it also persisted to a very late date in the arrangement whereby a practitioner was paid a certain sum per annum for attendance on all members of a particular family. This similarly provided the practitioner with an assured minimum income, but also involved an 'actuarial' estimate of risks. Competitive tendering, with the advantage lying with the buyer, was possibly last seen in the conditions under which medical officers of health and poor law medical officers were employed by local authorities and Boards of Guardians. Organised resistance to this disadvantageous version of a 'commercial' system was not wholly successful until the 1920s.[72] The persistence of commercial characteristics was exemplified in the panel system of National Health Insurance, and even in the systems of payment favoured by medical practitioners themselves for the National Health Service.

Opposition to some aspects of such systems was being offered in the earlier period by physicians and some surgeons.[73] Both saw the advantages of aiming at the kind of unconditional disembodied or verbal transactions with their clients which were usually associated with lawyers and the clergy. Thus, at its most extreme, there was neither substantial or even visual contact between the physician and his patient: advice was given through intermediaries. Even in hospitals, the physician was by his own definition to be more distant from his patients than the surgeon or the apothecary. At the refounded St Bartholomew's Hospital in London, under the regulations proposed by William Harvey in 1633, the physician (who was not resident) attended once a week and sat at a desk in the great hall flanked by the other officers of the hospital. The patients were then brought before him; there was no provision for his seeing the bedridden in their beds.[74] The collaborations entered into for mutual benefit by some apothecaries and physicians are in some ways reminiscent of the lawyer's use of his clerk, who still protects his principal from the material side of each transaction.

So far, many of the criteria of professionalisation under discussion may seem to relate to conditions in towns rather than to rural life. As has already been suggested, this is not surprising given that for some authors, stressing institutional developments, this becomes a matter of definition. Yet any discussion of professions in the early modern period must take into account the fact that around 1500 only about 6 per cent of the population could be classified as urban, and, even in 1700, only 20 per cent of the population were living in towns.[75] Without forgetting that a town also served those in the surrounding area to a greater or lesser degree, and that the population as a whole was relatively mobile, it must still be assumed that in considering urban conditions one is concerned very much with the minority rather than the majority. Although evidence is much harder to find than in respect of the largest centres, it has at least been demonstrated that orthodox practitioners were not uncommon even in small towns — which must be taken into account in conclusions about changing social conditions for the professions in towns in the early eighteenth century — and that, on the same quantitative basis already described, medical practitioners were present in well-populated rural areas at least, on a similar ratio to population of *c.* 1:400.[76]

The complexion of practice was of course different from that of towns. Although barbers could be present even in small villages, barbers, barber-surgeons and apothecaries did not form the dominant groups, and unlicensed practitioners were more common than the licensed. A major resource in the countryside (although they also flourished in London) were the cunning men and women who often used ritual, magic and prayer, leading in some cases to charges of witchcraft or conjuring. As might be expected from the structure of rural economies, medicine was very often practised either simultaneously or alternately with other employments, by, for example, blacksmiths. Both the clergy and the gentry were likely to be involved in medicine, balancing the idea of rural practice as being necessarily of low status. The influence of women of all classes on their sons is an under-explored aspect of medicine. An interesting example is Thomas Tyrell, a younger son of a strongly Protestant gentry family based at Gipping Hall in Suffolk. Tyrell was apprenticed to an apothecary in Norwich and made his life there in the same occupation, but when he died in 1644 he left bequests to his mother at Gipping which indicate that his choice of business could be seen as a commercial and urban extension of his mother's influence in a rural setting.[77]

Recent work by Ronald Sawyer on the case records of the Bedfordshire clergyman-physician Richard Napier (d. 1634) confirms the extent to which rural medicine proceeded outside the usual terms of historiographical definition.[78] Among Napier's wide circle of medical acquaintances, many moved through the different categories of practice in their own lifetimes. Sawyer identifies unofficial women practitioners as providing the most important stratum of care in Jacobean England. His finding that proximity was an important factor in choosing a practitioner reinforces the suggestion already made, that even in rural areas practitioners were likely to be present in large numbers. Many of these were provided from the 'internal resources' of rural communities, and Sawyer stresses the role of community sanction in the emergence of practitioners. This situation tended to create a 'system of competences', with the scope of practice defined largely by what the practitioner's skills were perceived to be.[79] Thus lay participation was even greater than in towns, and, while differences in levels of education might be very large, there was a more obvious role for shared traditional knowledge. Rather than the unbridled conflicts between practitioners which have been assumed to be typical of an allegedly deeply divided but less 'civilised' (and extra-institutional) medical system, Sawyer finds that in one rural area at least there was considerable harmony and co-operation among those engaged in medicine. This is a particularly striking finding for the area of Napier's practice, as one of his medical rivals was John Cotta, author of a well-known diatribe against unlicensed practitioners, which undoubtedly drew upon his own experience.[80] Sawyer's findings about rural practice reinforce points already made: harmony among members of an occupation is not necessarily dependent upon an institutional context or on 'uniformity', and local forms of control have their own historical importance.

One area of identifiable conflict detectable in Napier's circle was the hostility of London to provincial practitioners, a feature indicating both the extreme competitiveness of practice in the capital and the frequency of interchange between London and the surrounding counties. Another source of conflict emerged when the accepted division of labour was not respected. This tendency to specialism did not, however, place much restriction on patients. Napier's practice provides ample confirmation of the high level of consumption of medical care in the earlier period. Ill people 'shuttled' (Sawyer's term) ceaselessly from one kind of practitioner to another in search of relief, according to their own and their friends' judgement of their condition, and its persistence. Specialism as a 'refinement of skill' certainly existed at this time, just as specialism as an indication of limited (or entrepreneurial) skills is not unknown at later periods.[81] Among the more traditional specialists were the bonesetters, ophthalmologists, lithotomists and those specialising in the diseases of women and children. These could be itinerant but none the less respectable, travelling according to occasion from a fixed base. Many specialisms were recognised in licensing, although here restriction and recognition of special skills could overlap.[82] Licensing could also be a way of ensuring that useful

skills could be practised among the population without interference from other practitioners. It is important to stress that
neither experience nor formal education in medicine was
likely to produce uniformity at this time. The products even of
a single university tended to be heterogeneous. At the same
time many aspects of medical culture, far from 'emancipating'
the educated medical practitioner from the laymen, formed
part of a common philosophy which partly explains the level of
lay knowledge of, and interest in, medicine.[83]

So far this essay has stressed what seem to be neglected
features of the larger part of the whole population of medical
practitioners in the earlier period. These features stress the
interrelation of medicine with other occupational groups, and
point to some of the defects in the contrasts usually drawn
between the earlier and the later periods. It is perhaps
desirable to pay some attention to the various contexts in which
contemporaries showed that they themselves perceived a
difference between 'professions' and trades or crafts. The term
itself had a wide range of meanings derived from its use in the
religious context. A member of a religious order 'professed'
when he or she took in public the final vows of commitment to
the religious life. After the Reformation the term rapidly
acquired a range of secular applications, having as their
common denominator the theme of public commitment or
open avowal. The term 'professor', implying public teacher,
passed into English use as opposed to Latin in connection with
Henry VIII's Regius professorships (one of them in physic).
A neat summary of the history of the term is contained in
a recommendation of the nineteenth-century Royal Commission on Oxford which was trying to establish prestige lecturing
posts in 'liberal' (not applied) science in the university. The
Commissioners expressed the hope that in future a profes-
sorship would become a recognised profession.[84] Given the
sense of change in sixteenth-century society, it is not surprising
that the word almost immediately acquired a range of connotations implying insincerity or a distance between spoken
commitment and actual performance. This creates a difficulty
for the modern reader in distinguishing the literal and satirical
meanings in such sources as plays.

Undoubtedly literal is the reference of the printer and
author Robert Copland, who wrote in 1541 that 'the parts of
the art of medicine (that is to wit dietetic, pharmaceutic, and

surgery) be in such wise coupled and connected together that in no wise they cannot be separated one from the other without the damage and great detriment of all the medicinal profession'. However modern this may sound, it seems clear that Copland was referring in effect to all who *professed* medicine, and that his usage was affected by proximity to the Reformation. Francis Bacon, writing at the beginning of the seventeenth century, used the term 'profession' in a fairly pragmatic way to mean 'occupation'. An example from *The advancement of learning* serves as a reminder of points made earlier in this essay, as well as pointing to the relatively low social status and reputation of physicians:

> For in all times, in the opinion of the multitude, witches and old women and impostors have had a competition with physicians . . . And therefore I cannot much blame [them], that they use commonly to intend some other art or practice, which they fancy more than their profession. For you shall have of them antiquaries, poets, humanists, statesmen, merchants, divines, and in every of these better seen than in their profession; and no doubt on this ground, that they find that mediocrity and excellency in their art maketh no difference in profit or reputation towards their fortune; for the weakness of patients, and the sweetness of life, and nature of hope, maketh men depend upon physicians with all their defects.[85]

It is easy for the modern reader to understand a shift from a declaration made in the religious context to a different kind of public declaration based on learning and the verbal skills of the lawyer, clergyman, or even the physician. It is less easy to remember that in the earlier period, and to some extent even to the present day, learned men also declared themselves in public by their dress and accessories, and therefore that, as we have seen, they shared this mode of declaration with other occupations and trades. Thus a Shakespearean character *c.* 1601 could demand of an anonymous passer-by, 'you ought not walk / Upon a labouring day without the sign / Of your profession, . . . what trade art thou?'[86] The terms used in apprenticeship do not seem to have included 'profession', but it may not be too far-fetched to suggest that 'profession' referred to a state which has been achieved and can be publicly declared, rather than to what had to be learnt. It should be emphasised that, as has already been suggested in relation to guilds, the wearing or displaying of 'signs of profession' was not only necessary but honourable: individuals without identity were suspect. Important social changes had to occur before such signs were seen as demeaning and 'self-advertisement' a breach of the professional code.[87]

The self-consciousness of physicians in particular is illustrated by the physician Edward Jorden in the context of his treatise published in 1603 claiming that the subject of a celebrated witchcraft trial (Mary Glover) was naturally, not supernaturally, afflicted. Jorden considered that people had the wrong view of such cases, that is, cases of hysteria or suffocation of the mother, because they were either too little learned or lacked the humility to consult physicians. In a passage stressing the role of public avowal as made by the possessors of the whole range of manual and intellectual skills, Jorden asked:

> if . . . we do depend upon those which have been trained up in other particular subjects, believing men in their own professions: why should we not prefer the judgements of physicians . . . before our own conceits; as we do the opinions of divines, lawyers, artificers, etc., in their proper elements.[88]

The College, of which Jorden was then a fellow, was in the event unable to present the kind of united front implied by Jorden with respect to Mary Glover's case. Jorden also implies not only that the clergy and the lawyers were in a more favourable position to suppress competition than physicians, but that physic was less organised even than the trades.

The campaign for the reform of the learned professions conducted in the first half of the seventeenth century is significant not only for the increasing trend towards social polarisation, but also as indicating how the ideal of the full-time professional might have been strengthened later in the century as one result of the forces of reaction. In spite of its stress on idle and elaborate learning, this campaign, like other major moves affecting the regulation of the medical profession at this period, should be seen in a wider economic and social context: in this case, the continuing struggle against monopolies, which were, like the College of Physicians, dependencies of the crown. Contemporary critics saw a symmetry of exploitation in which the clergy monopolised the soul, physicians the body, and the lawyers property. Physicians were put together with the clergy as Latin-speaking and heathenish. As with the clergy, learning had made physicians idle. In the previous century both Vesalius and Paracelsus had strongly criticised physicians for abandoning their most useful and basic skills to uneducated artisans, who had subsequently, though despised, become much more useful and reliable as practitioners. However necessary learning might be, to regard it as the only necessary qualification was to deny the role of divine grace, without which learning itself became a mere trade. Lawyers were particularly criticised for elaborating the law to such a degree that it had become a full-time occupation, inaccessible to those whom it was designed to serve. Thus, occupational diversity, with the emphasis on 'honest' trades, was elevated to a moral principle. Moreover, any form of 'specialism' which involved the monopoly of knowledge or the hoarding of esoteric lore was to be deplored.[89]

Puritan reformers also suggested that the clergy should combine useful work with their vocation, and further that the clergy could themselves become the basis of an evenly distributed and responsible medical service.[90] The College of Physicians was hostile to the involvement of the clergy in medicine, but there was a convenience about transferring from one occupation to the other which had spiritual meaning, as well as the material justifications already mentioned. The sanitary reformer Thomas Southwood Smith is an example from the nineteenth century who deliberately combined the two vocations in the context of Unitarian belief. Smith practised as physician and minister in Yeovil around 1815, and his medical studies in Edinburgh, themselves partly motivated by his renunciation of a career as a Baptist minister, were supported by the Unitarian Fund.[91] It seems implausible that the College of Physicians, whatever its ambitions in the professional direction, and whatever its envy of the established state of the clergy in settled times, would ever have wished to create the equivalent of the church's wideflung administrative hierarchy with its army of underbred and often impoverished underlings. The College's indifference to the periphery, although striking from the mid-eighteenth century onwards, was hardly anything new.

Thus on the one hand physicians in particular were criticised for having achieved a state of empty scholarship — in Bacon's words, 'more professed than laboured'. They assumed social graces, and despised 'the meaner sort'. As part of this critique there was an attempt to 'rematerialise' the transactions between physicians and patients. Physicians should cease hiding behind their apothecaries, they should do their own prescribing, and their prescriptions should be written in English, so that the patients knew what they were getting. That is, the transactions of physicians should be made to bear a greater resemblance to the purchase of an agreed cure. At the same time critics pointed to discrepancies between the medical practitioners' professed claim to belong to a higher calling, and their economic behaviour. Clergy, lawyers and physicians were all abused as having the profit motives of tradesmen.[92] This charge had particular application in the context of early modern London, as the capital became increasingly a trading rather than a manufacturing centre, and a focus for the activities of middlemen. The upheavals of the first part of the seventeenth century thus lent great complexity and political significance to the concepts of trade and profession.

The surgeons, particularly the surgeons of London, were not exempt from similar criticism, especially with relation to high fees and a tendency to distance themselves from their patients. None the less, the generation of London surgeons that was dominant towards the end of the sixteenth century does provide a contrast with the physicians in respect of the means to be adopted to raise professional standards. These surgeons spoke strongly against idle knowledge and were conspicuous by their use of the vernacular, a move usually regarded as prejudicial to professional status as now defined.[93] Nor did surgeons like William Clowes, who was copious in his denunciation of intruders into surgery from other trades, necessarily despise the unlearned operator. In his indictment of Raseworme as lithotomist, Clowes was careful to make clear that he was speaking against 'this proud ambitious golden ass, and false deceiver' but not against 'any honest man which cutteth for the stone and ruptures'. It could not be denied, he stated, that many of these had performed 'honestly, carefully, painfully, and skilfully, to their great praise, and to the comfort and health of their patients, and to the honour and praise of almighty God'. At the same time,

> every science and faculty hath his own bonds and limits, in the which, good order willeth ... men to keep themselves without confusion, disorder or mingle mangle. Therefore I exhort all such, of what trade or faculty so ever they be, to profess only that art wherein they have most knowledge, best judgement, and greatest experience.

Clowes and his friends denied all motive for discrediting rival practitioners, 'for it is the comfort of every honest artist, to see the professors to flourish, and especially being of one body, and company, for one member not doing his duty, all the rest fareth the worse'.[94] Clowes proceeded to back up his attitude by making available to young practitioners instructions in the vernacular, both from the best sources, and as he had had experience of them himself. The surgeons and barber-surgeons, whose social utility took many forms, and whose practice best fitted the tangible, contractual model of patient–practitioner relations, continued to be regarded as useful, much more certain in principle, and less precarious in success.[95]

In a well-known article Lawrence Stone plausibly defined the period from 1550 to the mid-seventeenth century as one of great social mobility, characterised by a rise in population and an expansion of educational opportunities. He saw both the trades and the professions as rising in status relative to the landed classes. After the restoration land transfer was greatly reduced and opportunities for advancement via the professions were, more and more, open only to those with access to the educational ladder. This interpretation was compatible with Everitt's thesis concerning the rise of the 'pseudo-gentry' in towns. It also seems a plausible framework for the evolution of the numerous, competitive, self-improving and extremely various body of medical practitioners which emerges against a background of population increase and economic and social crisis in the period before 1660, and the relatively more uniform and familiar situation which was developing at the end of the seventeenth century. Stone also pointed to various features of the period before 1660 which analysts have regarded as concomitant with the emergence of the professions in the nineteenth century: increasing secularisation, population expansion, increases in demand, and a trend towards literacy. Further changes with respect to the medical profession after the restoration identified by Holmes confirm the other half of Stone's interpretation: the increased incidence of medical 'dynasties'; the payment of high premiums; the greater uniformity of more expensive education. Other changes underline the importance of social polarisation: in spite of their real usefulness and general viability, the barber-surgeons lost ground, as the concept of utility itself became discredited.[96]

In spite of the importance of these social changes, the degree of continuity into the eighteenth century was considerable. Uniformity was not a characteristic of the medical practitioners of even the nineteenth century.[97] The connections with the wider economic and social world changed but did not disappear. Even where these later connections have been recognised by historians, they tend still to be seen as deviations from professional norms.[98] It is a curious feature of much discussion of the professions which concentrates firmly on the industrial period that it has established little about medical personnel as full members of an industrial society. Economic language and concepts are used, but only as a different way of describing medicine itself.[99] In such an interpretation there is only one kind of view taken of such cases as the Tunbridge and London practitioner William Henry Cook, who was essentially supported by the unearned income of his wife's mother and sister, and also in part by the income earned by his wife in writing, teaching and lodging children who needed a good Christian upbringing while their parents were in the colonies. There is even less room for other examples, such as William Budd, physician and epidemiologist, who, at a time when he could earn less than £500 per annum for his practice, apparently lost £3,500 in an investment in shares. A strong believer in water carriage as a cause of disease, Budd was a member of the first Board of Directors of the Bristol Water Works Company. William Farr, the medical statistician, made extensive and usually unfortunate commitments in the world of commercial insurance. John Snow, anaesthetist to Queen Victoria, was prompted to enter this line by the example of a druggist who boasted to him of having built up an 'ether practice'. Disinfection was another area of combined medical and commercial enterprise.[100] These examples are not specially selected, but they do indicate that there was more to the economic life and occupation of even nineteenth-century men than remote and gentlemanly investment in land or consols, or desperate and ungentlemanly selling of pills and ointments.

It is usually assumed that it is professionalism which must be continuous: that, having once begun (whether, as has been variously proposed for medicine, in the middle ages, the eighteenth century, or the nineteenth), its progress is inevitable. The persistence of institutions (universities, hospitals) seems to provide a tangible basis for this. Yet, if professionalisation is to be linked to these institutions, its course must likewise be one not of linear development but of periodic weakness and strength. For example, the revival of Cambridge in particular as a centre of medical education in the sixteenth century must be contrasted with the nadir of English university faculties in the eighteenth century. Growth in the university context could take place largely outside the 'training' curriculum, as in the mid-seventeenth century at Oxford; and such 'training', as already suggested, could help maintain a common cultural experience, rather than dividing the layman from the professional. Similarly the College of Physicians of London could claim greater pretensions to professional leadership in the early sixteenth or early seventeenth centuries, than by the eighteenth, when religious tests had created separate nonconformist establishments rivalling the older institutions, and when fragmentation was a permanent feature of social life. By this time the College had cut itself off from the sectors of society most likely to go into medicine. The contrasting notions evolved during the Commonwealth did not simply disappear. As we have seen, medicine, with its combination of mental and manual skills, was peculiarly likely to reflect changing or conflicting attitudes to hierarchy and class structure.

Even historically based accounts of the rise of medicine since the nineteenth century end by presenting a kind of immutable monolith. Seen in this way, becoming a profession is a goal, and once this is achieved, it is not clear what happens subsequently. But is it actually true, as has been suggested, that 'the modern professions — whose archetype is medicine — fostered group solidarity, loyalty, and exclusiveness, regardless of differences in general education, ascribed social rank or economic standing'?[101] Or is medicine even in the twentieth century a larger field, more various, less controlled, and more fragmented in socio-economic terms than this suggests, and thus recognisably the product of much earlier developments?

Notes

Acknowledgements

I am grateful for the comments of Charles Webster, Jonathan Barry, Irvine Loudon and Wilfrid Prest on this essay, which is a revised version of a paper first given in a Society for the Social History of Medicine lecture series in 1983.

1. For a recent discussion and references see S. E. D. Shortt, 'Physicians, science and status: issues in the professionalization of Anglo-American medicine in the nineteenth century', *Medical History*, vol. 27 (1983), pp. 51–68. See also P. Wright and A. Treacher (eds), *The problem of medical knowledge: examining the social construction of medicine* (Edinburgh, 1984); J. H. Warner, 'Science in medicine', *Osiris*, 2nd ser., vol. 1 (1985), pp. 37–58.

2. M. S. Larson, *The rise of professionalism: a sociological analysis* (Berkeley, 1977), p. xi.

3. V. L. Bullough, *The development of medicine as a profession. The contribution of the medieval university to modern medicine* (Basle, 1966), p. 3. Throughout this essay I shall use 'medicine' to refer to all parts of practice, and not simply to 'physic' as opposed to surgery.

4. R. Gottfried, 'English medical practitioners 1340–1530', *Bulletin of the History of Medicine*, vol. 58 (1984), pp. 164–82.

5. G. N. Clark, *A history of the Royal College of Physicians of London* (2 vols, Oxford, 1964–6); J. H. Raach, *A directory of English country physicians 1603–1643* (1962); see also J. H. Raach, 'The English country doctor in the province of Canterbury, 1603–1643', Unpublished PhD thesis, Yale University, 1941.

6. See e.g. J. F. Kett, 'Provincial medical practice in England 1730–1815', *Journal of the History of Medicine*, vol. 19 (1964), p. 17; M. Jeanne Peterson, *The medical profession in mid-Victorian London* (Berkeley, 1978), pp. 5ff; I. Waddington, *The medical profession in the industrial revolution* (Dublin, 1984), p. 1; M. T. Walton, 'Fifteenth-century London medical men in their social context', unpublished PhD thesis, University of Chicago, 1979, pp. xiiff.

7. Bullough, *Development of medicine*, pp. 86–7; Gottfried, 'English medical practitioners', p. 165. For recent stress on the College of Physicians, see W. J. Birken, 'The fellows of the Royal College of

Physicians of London, 1603–1643: a social study', unpublished PhD thesis, University of North Carolina, 1977; H. J. Cook, *The decline of the old medical regime in Stuart London* (Ithaca, NY, 1986).

8. Cf. Walton, 'Fifteenth-century London medical men', p. viii.

9. Cf. K. Charlton, 'The professions in sixteenth century England', *University of Birmingham Historical Journal*, vol. 12 (1969), p. 27. Cf. C. M. Cipolla, 'The professions. The long view', *Journal of European Economic History*, vol. 2 (1973), p. 39.

10. There are historical reasons for this: cf. C. Webster, 'Medicine as social history: changing ideas on doctors and patients in the age of Shakespeare' in L. G. Stevenson (ed.), *A celebration of medical history* (Baltimore, 1982), pp. 108–9.

11. W. Munk, *The roll of the Royal College of Physicians of London . . . 1518 to . . . 1825* (1878), p. iv. The interpretive stress on the private relationship between practitioner and patient in the modern profession goes back at least to publications of the 1940s: see Larson, *Rise of professionalism*, pp. 22–3, 25; J. Woodward and D. Richards, 'Towards a social history of medicine', in J. Woodward and D. Richards (eds), *Health care and popular medicine in nineteenth century England* (1977), pp. 36–7, 53. For incisive comment on different attitudes towards the individual client and to the community, see A. M. Carr-Saunders and P. A. Wilson, *The professions* (Oxford, 1933), pp. 471–7. That medicine in the eighteenth century was dominated by patronage relationships was asserted by S. W. F. Holloway, and developed by N. D. Jewson; different stresses on 'low demand' have been placed by e.g., Holloway, Freidson and, especially, Starr: see sources cited in Waddington, *The medical profession*, pt. III.

12. Cf. T. J. Pettigrew, *Medical portrait gallery* (1840); T. J. Pettigrew, *On superstitions connected with the history and practice of medicine and surgery* (1844); C. Allbutt, *The historical relations of medicine and surgery to the end of the sixteenth century* (1905); J. F. South, *Memorials of the craft of surgery in England*, ed. D'A. Power (1886).

13. See note 11 above.

14. G. Holmes, *Augustan England: professions, state and society, 1680–1730* (1982), esp. Chs. 6 and 7.

15. Gottfried, 'English medical practitioners', pp. 166–7, 181. This argument is put more cautiously, and with respect to Continental cities, by Cipolla, 'The professions', pp. 37–52. Cf. W. J. Birken, 'The Royal College of Physicians of London and its support of the parliamentary cause in the English Civil War', *Journal of British Studies*, vol. 23 (1983), pp. 47–62.

16. Holmes is the latest to adopt this approach: cf. *Augustan England*, pp. 169, 202ff. For an earlier example, see R. Shryock, 'Public relations of the medical profession in Great Britain and the United States, 1600–1870', *Annals of Medical History*, n.s., 2 (1930), p. 310.

17. The stress on institutions has received a new lease of life from the adventurous work of Michel Foucault, especially his *Naissance de la clinique: une archéologie du regard médical* (Paris, 1963); *Folie et déraison* (Paris, 1961); *Surveiller et punir* (Gallimard, n. p., 1975). Cf. E. H.

Ackerknecht, *Medicine at the Paris Hospital, 1794–1848* (Baltimore, 1967).

18. Larson, *Rise of professionalism*, p. x.

19. Holmes, *Augustan England*, pp. 183–4, 199–202.

20. Cf. C. Webster, 'The crisis of the hospitals during the industrial revolution' in E. Forbes (ed.), *Human implications of scientific advance* (Edinburgh, 1978), pp. 214–23; F. Honigsbaun, *The division in British medicine: a history of the separation of general practice from hospital care 1911–1968* (1979). Poor law (later municipal) hospitals and specialist hospitals represented further divisions within the profession: see M. A. Crowther, *The workhouse system 1834–1929* (1981), Ch. 7; Peterson, *Mid-Victorian medical profession*, pp. 259–82; R. Stevens, *American medicine and the public interest* (New Haven, Conn., 1971).

21. Exceptions are J. J. Keevil, 'The seventeenth-century English medical background', *Bulletin of the History of medicine*, vol. 31 (1957), pp. 408–24; R. S. Roberts, 'The personnel and practice of medicine in Tudor and Stuart England', *Medical History*, vol. 6 (1962), pp. 363–82; vol. 8 (1964), pp. 217–34; R. M. S. McConaghey, 'The history of rural medical practice' in F. N. L. Poynter (ed.), *The evolution of medical practice in Britain* (1961), pp. 177–43; C. Webster (ed.), *Health, medicine and mortality in the sixteenth century* (Cambridge, 1979); I. S. L. Loudon, 'The nature of provincial medical practice in eighteenth-century England', *Medical History*, vol. 29 (1985), pp. 1–32; M. Pelling, 'Healing the sick poor: social policy and disability in Norwich, 1550–1640', *Medical History*, vol. 29 (1985), pp. 115–37; R. Porter (ed.), *Patients and practitioners: lay perceptions of medicine in pre-industrial society* (Cambridge, 1985). The debate over the effects of the dissolution is of long standing: see e.g. S. and B. Webb, *English local government: English poor law history Part 1: the old poor law* (1927), pp. 17–19. A more realistic view is now generally taken by historians: see J. Youings, *Sixteenth-century England* (Harmondsworth, 1984), pp. 256–9, 264.

22. Cf. Clark, *History of the Royal College*; S. Young, *Annals of the barber-surgeons of London* (1890); C. R. B. Barrett, *The history of the Society of Apothecaries of London, Vol. I, 1617–1815* (1963). Cf. R. S. Roberts, 'The London apothecaries and medical practice in Tudor and Stuart England', Unpublished PhD thesis, University of London, 1964; R. T. Beck, *The cutting edge. Early history of the surgeons of London* (1974).

23. See e.g. G. Parker, 'Early Bristol medical institutions, the medieaval hospitals, and barber surgeons', *Transactions of the Bristol and Gloucestershire Archaeological Society*, vol. 44 (1922), pp. 155–78; F. C. Pybus, 'The Company of Barber Surgeons and Tallow Chandlers of Newcastle-on-Tyne', *Newcastle Medical Journal*, vols 9–10 (1928–30), pp. 147–63; F. Simpson, 'The city gilds or companies of Chester, with special reference to that of the barber-surgeons', *Journal of the Chester Archaeological Society*, vol. 18 (1911), pp. 98–203; D. Embleton, 'The Incorporated Company of Barber-Surgeons and Wax and Tallow Chandlers of Newcastle-upon-Tyne', *Archaeologia Aeliana*, vol. 15 (1892), pp. 228–69; W. A. Leighton, 'The guilds of Shrewsbury', *Shropshire Archaeological and Natural History Society Trans-*

actions, vol. 5 (1882), pp. 265–97; F. J. Furnivall and P. Furnivall (eds), *The anatomie of the bodie of man by Thomas Vicary* (1888), esp. pp. 243–87.

24. C. Phythian-Adams, 'The economic and social structure' in *The fabric of the traditional community* (Milton Keynes, 1977), p. 17.

25. T. D. Whittet, 'The apothecary in provincial guilds', *Medical History*, vol. 8 (1964), pp. 245–73; cf. Holmes, *Augustan England*, pp. 184–92, 210–13; Charlton, 'Sixteenth-century professions', pp. 24–5.

26. Cf. J. Toulmin Smith, *English gilds* (1870). See also G. Unwin, *The gilds and companies of London*, 3rd edn (1938); E. Power, 'English craft gilds in the middle ages. Historical revisions, 12', *History*, vol. 4 (1919–20), pp. 211–14.

27. G. Unwin, *Industrial organization in the sixteenth and seventeenth centuries* (Oxford, 1904); T. H. Marshall, 'Capitalism and the decline of the English gilds', *Cambridge Historical Journal*, vol. 3 (1929–31), pp. 23–33; Holmes, *Augustan England*, p. 3; Clark, *History of the Royal College*, vol. 1, pp. 7–11.

28. Larson, *Rise of professionalism*, pp. 61–3.

29. Clark, *History of the Royal College*, vol. 1, pp. 34, 62–3. Cf. C. Webster, 'Thomas Linacre and the foundation of the College of Physicians' in F. R. Maddison *et al.* (eds), *Essays on the life and work of Thomas Linacre* (Oxford, 1977), pp. 198–222.

30. Clark, *History of the Royal College*, vol. 1, p. 16.

31. M. Pelling, 'Occupational diversity: barber-surgeons and the trades of Norwich, 1550–1640', *Bulletin of the History of Medicine*, vol. 56 (1982), pp. 490, 492; D. M. Palliser, *Tudor York* (Oxford, 1979), p. 177; C. F. Bradshaw, 'The craft gilds of Canterbury', *Good Books* (Canterbury Central Library), vol. 5 (1948), pp. 8–11; Furnivall and Furnivall, *Anatomie*, p. 274; Keevil, 'Medical background', p. 410.

32. Whittet, 'The apothecary in provincial gilds', p. 256. Clark himself cites the example of a physician and mercer of Colchester: *History of the Royal College*, vol. 1, p. 16, note.

33. Holmes, *Augustan England*, pp. 17–18.

34. M. Pelling and C. Webster, 'Medical practitioners' in Webster, *Health, medicine and mortality*, p. 203; K. Dewhurst, *Dr Thomas Sydenham* (1966), pp. 17, 47–8, 56–9; Webster, 'Medicine as social history', p. 109. I am grateful to Ronald Sawyer for allowing me to consult his draft University of Wisconsin PhD thesis on health, disease and medicine in the south-east Midlands, 1597–1634.

35. C. Phythian-Adams, 'Sources for urban history. 3: Records of the craft gilds', *The Local Historian*, vol. 9 (1971), pp. 267–74. For the persistence of provincial guilds in particular up to the eighteenth century, see D. Palliser, 'The trade gilds of Tudor York' in P. Clark and P. Slack (eds), *Crisis and order in English towns 1500–1700* (1972), pp. 86–116. Young, *Annals*, pp. 423–30.

36. Cameron and Wall, *Worshipful Society of Apothecaries*, pp. 13–14, 41–57; W. L. Sachse (ed.), *Minutes of the Norwich Court of Mayoralty 1630–1631*, Norfolk Record Society, vol. 15 (1942), pp. 39–41 and *passim*; Palliser, 'Trade gilds of Tudor York', pp. 95–6, 101–2.

37. It has not been clearly established that the Hippocratic oath was taken in any context in either England or Scotland in the sixteenth or

seventeenth centuries. Clark implies its relevance to the ideals of London physicians without establishing any actual connection: Clark, *History of the Royal College*, vol. 1, pp. 32–4. I am grateful to Charles Webster for his guidance on this point. The most authoritative discussion in print of the oath is L. Edelstein, *The Hippocratic oath, text translation and interpretation* (Baltimore, 1943). For examples of guild and municipal oaths see W. Hudson and J. C. Tingey (eds), *The records of the City of Norwich* (2 vols, 1906–10), vol. 2, pp. 313, 315–16, 382ff; Young, *Annals*, pp. 142, 254.

38. Cf. J. H. Thomas, *Town government in the sixteenth century* (1933); A. Everitt, 'The marketing of agricultural produce' in J. Thirsk (ed.), *The agrarian history of England and Wales, Vol. IV: 1500–1640* (Cambridge, 1967), pp. 577–86; Sachse, *Minutes of the Norwich Court*, pp. 39–43, 46–8 and *passim*. See also under the heading of 'nuisances' in S. and B. Webb, *English local government: the manor and the borough* (1908).

39. See for example, Waddington, *The medical profession*, pp. 183–5.

40. Pelling and Webster, 'Medical practitioners', pp. 168–77; C. Webster, *The great instauration: science, medicine and reform 1626–1660* (1975), pp. 308–14.

41. Pelling and Webster, 'Medical practitioners', p. 205. For Raach, see above, note 5.

42. Pelling and Webster, 'Medical practitioners', pp. 166, 188, 186.

43. Pelling, 'Occupational diversity', esp. pp. 495, 507–8.

44. P. Clark, *The English alehouse: a social history 1200–1830* (1983), Chs. 4–7.

45. Pelling, 'Healing the sick poor', pp. 115–37.

46. Pelling and Webster, 'Medical practitioners', p. 209.

47. Palliser, *Tudor York*, p. 20; J. T. Evans, *Seventeenth-century Norwich* (Oxford, 1979), p. 6.

48. Holmes, *Augustan England*, pp. 11–18.

49. Cf. my 'Occupational diversity' and 'Appearance and reality: barber-surgeons, the body and disease' in L. Beier and R. Finlay (eds), *London 1500–1700: the making of the metropolis* (1986), pp. 82–112.

50. F. W. Steer, 'The possessions of a Sussex surgeon', *Medical History*, vol. 2 (1958), pp. 134–6; R. S. Roberts, 'The early history of the import of drugs into England' in F. N. L. Poynter (ed.), *The evolution of pharmacy in Britain* (1965), pp. 165–86.

51. T. R. Forbes, 'Apprentices in trouble: some problems in the training of surgeons and apothecaries in seventeenth century London', *Yale Journal of Biology and Medicine*, vol. 52 (1979), p. 230. Webster, *Great instauration*, pp. 253–4; Young, *Annals*, p. 338; Cameron and Wall, *Worshipful Society of Apothecaries*, p. 57.

52. Holmes, *Augustan England*, p. 197.

53. Richard Argentine, a sixteenth-century physician and divine, graduate of Cambridge, during a period in Ipswich practised medicine, held ecclesiastical appointments, and taught at the grammar school: cf. *DNB*; Pelling and Webster, 'Medical practitioners', pp. 227–8. See also McConaghey, 'History of rural medical

practice', pp. 118–21; D. W. Amundsen, 'Medieval canon law on medical and surgical practice by the clergy', *Bulletin of the History of Medicine*, vol. 52 (1978), pp. 22–44; C. Webster, 'English medical reformers of the puritan revolution: a background to the "Society of Chymical Physitians"', *Ambix*, vol. 14 (1967), pp. 21–3; C. H. Talbot, *Medicine in medieval England* (1967), p. 196. In the sixteenth century, the London Barber-Surgeons' Company included citizen-scrivener-surgeons: Furnivall and Furnivall, *Anatomie*, pp. 200–1. On relations between Continental medical personnel and notaries, see Cipolla, 'The professions', p. 50.

54. See J. K. Mustain, 'A rural medical practitioner in fifteenth-century England', *Bulletin of the History of Medicine*, vol. 46 (1972), pp. 469–76. Cf. the case of Edward Rigby, distinguished provincial physician/surgeon/lithotomist/farmer and agricultural writer, d. 1822: *DNB*; A. Batty Shaw, 'The Norwich school of lithotomy', *Medical History*, vol. 14 (1970), pp. 247–8. See also F. Neale, 'A seventeenth-century country doctor. John Westover of Wedmore', *Practitioner*, vol. 203 (1969), pp. 699–704; Waddington, *The medical profession*, pp. 187, 189–90.

55. On Dee see J. H. Appleby, 'Dr Arthur Dee: merchant and litigant', *Slavonic and East European Review*, vol. 57 (1979), pp. 32–55; J. H. Appleby, 'Some of Arthur Dee's associations before visiting Russia clarified, including two letters from Sir Theodore Mayerne', *Ambix*, vol. 26 (1979), pp. 1–15.

56. Bullough, *Development of medicine*, pp. 2, 5; Waddington, *The medical profession*, pp. 186–91.

57. See above, note 49.

58. Pelling, 'Occupational diversity', pp. 505, 506. Little attention has been paid to the connections between medicine and the food trades; but see J. O'Hara May, *Elizabethan dietary of health* (Lawrence, Kan., 1977); C. Webster, 'The College of Physicians: "Solomon's House" in Commonwealth England', *Bulletin of the History of Medicine*, vol. 41 (1967), pp. 406, 407; Webster, *Great instauration*, pp. 248, 249.

59. See e.g. the inventory of Samuel Newboult of Lichfield (1666): D. G. Vaisey (ed.), *Probate inventories of Lichfield and district 1568–1680*, Staffordshire Records Society, Collections, 4th ser., vol. 5 (1969), pp. 155–61; and M. Rowe and G. E. Trease, 'Thomas Baskerville, Elizabethan Apothecary of Exeter', *Transactions of the British Society for the History of Pharmacy*, vol. 1 (1970), pp. 3–28. See also the complaints made by the Grocers' Company of London against the claims of the apothecaries: Cameron and Wall, *Worshipful Society of Apothecaries*, p. 37.

60. A. Clark, *Working life of women in the seventeenth century* (1982; first published 1922), pp. 197–235, 242–89; D. Willen, 'Guildswomen in the city of York, 1650–1700', *The Historian* (USA), vol. 46 (1984), pp. 204–18; Palliser, *Tudor York*, p. 150; M. Prior (ed.), *Women in English society 1500–1800* (1985), pp. 70–1, 106–7; Pelling and Webster, 'Medical practitioners', pp. 183–4, 186–7 and *passim*; A. L. Wyman, 'The surgeoness: the female practitioner of surgery 1400–1800', *Medical History.*, vol. 28 (1984), pp. 22–41; Pelling, 'Occupa-

tional diversity', pp. 508–9. Women barbers appear in their own right in formal records to the end of the fifteenth century: L. Fox, 'The Coventry gilds and trading companies with special reference to the position of women', *Birmingham Archaeological Society Transactions*, vol. 78 (1962), p. 17.

61. J. O'Hara May, 'Foods or medicines? A study in the relationship between foodstuffs and materia medica from the sixteenth to the nineteenth century', *Transactions of the British Society for the History of Pharmacy*, vol. 1 (1971), esp. pp. 61–8.

62. See Holmes, *Augustan England*, p. 215; Waddington, *The medical profession*, pp. 187–9.

63. This paragraph is necessarily speculative. The major shifts proposed by Jewson and others (e.g. from 'bedside' to 'hospital' medicine) are essentially based on medical ideas: see note 11 above; N. D. Jewson, 'The disappearance of the sick-man from medical cosmology, 1770–1870', *Sociology*, vol. 10 (1976), pp. 225–44. N. Elias, *The history of manners*, trans. E. Jephcott (Oxford, 1983), pp. 163–8, is suggestive but Elias does not deal with the conventions of sickness. Adrian Wilson stresses the public and ritual aspects of midwifery in his *A safe deliverance: changing rites of childbirth in early modern England* (Cambridge, forthcoming). See also M. MacDonald, *Mystical Bedlam: madness, anxiety and healing in seventeenth century England* (Cambridge, 1981); G. Smith, 'The physiology of air: eighteenth-century fever therapy in the advice literature', *Bulletin of the Society for the Social History of Medicine*, vol. 35 (1984), p. 22; D'A. Power, 'John Halle and sixteenth-century consultations', *Proceedings of the Royal Society of Medicine, Section for the History of Medicine*, vol. 11 (1981), p. 60.

64. See Furnivall and Furnivall, *Anatomie*, pp. 208–9, 274; Pelling and Webster, 'Medical practitioners', p. 213; Foster, 'Dr William Henry Cook', pp. 47–8.

65. Clowes, *Morbus Gallicus*, fo. 10. The operation took place 'in the presence of divers honest persons'.

66. E. A. Hammond, 'Incomes of medieval English doctors', *Journal of the History of Medicine*, vol. 15 (1960), pp. 154–69; Talbot, *Medicine in medieval England*, p. 138; Pelling, 'Healing the sick poor', pp. 122–3, 129.

67. For ordinances and examples, see Young, *Annals*, pp. 182 and *passim*; Furnivall and Furnivall, *Anatomie*, p. 255; C. Williams, *The barber-surgeons of Norwich* (Norwich, 1897).

68. For the Levine case see T. R. Forbes, 'The case of the casual chirurgeon', *Yale Journal of Biology and Medicine*, vol. 51 (1978), pp. 583–8. For other examples see Young, *Annals*, pp. 316, 319; C. H. Talbot and E. A. Hammond, *The medical practitioners in medieval England. A biographical register* (1965); references as given in J. B. Post, 'Doctor versus patient: two fourteenth century lawsuits', *Medical History*, vol. 16 (1972), pp. 296–300. Cf. M. P. Cosman, 'Medieval medical malpractice: the dicta and the dockets', *Bulletin of the New York Academy of Medicine*, vol. 49 (1973), pp. 22–47; Walton, 'Fifteenth-century London medical men', pp. 150–65.

69. *OED*, s.v. 'profession', citing a lecture on middle-class

education by F. D. Maurice.

70. Cf. Larson, *Rise of professionalism*, pp. 14ff, 209–19; K. Figlio, 'Sinister medicine? A critique of left approaches to medicine', *Radical Science Journal*, vol. 9 (1979), pp. 14–68.

71. See Pelling, 'Healing the sick poor'. Pelling, 'Old people and poverty in early modern towns', *Bulletin of the Society for the Social History of Medicine*, vol. 34 (1984), p. 45; E. Clark, 'Some aspects of social security in medieval England', *Journal of Family History*, vol. 7 (1982), pp. 307–20.

72. The most extended discussion of the incomes and conditions of medical practitioners in the later period is Peterson, *Mid-Victorian medical profession*, Chs. 3 and 5, but 'tendering' is mentioned only in passing. More detail should be provided by I. S. L. Loudon, *Medical care and the general practitioner 1750–1850* (Oxford, forthcoming). See also H. Marland, 'Medicine and society in Wakefield and Huddersfield 1780–1870', unpublished PhD thesis, University of Warwick, 1984, Ch. 7, section II; M. A. Crowther, 'Paupers or patients? Obstacles to professionalisation in the poor law medical service before 1914', *Journal of the History of Medicine*, vol. 39 (1984), pp. 33–54; D. Watkins, 'The English revolution in social medicine, 1889–1911', unpublished PhD thesis, University of London, 1984. On incomes and fees in the earlier period see Walton, 'Fifteenth-century London medical men', pp. 171–92; W. R. LeFanu, 'A North-Riding doctor in 1609', *Medical History*, vol. 5 (1961), pp. 178–88; McConaghey, 'History of rural medical practice', pp. 126–9; Raach, 'The English country doctor', Ch. 5; and note 66 above. On contracting, tendering and 'farming' in poor relief from the eighteenth century, see S. and B. Webb, *English poor law history Part 1*, pp. 277–313.

73. In relation to the serious conditions caused by syphilis, Clowes can be seen attempting to modify the usual contractual terms: Clowes, *Morbus Gallicus*, fos. 39r, 42v.

74. J. Paget, *Records of Harvey* (1846), p. 16.

75. P. Clark and P. Slack, *English towns in transition 1500–1700* (1975), pp. 11–12. See pp. 5ff for definition of towns. These percentages are based on populations of around 4,000 and over. On rural medical practice see McConaghey, Sawyer, MacDonald, Neale, Raach and Mustain (notes 21, 34, 63, 5 and 54 above). Except for McConaghey these sources are dealing primarily with the comparatively prosperous practitioner of physic; cf. Pelling and Webster, 'Medical practitioners', pp. 230–4; K. Thomas, *Religion and the decline of magic* (Harmondsworth, 1980), esp. pp. 209–27.

76. Pelling and Webster, 'Medical practitioners', p. 235.

77. For Tyrell's will, see Norfolk RO, NCC 129 Amyson (1644).

78. See above, note 34.

79. Cf. William Clowes's observation made in an urban context, quoted above, pp.115–16.

80. For Cotta, see *DNB*.

81. See Peterson, *Mid-Victorian medical profession*, pp. 259–82.

82. See Young, *Annals*, pp. 178, 313, 317, 324, 325, 329, 331, 340.

Men as well as women could be licensed specifically for the treatment of women: ibid., pp. 330–1 (male practitioner, generative parts of women, including midwifery, 1611) and Pelling and Webster, 'Medical practitioners', p. 209 (female practitioner, the art of physic on women and children and others, 1596).

83. Pelling and Webster, 'Medical practitioners', p. 198; C. Webster, 'Alchemical and Paracelsian medicine' in Webster, *Health, medicine and mortality*, pp. 301–34; C. Webster, *From Paracelsus to Newton: magic and the making of modern science* (Cambridge, 1983), introduction.

84. See *OED*, s.v. 'profession'.

85. R. Copland, *The questyonary of cyrurgyens . . .* (1541), sig. [2] Ai v; F. Bacon, *The advancement of learning*, ed. G. W. Kitchin (1965), Bk. 2, X, 2.

86. *Julius Caesar*, I.i.3–5.

87. Cf. Holmes, *Augustan England*, pp. 194, 197; Peterson, *Mid-Victorian medical profession*, pp. 252–9.

88. E. Jorden, *A briefe discourse of a disease called the suffocation of the mother* (1603), Epistle Dedicatory, sig. A2.

89. See Webster, 'English medical reformers'; Webster, *The great instauration*, section IV, 'The prolongation of life'; C. Hill, 'The medical profession and its radical critics', in C. Webster, *Change and continuity in seventeenth-century England* (1974), pp. 157–78.

90. Webster, *The great instauration*, pp. 259–60, 282–3.

91. F. N. L. Poynter, 'Thomas Southwood Smith — the man (1788–1861)', *Proceedings of the Royal Society for Medicine*, vol. 55 (1962), pp. 383–5.

92. Bacon, *Advancement of learning*, Bk. 2, X, 3; Webster, *The great instauration*, pp. 256ff.

93. On different attitudes to the vernacular see Bullough, *Development of medicine*, p. 4; Larson, *Rise of professionalism*, pp. 3–4. Cf. Pelling and Webster, 'Medical practitioners', pp. 176, 177; Webster, *The great instauration*, pp. 256–73. See also P. Slack, 'Mirrors of health and treasures of poor men: the uses of the vernacular medical literature of Tudor England' in Webster, *Health, medicine and mortality*, pp. 237–73. On the literacy of barber-surgeons, see also Walton, *Fifteenth-century London medical men*, pp. 72–7; Young, *Annals*, pp. 309–10, 312; Talbot, *Medicine in medieval England*, pp. 186–97. On increasing literacy among apprentices in general in the sixteenth century, see Palliser, 'Trade gilds of Tudor York', p. 99.

94. Clowes, *Morbus Gallicus*, fos. 10r, 13v–14r; George Baker, 'The nature and property of quicksilver' in ibid., fo. 49r.

95. Holmes, *Augustan England*, p. 194.

96. L. Stone, 'Social mobility in England, 1500–1700', *P & P*, no. 33 (1966), pp. 16–55; A. Everitt, 'Social mobility in early modern England', ibid., pp. 56–73. M. Espinasse, 'The decline and fall of restoration science', *P & P*, no. 14 (1958), pp. 71–89.

97. This is rightly stressed by Peterson, *Mid-Victorian medical profession*. For a reassertion of the professional differences between the 'ordinary practitioner' of the eighteenth century (in France) and the

nineteenth-century general practitioner, see T. Gelfand, 'The decline of the ordinary practitioner and the rise of a modern medical profession' in M. S. Staum and D. E. Larsen (eds), *Doctors, patients, and society: power and authority in medical care* (Waterloo, Ontario, 1981), pp. 105–29.

98. This is true even of Peterson, *Mid-Victorian medical profession*, who is unusually broad and detailed in her coverage of the economic circumstances of the London profession.

99. There has consequently been only limited response to Inkster's charge of 'neglect of the economic function of the profession': I. Inkster, 'Marginal men: aspects of the social role of the medical community in Sheffield 1790–1850' in J. Woodward and D. Richards (eds), *Health care and popular medicine in nineteenth century England* (1977), p. 154. Hence the vagueness in application of terms such as 'supply', 'demand' and 'market', and the lack of reference to areas outside medicine itself. Similar limitations apply to the criticism made by Paul Starr, and to his own attempt to supply the deficiency, even though his interpretation is regarded by many as extreme: P. Starr, 'Medicine, economy and society in nineteenth-century America' in P. Branca (ed.), *The medicine show* (New York, 1977), p. 47; P. Starr, *The social transformation of American medicine* (New York, 1982). For an attempt to go outside 'professional' issues in this respect, see J. Pickstone, 'The professionalisation of medicine in England and Europe: the state, the market and industrial society', *Nihon Ishigaku Zasshi [Journal of the Japan Society of Medical History]*, vol. 25 (1979), pp. 520–50.

100. Foster, 'Dr William Henry Cook: the finances of a Victorian general practitioner', *Proceedings of the Royal Society of Medicine, Section for the History of Medicine*, vol. 66 (1973), pp. 12–50; William Budd to Richard Budd, 16 Nov. 1845, Autograph Letter Collection: William Budd, Wellcome Institute for the History of Medicine, London; E. W. Goodall, *William Budd* (Bristol, 1936), p. 64; *DNB*, s.v. 'Farr, William'; J. Snow, *Snow on Cholera*, ed. W. H. Frost (New York, 1965), p. xxxi; D. Palfreyman, *John Jeyes . . . The making of a household name* (Thetford, 1977). For other possible examples see Holmes, *Augustan England*, p. 222; Inkster, 'Marginal men', p. 162.

101. Peterson, *Mid-Victorian medical profession*, p. 287.

5

A Drudgery of Schoolmasters: the Teaching Profession in Elizabethan and Stuart England

David Cressy

Was schoolteaching a profession or simply an occupation? Sixteenth- and seventeenth-century schoolmasters belonged to no professional association, experienced no uniform training, and enjoyed little of the social standing or financial reward of their contemporaries in the law or the church. Professional solidarity among schoolteachers was virtually impossible since their incomes, circumstances, quality and expectations varied so much. While some teachers dedicated their lives to educating children, many more treated time in the classroom as a temporary job. Schoolteaching could be a career, but it could also be undertaken begrudgingly as a lowly stopgap employment on the way to something else. Given the breadth of the educational spectrum, it is not unreasonable for historians to have characterised 'schoolteaching' as a 'grey area' replete with 'apparent anomalies' when contrasted to the mainstream professions. Even contemporaries, like the Jacobean schoolmaster John Brinsley, could barely decide whether they were engaged in a 'worthy profession' or a 'moiling and drudging life'.[1]

Seventeenth-century grammar school masters talked of their 'office', their 'function', a toilsome 'employment' and 'the most laborious calling' as well as of their 'profession'. John Brinsley's *Ludus literarius* (1612) presents a dialogue between two teachers, *Spoudeus*, who seems to have been labouring in a country grammar school, and *Philoponus*, a successful master teacher. Spoudeus has found schoolmastering to be 'a fruitless, wearisome and unthankful office'. He is wearied — today we might say burned out — by the 'discouragements and vexations' of his difficult and unrewarding task. Philoponus responds sympathetically, agreeing that teaching is 'too unthankful a calling'. For Brinsley, speaking through Philoponus, the remedy includes stoic endurance: 'we must look for thanks and the rewards of our labours from God when the world is unthankful'. Spoudeus asks how a schoolmaster should be qualified, but instead of discussing university training, degrees or other courses of preparation Philoponus discourses on the teacher's moral qualities. The ideal teacher should be conscientious, painstaking and diligent, loving, gentle and grave, 'a godly man, of good carriage in his conversation'.[2] Brinsley's schoolmaster may have belonged to a quasi-profession, but he was to be judged more by God than by his colleagues or peers.

Henry Peacham noted in *The truth of our times* (1638) that 'there is no profession more necessary to the erecting of a famous commonwealth than that of schoolmasters, yet none in more dis-esteem'.[3] Thomas Fuller in *The holy state* (1648) judged that 'there is scarce any profession in the commonwealth more necessary, which is so slightly performed'.[4] Marchamount Nedham in his *Discourse concerning schools and school-masters* (1663) repeated the charge that there was 'no employment more publicly useful, none more toilsome and painful, yet no one more sleighted even to reproach, no one else rewarded or regarded'. Nedham even went so far as to liken schoolmastering to labouring in the galleys, quoting '*Quem Jupiter odit, Paedagogum facit.*'[5]

A brief review of educational provision in Elizabethan and Stuart England will set the scene. High in the firmament were the great schools of England, notably Eton, Winchester and Westminster. These rich establishments served a national and privileged clientele. They enjoyed close connections with Oxford and Cambridge colleges and employed masters whose academic and social standing was comparable to that of university dons.[6] Stars of the second magnitude included the major endowed grammar schools like St Paul's and Merchant Taylors' in London, Bury St Edmunds in Suffolk and St Bee's in Cumberland. Founded to teach the classical curriculum, these schools sent a regular succession of boys to the universities. Pupils came from gentle, professional and commercial families over a wide geographical area. Generously endowed and usually well organised, the major grammar schools sought out the best qualified schoolmasters and ushers. Most of their teachers were graduates, and among them could be found the most dedicated *ludimagistri*. Several dozen schools might be grouped in this category.[7]

Typically the grammar school master supervised a school of fifty to a hundred pupils, divided into forms according to their numbers, age and ability. The master employed an usher or two to assist with the teaching, and recruited senior boys or servants to perform such chores as preparing the ink, stoking the fire, sweeping the room and emptying the soil buckets. The master was a manager as well as an instructor. He kept the accounts, registered admissions, and dealt with trustees and parents. He drilled his pupils with Nowell's *Catechism*, dealt out double translation of Cicero (from Latin to English, then back to Latin again), and laboured with Livy and Horace. The best schools also taught Greek, using the *Clavis Graecae linguae* as an introduction. Some even made a beginning with Hebrew.[8]

Overshadowed by the major grammar schools were the local grammar schools, perhaps two or three hundred in number.[9] Like the prestigious grammar schools on which they were modelled, these country grammar schools offered a Latin curriculum but often added vocational or even elementary subjects to meet the needs of local inhabitants. Typically they served the lesser gentry, yeomen and trading families of the surrounding parishes, preparing children for apprenticeships but intermittently sending boys up to Oxford or Cambridge. The value of their endowments varied as much as the quality of the teaching. The masters were usually university graduates, although men without academic credentials might serve at a pinch. The success of these schools depended less on the quality of the institution than on the talents of any individual teacher. Their reputations rose and fell briskly as teachers came and went. An ambitious man such as William Dugard at Colchester (1637–42) or Thomas Hall at King's Norton (1629–62) could transform such a school by the success of his teaching or by catering to a particular fee-paying clientele.[10] Henry Rix brought fresh ideas to the old free grammar school at Saffron Walden, Essex, in 1674. Taking advantage of the new communications media, he advertised in *The London Gazette* his offering of 'the Latin, Greek and French tongues' and also 'arithmetic, merchant accounts, and the writing of twelve several hands . . .'[11] Local grammar schools could just as easily decay through bad management, lax instruction, or a failure to attend to local needs. Their chronicles are filled with disputes between masters, parents and trustees, revealing conditions of flux and frustration.[12]

Somewhat murkier is the history of the so-called general schools, sometimes marginally endowed but more often supported by subscriptions and fees. These schools, perhaps a thousand or more in number, operated fitfully in both rural and urban areas. They usually depended for their existence on the presence of a freelance schoolmaster who was willing to teach what he could to all who chose (and could afford) to attend.[13] Instruction ranged from the rudiments of ABC to arithmetic and Latin, depending on the skills of the master and the demands of his clientele. The teacher might be a graduate clergyman, but was more often an enterprising layman. Some of his pupils would graduate to the grammar schools, and a few might go direct to university, but the majority would be recruited to trades. Some general schoolmasters turned their schools into successful commercial establishments, augmenting or even abandoning the antique curriculum and offering instead a battery of useful modern subjects. Such transformations were more common in the latter half of the seventeenth century. Edmund Whitside became schoolmaster at Wells, Norfolk, in 1673 with a curriculum of 'reading, writing, arithmetic, navigation, astronomy, the art of dialling, surveying of land, lagging of cask, making of all sorts of sea instruments, modelising of all sorts of ships, geography, trigonometry the first and second part'.[14] Whitside was evidently a talented and well-organised man, a professional instructor, but not a *ludimagister* of the traditional kind.

In the darkest reaches of educational activity we can glimpse the activities of the petty schools. Teaching reading, with perhaps some writing and ciphering, the petty teachers struggled to bring their charges across the threshold of literacy. Their own education and competence varied greatly, and brought little credit to the teaching 'profession'. Francis Clement described them in 1587 as 'men or women altogether rude, and utterly ignorant of the due composing and just spelling of words'.[15] The churchwardens of Sherwell, Devon, reported in 1665 that they had no public schoolmasters, but 'only the clerks of some parishes, and some poor people who would otherwise in likelihood be burdensome to the parishes. They teach ABC, to spell and read'.[16] One of this type, Richard

Roach, appeared in 1671 to request a schoolmaster's licence to teach English in the parish of Stepney, Middlesex. The testimonial on his behalf told a sad tale of injury and indigence, and further certified 'that the said Richard hath not so much of scholarship whereby to prejudice any Latin schools whatsoever, but what he can do is only for his present subsistence'.[17] Only the most generous interpretation could link these people with grammar masters like John Brinsley or Henry Rix as colleagues in a 'worthy profession'.

Almost anyone could serve as a schoolteacher in Tudor and Stuart England provided they met the requirements of the church, their patrons and their clientele. Standards varied enormously in a loose free market of talent and incompetence. Except informally and occasionally, schoolmasters experienced no peer review. They were, however, subject to inspection by the church.

Like midwives and preachers, whose activities were similarly considered to impinge on things spiritual, schoolteachers were supposed to obtain formal licences from the church. As late as 1700 the Lord Keeper declared in Chancery, 'I always was, and still am of opinion, that keeping of school is by the old laws of England of ecclesiastical cognisance.' The licensing requirement applied equally to grammar school masters and petty teachers, although in practice elementary teachers were more likely to escape ecclesiastical attention.[18]

Throughout the sixteenth and seventeenth centuries the church vetted applicants for teaching licences and then kept track of schoolmasters through periodic visitations. Elizabeth's Injunctions of 1559 repeated the Marian provision 'that no man shall take upon himself to teach but such as shall be allowed by the ordinary'. (The ordinary was the archbishop, bishop, archdeacon or commissary who exercised local ecclesiastical jurisdiction.) The Canons of 1604, following those of 1571, laid down the rules that were to be followed for the rest of the seventeenth century: 'No man shall teach either in public school or private house, but such as shall be allowed by the bishop of the diocese or ordinary of the place, under his hand and seal.' Intending teachers had to subscribe to the Oath of Supremacy and to the Oath of Allegiance. The Canons of 1604 also required them to subscribe to the articles of religion. The Act of Uniformity of 1662 required schoolteachers to acknowledge the unlawfulness of taking up arms against the

King and to renounce the Solemn League and Covenant. Schoolmasters performed these subscriptions in front of officers of the church.[19]

Episcopal visitors frequently took stock of the teachers within their jurisdiction. Richard Montague, visiting the diocese of Norwich in 1638, demanded of the church-wardens, 'is there any school-master in your parish, who teacheth public grammar, to write or read, or in private house? Who are they, in whose houses do they teach, with license from the ordinary or without?' Bishop Anthony Sparrow issued similar instructions in 1677:

> You shall also cite all parsons, vicars, curates and school-masters of every parish church or chapel . . . to exhibit their letters of orders, licences to preach, serve cure or teach school, if they have any, or else come and show cause why they officiate without.[20]

This machinery of ecclesiastical control operated everywhere in England as the only register of schoolmasters. Although diocesan administrations varied in efficiency, allowing all sorts of irregularities of compliance, the principle was clearly established: schoolteachers were answerable to the church.

The following tables indicate the educational qualifications and teaching subjects of schoolmasters known to the ecclesiastical authorities of the dioceses of London and Norwich. The London figures are drawn from the vicar-general's licensing register and refer to schoolmasters in the City, Middlesex, Essex and part of Hertfordshire. The Norwich figures are based on episcopal visitations and cover Norfolk, Suffolk and part of Cambridgeshire. A more complete picture can be obtained by synthesising visitation comperta and consignations, testimonials, licensing and subscription books, as well as school histories, but the coverage and the results are not susceptible to a simple statistical presentation.[21] Some records do not survive and others were poorly put together in the first place. The revolutionary decades of the mid-seventeenth century are not represented here since episcopal administration first collapsed and was then temporarily abolished in the 1640s. Although the tables are based on the most complete set of licensing records and the most comprehensive visitations, they represent only the minimum number of schoolmasters practising at any one time.

Table 5.1: Schoolmasters in the diocese of London, 1580–1700

Decade	Total	BA	MA	hd	lit	%gd	%lit	gr	gr+	ng	unk	%gr
1580s	156	24	18	0	0	27	0	59	10	62	25	38
1590s	193	33	35	0	59	35	31	97	3	83	10	51
1600s	127	27	27	0	35	43	28	70	10	46	1	55
1610s	202	38	47	3	85	44	42	123	3	60	14	61
1620s	160	33	46	0	53	49	33	100	4	48	8	62
1630s	148	33	55	0	45	59	30	117	1	27	3	79
1660s	150	19	26	1	20	30	13	93	9	13	35	62
1670s	121	11	18	1	29	25	24	85	0	13	23	75
1680s	91	2	4	0	42	8	46	70	1	10	10	77
1690s	71	2	5	0	7	10	10	64	1	5	1	90
Total	1,419	222	281	5	375	36	26	878	42	367	130	62

Key to Tables 5.1 and 5.2: BA: Bachelor of Arts; MA: Master of Arts; hd: higher degree; lit: 'literatus'; gd: graduate; gr: offering grammar; gr+: offering grammar and other subjects; ng: not offering grammar; unk: unknown whether offering grammar.

Table 5.2: Schoolmasters in the diocese of Norwich, 1605–92

Year	Total	BA	MA	hd	lit	%gd	gr	gr+	ng	unk	%gr
1605	65	17	11	0	2	43	36	21	8	0	55
1627	64	5	21	0	0	41	35	17	8	4	55
1636	80	10	37	0	0	58	57	8	10	5	71
1662	46	2	14	0	0	35	35	2	4	5	76
1677	42	7	9	0	0	38	8	18	7	9	19
1692	54	6	6	0	0	22	24	6	8	16	44

See Table 5.1 for key to abbreviations.

More than a third of the licensed schoolmasters in London and East Anglia had university degrees and half of them had some kind of university experience. The London register shows a steady improvement in the educational background of teachers from 27 per cent graduates in the 1580s to 59 per cent in the decade before the Civil War. The diocese of Norwich visitations also show an expanding proportion of graduates in the 1630s. These figures correspond with the growth of the universities, and may also reflect the scarcity of alternative employment for graduates. Schoolmastering became an interim employment for men down from Oxford or Cambridge. A smaller proportion of graduate teachers appeared in the records in the decades following the Civil War. Fragmentary Norwich licensing records (not tabulated) tell a similar story, with 30 per cent of schoolmasters holding degrees in the 1580s, 49 per cent in the 1630s, 31 per cent in the 1660s and just 6 per cent in the 1690s. Twenty-five per cent of schoolmasters making subscriptions in the diocese of Norwich in the period 1660 to 1700 were university graduates.[22]

A quarter of all schoolmasters licensed in the diocese of London were recorded as *literati*. Nearly half the schoolmasters licensed in the diocese of Norwich in the 1580s were similarly designated, as were 11 per cent of those who signed subscriptions later in the seventeenth century. The designation *literatus* applied to someone who had attended one of the universities but who left before taking a degree. In fact 50 per cent of all entrants to Cambridge went down without graduating, so there were plenty of job-seeking *literati* in the pool.[23]

Unless ill-educated general schoolmasters evaded ecclesiastical attention — a possibility which has yet to be adequately demonstrated — we must conclude that the educational credentials of the known teaching force were impressively high. However, a degree was by no means a necessary part of a schoolmaster's qualifications, and apparently became less common towards the end of the seventeenth century.

The ecclesiastical records also indicate the subjects which particular teachers taught, although this information is not wholly reliable. For example, we know from other sources that the Londoner John Clarke taught 'the art of writing and arithmetic, grammar and the English tongue', but his licence makes no mention of arithmetic. Edmund Whitside of Wells,

Norfolk, taught a range of useful subjects including reading, writing and surveying; the bishop recorded him as a grammar teacher although Whitside made no such claims.[24] Underlying these adjustments may have been an assumption that schoolmasters naturally taught the classical curriculum, and a supposition that grammar teaching should be monitored because it was ideologically sensitive.

The London licensing register shows a substantial increase in the proportion of schoolmasters teaching grammar, from 38 per cent in the 1580s to 90 per cent in the 1690s. The rise in the first part of the seventeenth century roughly parallels the rise in the proportion of graduate teachers and probably reflects their pedagogic expectations. Men with degrees would most likely want to teach grammar.[25] The renewed expansion after 1660 is more difficult to explain since the proportion offering grammar increased as overall numbers and the graduate percentage declined. Perhaps only grammar teachers thought it necessary to obtain licences in the post-Restoration era. Perhaps too the figures mask a number of elementary or petty teachers whose credentials were upgraded to grammar. It is hard to believe that grammar teaching held such sway at the end of the seventeenth century when all other indications point to an upsurge of non-classical instruction.[26]

The evidence from the diocese of Norwich, by contrast, shows a falling off in the proportion of schoolmasters offering grammar from 78 per cent in the 1580s, 72 per cent in the 1630s, to 47 per cent in the 1660s and 21 per cent in the 1690s. Visitations of the diocese found a varying proportion licensed for grammar — from 19 per cent to 76 per cent — but no apparent pattern.[27]

The Elizabethan Injunctions required a teacher to be 'found meet as well for his learning and dexterity in teaching, as for sober and honest conversation and also for right understanding of God's true religion'.[28] This test of ideology and character was important since the schoolmaster employed the church catechism as a teaching tool (in English or Latin), and was critically positioned to shape his children's minds.[29] Schoolteachers often tendered testimonials to show their suitability for a licence. The testimonials usually addressed the issue of 'honest conversation'. For example, the rector and two principal inhabitants certified in 1676 that:

James Andrews of Chelsworth in the county of Suffolk, being desirous to have a licence to teach young ones the art of reading English as also the grammar, is one very orthodox in his judgement, honest in his life and conversation, exactly complying with the discipline of the Church of England, and one that gives us very good hopes that he will be very serviceable in the work and service that he desires to meddle with and engage in.

The bishop's chancellor duly endorsed this testimonial, 'fiat licentia ad docendam gramaticam'.[30]

The church had authority to scrutinise a teacher's competency for the classroom, but in practice the bishop's licensing clerks paid scant attention to anything but religious conformity. Sixteen neighbours (five of them illiterate) testified on behalf of Richard Roach, the crippled petty teacher, 'that he is a man of civil demeanour amongst us and also that he constantly and duly frequenteth the protestant church'. It was enough to be orthodox in religion.[31]

If the licensing authorities were more interested in religious probity than professional competence, who would oversee the personal and pedagogic qualities of the teaching profession? The burden lay with employers and patrons, who bore it with uneven effect. The trustees of Ipswich school in 1580 inspected a prospective schoolmaster equipped with 'all such endowments and ornaments requisite to such a function as true religion, learning, diligence and practice'. Lord Burghley advised the governors of Bury St Edmunds school in 1581 that someone exhibiting 'soundness in religion . . . manners and conversation' would satisfy their requirements.[32] Personal qualities usually outweighed 'professional' attributes. There was little more than a loose consensus about the criteria for schoolmasters, even in the established grammar schools.

Founders and benefactors of endowed grammar schools often specified the kind of man they wanted, leaving school governors or trustees to find an applicant to fit the bill. The following three examples may be regarded as representative. At Sir John Deane's Free Grammar School at Witton, Chester, founded in 1558, the master was supposed to be 'learned, sober, discreet and unmarried; such a one as hath taken a degree or degrees in the Universities of Oxford or Cambridge; undefamed, and of the age of thirty years at the least'. If, despite these qualifications, he proved 'dissolute in manners, a drunkard, a whoremonger, or intangled with other occupations repugnant to his vocation, a dicer, or a common gamester' the feoffees had authority to remove him.[33]

Sir Roger Manwood's 1580 statutes for Sandwich school, Kent, invoked the university as well as the church in the process of selecting a teacher. The Rector and Fellows of Lincoln College, Oxford, were to assist the school trustees in their search. The successful candidate could become master provided he:

> be well reported of, Master of Arts in degree if it may be conveniently . . . and that the schoolmaster be first allowed by the ordinary, and by examination found meet both for his learning and discretion of teaching, as also for his honest conversation and right understanding of God's true religion now set forth by public authority.

Like his counterpart at Witton, the Sandwich schoolmaster would be disqualified if he proved to be 'a common gamester, and haunter of taverns, nor by an extraordinary or unnecessary expenses in apparel or otherwise become an infamy to the school'.[34]

The orders for Archbishop Samuel Harsnet's school at Chigwell, Essex, founded in 1631, specified that:

> the Latin schoolmaster be a graduate of one of the universities, not under seven and twenty years of age, a man skilful in the Greek and Latin tongues, a good poet, of a sound religion, neither papist nor puritan, of a grave behaviour, of a sober and honest conversation, no tippler nor haunter of alehouses, and above all, that he be apt to teach and severe in his government.

In this case the founder was adamant that his schoolmaster should not be a cleric, a pluralist who would divide his attentions and perhaps neglect the school: 'As soon as the schoolmaster do enter into holy orders, either as deacon or priest, his place to become void *ipso facto*, as if he were dead.'[35]

Founders and governors of grammar schools shared a preference for university men, graduates at least and Masters of Arts if possible. Possession of a degree from Oxford or

Cambridge signified a command of the grammar curriculum and also encouraged confidence that the teacher could train schoolboys to follow in his footsteps. Graduate teachers often presented a testimonial from their college in praise of their learning. No one taught teachers how to teach, yet they had to satisfy their employers of their aptitude and 'discretion of teaching'. This could be a baptism of fire, unless the master had worked as an usher or junior teacher before. The master in charge of a grammar school was supposed to be a man of maturity, able to command respect among schoolboys and their parents. A schoolmaster needed dignity in the same way that a school needed 'reputation'. Moral character was vitally important. Underlying these provisions was a sense that certain types of behaviour were 'repugnant' to a schoolmaster's 'vocation', and that desirable 'professional' standards might best be achieved by prohibiting their opposites.

In practice, of course, some schoolmasters fell short of these desired specifications. The age specifications were not always enforced. Nor did every teacher possess a degree. John Langley, who taught grammar at Edmonton, Middlesex, in 1611, 'performeth not the duty of a schoolmaster according to the Canons and is not of sober conversation but very often shamefully and most offensively drunk'. Schoolmasters, no less than men in other professions, fell victim to lassitude, gluttony, corruption and vice.[36]

School governors sometimes listened to the advice of well-respected schoolmasters when selecting a candidate for a teaching post. This created a limited kind of peer review. In 1646, for example, the Fishmongers' Company of London consulted another John Langley, the Master of St Paul's School, and William Dugard, master of Merchant Taylors', when hiring a teacher for Gresham's grammar school at Holt, Norfolk, which lay in their charge. The two London teachers persuaded the company to drop their chosen candidate, reporting:

> that Mr. Richard Breviter is so far below their expectation and in such a condition as made them wonder he should offer himself to the employment of a schoolmaster's place in a public grammar school, which would prove a discontent to his mind and to others unsatisfactory.[37]

Whatever the reason (in 1646 it may well have been politics) the masters of the prestigious London schools felt qualified to judge the credentials of a fellow schoolmaster. But they never went so far as to establish a 'society of schoolmasters' to formalise such judgements or to provide any centralised regulation for their profession.

A few seventeenth-century grammar school masters sought to upgrade the low status of teachers by advocating higher standards of pedagogy, more dignified behaviour, long years of career dedication, and higher pay. After reviewing the 'weariness and discontent' of schoolmasters, the fruitlessness of their labours, and the lack of gratitude among parents and children, John Brinsley considered how 'to take away all this reproach, and to begin to recover the credit of our worthy profession'. The best way was simply to be good at the job, so that 'masters may teach with much delight and comfort, and scholars learn with an ingenuous emulation'. The master should have command of classical grammar and be systematic and forceful in its application. Schoolmasters who took their work seriously would model their curriculum on that of the finest London schools. Brinsley also suggested that one way of enforcing respect was to insist on prompt and proper payment: 'It is wisdom ever to call for our due at the quarter's end.'[38]

Marchamount Nedham adduced another factor which detracted from the teacher's professional standing. Schoolmasters beat children, sometimes savagely, and their violence 'hath brought a very great contempt and hatred upon the profession'. Whipping and flogging, thought Nedham, were 'not at all beseeming either gentleman or divine', so that if a schoolmaster wished to enjoy a superior social status he should delegate the thrashing to the hands of a beadle or servant.[39] Everyone knew that schoolmasters had to be severe, but there came a point where severity descended to ferocity, a point of diminishing returns.

What other ways were there for schoolmasters to lay claim to a 'professional' standing? Like Brinsley, they could take pride in their learning and in the effectiveness of their pedagogy. Like the London schoolmasters advising the Fishmongers' Company, they could insist that the better grammar schools at least hired university graduates or men whose own education would not be a reproach to them all. As masters of endowed schools, subject to school statutes and ordinances and answerable to governors or trustees, they might in some cases claim career security, with lifetime tenure and even sickness pay.[40]

Security of tenure varied like everything else. The master of Sandwich school enjoyed exceptionally generous terms of employment besides his house and his stipend. Once appointed, he could look forward to a lifetime of security, so long as he conformed to the statutes. If he became sick of 'the ague or any curable sickness' he was to be 'tolerated for the time and his stipend allowed fully'. Even in his old age the school would look after him, 'so that his office be furnished by his sufficient deputy, although he himself be not able'. The master at Merchant Taylors' School enjoyed similar sickness leave, but no security of tenure. The statutes admonished him,

> this is no room of continuance and perpetuity, but upon the doing of your duty in the school. And every year when [the governors] shall be assembled in the school house, concerning the visitation thereof, you shall submit you to their examination, and, found doing your duty accordingly, you shall continue, otherwise, reasonably warned, you shall content you to depart.

Professional schoolmasters could insist on certain privileges, such as the right to control school admissions or the right to collect additional fees. At Alford Grammar School, Lincolnshire, the statutes promised a certain dignity: 'No man shall have authority to taunt and check the schoolmaster or to intermeddle with anything pertaining to his duty but only the governors of the school.'[41] Through such means the masters could compensate for their atrociously low salaries and ambiguous social standing. Teachers in our day have been told that these rewards constitute 'psychic income'.

Another professional inducement was the promise of an educational monopoly, the exclusion of competing licensed teachers from a particular location. At Hereford school the governors ordered, 'for the better encouragement of the said master and usher, and for the better advancement of the school . . . that no Latin school shall be kept within the said city other than the school aforsaid'. Richard Reynolds refused to accept his appointment as master of Colchester Grammar

School in 1691 unless the licence of a competing independent schoolmaster, Peter Noblet, was revoked. Thomas Bainbrigg, schoolmaster at Holt, Norfolk, complained in 1686 of his inability to conduct a monopoly operation, 'for that most of the curates in the country did teach school for their better maintenance', thereby undercutting his own income. Schoolmasters' monopolies became more jealously guarded in the competitive climate of the late seventeenth century, with disputes over alleged encroachments.[42]

Marchamount Nedham came right to the heart of the matter: "Tis the salary which makes schools and learning flourish.' Fine teaching (*pace* Brinsley) and long service (*pace* Peacham and Fuller) were all very well, but 'the conscience of doing public service, and satisfaction of discharging one's duty, is not a sufficient recompense for the toil of teaching'. Money alone was the answer. If schools paid better stipends 'young scholars at the university would prepare themselves for school, as for a handsome preferment; whereas now nothing but pure necessity can put them upon that way'. Adequate salaries, achieved perhaps by better management of school endowments,

> would invite men of eminent parts and abilities into school work; whereas now tis made the sanctuary of many idle insufficient persons who have no hopes elsewhere, or by those, which have any merit, design'd a step to some church preferment.[43]

Some teachers were desperately poor. Mathew Elwald, who taught grammar at St Dunstan's-in-the-West in London, protested in 1661 that he had 'lost his whole estate and his posterity, ruinated without recovery' in the service of the late King. Now, as a city schoolmaster in charge of a general school, he could not even afford a licence, 'his incomes at the most exceed not five shillings weekly'. Five shillings a week represented an income in the order of £10–£12 a year, which was pitiful even by seventeenth-century standards. Ralph Josselin, on the other hand, could congratulate himself on his income from teaching, which supplemented his clerical stipend and other enterprises. In 1657 he estimated his school at Earls Colne, Essex, to be 'worth near £70 yearly to me'.[44]

Masters of Elizabethan endowed grammar schools could

expect a salary in the neighbourhood of £20 a year, but remuneration varied without apparent pattern. The stipend from the foundation formed merely the teacher's base pay, to be supplemented by a miscellaneous collection of fees. Sir John Deane's school at Witton, Cheshire (founded in 1558), offered just £12 as wages, but the teacher could charge each pupil 4d at admission and 1d at Christmas. These additional fees were known as 'vails'. Twenty pounds a year was specified as the master's salary at St Albans' Grammar School, Hertfordshire, in 1570, an authorised payment which had not increased by the beginning of the seventeenth century, despite three decades of ruinous inflation. The governors graciously permitted the teacher to charge quarterly 'vails' of 4d per pupil from the borough and 12d for non-residents. Coventry Grammar School, Warwickshire, endowed in 1573, paid £20 to the master, £10 to 'a learned usher', and provided them both with houses. New orders for the school in 1628 did nothing to improve the salary but authorised the teachers to collect 12d per pupil on admission and to charge what the market would bear for boys who were not inhabitants of Coventry. The master of Sandwich school, Kent (founded in 1580), drew £20 a year. But the foundation also provided him with a house, allowed him to charge rent to boarders and to collect fees from pupils from out of town, so an enterprising master could boost his income. At St Bees, Cumberland (founded in 1583), the master received £20 a year plus admission fees. The usher, described as 'some poor scholar', earned £3 6s 8d, with 2d for each pupil entered and 4d for every one he taught to write. The low-paid master of Hartlebury school, Worcestershire, was permitted to augment his wages with 'the profits of all such cock-fights and potations as are commonly used in schools, and such other gifts as shall freely be given them by any of the friends of their scholars'. The master of Guisborough school, Yorkshire, could supplement his meagre income by demanding his 'vails' of 4d per pupil registration, but could charge no more 'of duty'. Benevolences, however, were another matter: 'If any of the parents or friends of the scholars give him anything of their free will he may take it thankfully.' This dependence on handouts was no way to build up professional self-respect.[45]

Quite often the original Elizabethan or early Stuart payment schedules persisted through the seventeenth century.

Marchamount Nedham complained that schoolmasters' salaries did not keep pace with improvements in the value of endowments. 'The trustees and governors in the several corporations share the improvements amongst themselves, take all above the salary for lawful prize, and leave the master to the bare old allowance, notwithstanding the vast increase of the old rents.'[46] The governors of Hereford school recognised this problem in 1665, but instead of drawing on the endowment they encouraged the master to open his doors and charge what the traffic would bear:

> In regard of the smallness of the annual salary and stipends belonging to the school, being £20 to the master and £10 to the usher . . ., the schoolmaster may demand and require what he thinks fit, not exceeding 5s for entrance and 20s per annum . . . of all free citizens of the said city . . . And as for foreigners, the schoolmaster is left to his own discretion for compounding with them for his salary[47]

The average salary (without fees) for a schoolmaster in the West Midlands in the 1640s was £17 2s, at a time when vicarages brought £42 or more a year and rectories were worth an average of £78.[48] At Gresham's Grammar School, Holt, Norfolk, the master was still receiving a bare £20 year in the late seventeenth century. Thomas Bainbrigg, an MA who spent 25 years teaching at Holt, supplemented his salary with the pluralist stipends from four church livings, and still needed the shilling per pupil he charged on admission.[49] Francis Brokesby observed in 1701 that many grammar masters in underendowed schools received 'mean and sordid' salaries, and there were examples before him of grammar school teachers with incomes from the foundation of just £10.[50] Professional solidarity was unlikely to develop, even among grammar school masters, in the face of such unevenness of remuneration.

Some schools paid well, with salaries that kept abreast of inflation. Norwich Grammar School, for example, paid just £10 to the master and £6 8s 4d a year to the usher in the middle of the sixteenth century but by 1586 the master was earning £25 a year and the usher's salary was £13 6s 8d. At the outbreak of the Civil War the master at Norwich drew £50 a year and the usher £24, respectable salaries befitting an important urban institution. Birmingham Grammar School, blessed with a developing endowment and good management, paid the master £50 a year in 1655 and £65 in 1676. To this should be added the income from benevolences and fees, and all the advantages of superior social contacts. Not surprisingly, these schools were more likely to attract and keep good teachers.[51]

Critics agreed that education suffered from a rapid turnover of teachers. Henry Peacham thought that some of the low esteem experienced by schoolmasters could be avoided if they would stick longer to the job. Unfortunately, given the poor rewards, most masters made teaching 'a shift but for a time, till a better fortune falleth'. Peacham wished (and wished in vain) that 'those who took that profession upon them, and found themselves able to endure it, should follow none other calling so long as they lived'. Thomas Fuller agreed with Peacham's analysis, observing that some teachers 'use it only as a passage to better preferment, to patch their rents in their present fortune till they can provide a new one and betake themselves to some more gainful calling'.[52] How could there ever be professional standing without professional career dedication? Marchamount Nedham, in his usual forthright manner, emphasised the primacy of 'Stipends, reward being the very life of action'.[53]

Length of service, like everything else associated with school-masters, varied with circumstances. The careers of masters of grammar schools in seventeenth-century Warwickshire and Worcestershire belied the gloomy estimates of contemporary critics. Their teaching lives can be traced over an average period of 27 years, with 15 years the mean length of stay at one establishment. At King Edward's School, Birmingham, which enjoyed the best salary and highest reputation in the region, the average length of service was 23 years.[54] The weaker endowed schools saw a rapid turnover of schoolmasters, and sometimes their posts remained unfilled. Wenhaston school in Suffolk, for example, saw ten teachers come and go between 1597 and 1633. Their annual salary was a meagre £7.[55] The ephemeral general schools saw even more mobility. Of 148 'schools' identified in Elizabethan Norfolk, 70 per cent existed for no more than six years. Only 18 per cent kept going for more than a decade.[56]

General schoolmasters and freelance teachers drifted in and

out of teaching, and often combined school work with other employment. John Butte of Elmham, Essex, augmented his income in 1637 by 'barbering men upon the Sundays'. John Cooke, the versatile schoolmaster of Brentwood, was presented in 1637 for being an irregular schoolmaster, also 'a disordered alehouse keeper . . . a tailor and a gardener and an underbailiff for arrest, and being also defamed for keeping company with two sisters and the mother of them'.[57] Most country schoolmasters probably engaged in farming, while others worked occasionally as scriveners or surveyors, according to their skills.[58]

Some of the better teachers combined service in the classroom with service in the church. Priests, however, formed only a minority of the teaching force in Elizabethan and Stuart England. Only 12 per cent of the schoolmasters licensed in the diocese of London between 1580 and 1700 were clergymen. Some of the lay teachers may subsequently have taken holy orders, but there was less of an overlap between schoolteaching and God's work than might be expected. Clerical school-masters also formed a distinct minority in the diocese of Norwich. Only 8 per cent of schoolmasters' licences went to clergymen; only 11 per cent of the schoolmasters who subscribed between 1660 and 1700 were also priests.[59]

Curates 'desirous to teach' would be licensed in preference to anyone else. The church canons promised them a monopoly of teaching unless there was already an established school in the parish.[60] Anthony Boughton, curate of St Andrew Under-shaft in London in 1610, also taught a school in the parish. John Stanhaw, a Cambridge graduate, was licensed to teach grammar at Kelsale, Suffolk, in 1619, was ordained as a priest in 1622, and was serving as a schoolmaster at Bawdsy, Suffolk, in 1629. In 1635 he became curate of Playford, Suffolk, but in the visitation the following year he displayed his old teaching licence and paid 12d for its consignation. The vicar of Stansted Mountfichet in Essex acknowledged in 1605 'that he is licensed to teach . . . this sixteen or eighteen years, and he sayeth he teacheth but two or three in his house'. Ralph Josselin served as a schoolmaster in Bedfordshire while waiting for a curacy, and later ran the school at Earls Colne, Essex, in tandem with his ministry.[61] Most of these men were clergy who supplemented their clerical income by teaching, rather than schoolmasters who doubled as priests. For them schoolmastering was a sideline, not a career.

The teaching irregulars and the ill-paid drudges, those who were drifting and those who were marking time, shared the burden of schoolmastering with dedicated and well-educated career *ludimagistri*. Society continued to treat schoolteachers as if they were inferior tradesmen. In most places the psychic rewards and the cash income were both poor. If we restricted our attention to the better grammar school masters like John Brinsley and William Dugard, we might consider school-teaching in the seventeenth century as an incipient profession, an activity whose prime practitioners were struggling for standards and recognition. However, they were compromised by the John Cookes and Richard Roaches, teachers who were utterly undeserving of 'professional' esteem. The anomalies noted by the historians and the ambivalence revealed in John Brinsley's dialogue would last for at least a couple of hundred years. Consider this appraisal of the teaching profession in the 1980s:

> We have no agreed definition of competence or agreed way of assessing it. There is very little involvement of professional practitioners in the training of aspirants. Following initial training, there is no uniform pattern or validation of the induction process, and no subsequent requirement for updating and for professional retraining. There is no overall body concerned with and publicly accountable for the discipline of the profession and the competence of its members. We still have a lot to do to establish our professional identity and authority.[62]

Add to this the perennial complaint about the paucity of teachers' pay, downplay the modern emphasis on training, and we have an indictment which might have come from Peacham or Nedham. Teachers today display an insecurity of status, an anxiety about professional position, akin to that of their predecessors in early modern England.

Notes

1. G. Holmes, *Augustan England: professions, state and society, 1680–1730* (1982), pp. 5, 7, 8, 34, 76. P. K. Orpen, 'Schoolmastering as a

David Cressy

profession in the seventeenth century: the career patterns of the grammar schoolmaster', *History of Education*, vol. 6 (1977), pp. 183–5. John Brinsley, *Ludus literarius: or the grammar schoole*, ed. E. T. Campagnac (Liverpool, 1917), pp. 1–3. John Brinsley, *A consolation for our grammar schools* (1622), pp. 7, 44–5. Cf. Kenneth Charlton, 'The professions in sixteenth-century England', *University of Birmingham Historical Journal*, vol. 12 (1969), pp. 34–40.

2. Brinsley, *Ludus literarius*, pp. 1–3, 267, 305–6.

3. H. Peacham, *The truth of our times: revealed out of one mans experience* (1638), pp. 14–15.

4. T. Fuller, *The holy state*, 2nd edn (Cambridge, 1648), p. 98.

5. M. Nedham, *A discourse concerning schools and school-masters* (1663), pp. 4, 9, 10. For more in this vein see Peacham, *Truth of our times*, pp. 19–20, and T. Morrice, *An apology for school-masters* (1619), sig. B2.

6. 'Some few prime schools in England serve as a foil for the rest; I mean Westminster, Winchester, Eton, Paul's, with some few others': Peacham, *Truth of our times*, p. 16. W. Harrison, *The description of England*, ed. G. Edelen (Itaca, New York, 1968), p. 76. E. Chamberlayne, *The second part of the present state of England* (1682), p. 320.

7. C. Hoole, *A new discovery of the old art of teaching schoole* (1660), p. 215. The life of these schools is described in F. Watson, *The English grammar schools to 1660: their curriculum and practice* (1908), and W. A. L. Vincent, *The grammar schools, their continuing tradition, 1660–1714* (1969).

8. D. Cressy, *Education in Tudor and Stuart England* (1975), pp. 48–53, 80–6.

9. Hoole, *New discovery*, pp. 213–14. Counting schools is a contentious business and classifying them even more troublesome. Estimates are obtained from Vincent, *Grammar schools*, pp. 6–7, from the 'Schools Inquiry Commission', *Parliamentary Papers* (1867–8), p. 108, and Appendix, pp. 150–1, from P. J. Wallis, 'The Wase school collection', *Bodleian Library Record*, vol. 4 (1952–3), pp. 78–104, and from charitable bequests such as those analysed in W. K. Jordan, *Philanthropy in England, 1480–1660* (1959). See also P. J. Wallis, *Histories of old schools: a revised list for England and Wales* (Newcastle upon Tyne, 1966).

10. Dugard, a graduate of Sidney Sussex College, Cambridge, taught at Oundle and Stamford before taking over the school at Colchester. His success brought him to the attention of the managers of Merchant Taylors' School, where he served as master from 1644 to his retirement in 1661: *DNB*; Colchester MS Register, Essex RO, Microfilm T/B 217. For Hall see Orpen, 'Schoolmastering as a profession', p. 191.

11. *London Gazette*, no. 879 (20–23 April 1674).

12. Vincent, *Grammar schools*, pp. 139–52, and references in Wallis, *Histories of old schools, passim*.

13. General schoolmasters often appear in the ecclesiastical records, as reported in A. Smith, 'Private schools and schoolmasters in the diocese of Lichfield and Coventry in the seventeenth century',

History of Education, vol. 5, (1976), pp. 117–26. See also D. Cressy, 'Education and literacy in London and East Anglia 1580–1700', unpublished PhD thesis, University of Cambridge, 1973, Appendix.

14. Norfolk RO, MS TES/1. The later seventeenth century saw an expansion of useful private enterprise education; see Vincent, *Grammar schools*, pp. 202–14, and Holmes, *Augustan England*, pp. 43, 48–50.

15. F. Clement, *The petie schole* (1587), p. 4. Cf. C. Hoole, *The petty schoole* (1659), incorporated in his *New Discovery*, pp. 1–41.

16. Lambeth Palace Library, MS 639, fo. 408.

17. Guildhall Library, MSS 11,016, 11,017.

18. 'Cox's case', *The English Reports*, vol. 24 (1903), pp. 281–2.

19. Injunctions, canons and other instruments of ecclesiastical control quoted in Cressy, *Education in Tudor and Stuart England*, pp. 28–40.

20. Richard Montague, *Articles of enquiry and direction for the diocese of Norwich* (Cambridge, 1638). Sparrow's visitation articles, Norfolk RO, MS VIS/7. See also W. H. Frere, *Visitation articles and injunctions of the period of the Reformation* (3 vols., 1910).

21. Greater London RO, MSS DL/C 33–45 (licences); Guildhall Library, MSS 9532/1 (licences), 9539A, 9539B, 9539C, 9540/1–6, 10, 114A (subscriptions), 10, 116–1–16, 10, 116A (testimonials), 9537/4–15, 9583D (visitations); Essex RO, MSS D/ABV2, D/ACV2–16, D/AEV2–16, D/ALV1, 2, D/AMV1–9 (visitations); Norfolk RO, MSS VSC/1–4, VIS/1–9, REG/16 (visitations), SUN/2, 4, COS/1, 2 (licences), SUB/1–4 (subscriptions), TES/1–8 (testimonials).

22. Norfolk RO, MSS SUN/2, COS/1, VSC/4.

23. John Browne subscribed in 1634 as 'literatus, alumnus Oxiensis'; Joshua Bowes, 'late of Oxford' according to his testimonial, was registered as 'literatus'. Guildhall Library, MSS 9539A/1, fo. 45 and 10,116/6; Greater London RO, MS DL/C 345, fo. 62v. For more examples of 'literati' see Smith, 'Private schools and schoolmasters', p. 124. Cambridge admissions, matriculations and graduations are tabulated in Cressy, 'Education and literacy', p. 237.

24. Guildhall Library, MSS 10,116/2 and 9539A, fos. 126, 127; Greater London RO, MS DL/C 344, fos. 177v, 220; Norfolk RO, MSS TES/1, SUB/1.

25. A rare graduate schoolmaster offered exclusively non-grammar subjects; Valentine Bankes, MA, was licensed to teach reading and writing at Uxbridge, Middlesex, in 1597 (Greater London RO, MS DL/C 336, fo. 164). Cf. Mark Curtis, 'The alienated intellectuals of early Stuart England', no. 23 (1962), pp. 25–41.

26. E.g. Holmes, *Augustan England*, pp. 47–8.

27. Sources as in note 22 above; discussion in Cressy, 'Education and literacy', pp. 166–7.

28. *Injunctions given by the Queen's Majesty* (1559), no. 40.

29. In 1580, for example, the privy council blamed 'lewd school-masters' for 'the corruption in religion grown throughout the realm', J. Strype, *History of . . . Edmund Grindal* (Oxford, 1821), p. 378. Cf. Edward Chamberlayne's views a century later in *The second part of the*

present state of England, pp. 320–2, quoted in Cressy, *Education in Tudor and Stuart England*, pp. 25–6.

30. Norfolk RO, MS TES/1.

31. Guildhall Library, MS 10, 116, file 7.

32. *Victoria County History, Suffolk*, vol. 2, p. 333. West Suffolk RO, MS E5/9/103 (Bury Grammar School papers).

33. N. Carlisle, *A concise description of the endowed grammar schools in England and Wales* (2 vols, 1818), vol. 1, p. 130.

34. Ibid., pp. 597–9.

35. Ibid., pp. 417–18.

36. Greater London RO, MS DL/C 309, fo. 116. James Carkesse had to be removed from his teaching position at Chelmsford, Essex, in 1677 'by reason of distempers in body and mind' (ibid., D/C 345, fo. 181v).

37. Guildhall Library, MS 5570, p. 928 (Fishmongers' Ledger).

38. Brinsley, *Ludus literarius*, p. 306. Cf. Hoole, *New discovery*, pp. ix–xi (complaints about status), pp. 129–209 (the master's method).

39. Nedham, *Discourse concerning schools*, p. 14. Cf. Hoole, *New discovery*, pp. 277–8.

40. Carlisle, *Endowed grammar schools*, vol. 1, pp. 599–600, vol. 2, pp. 50, 52.

41. Ibid., vol. 1, p. 785.

42. Ibid., vol. 1, p. 492. Guildhall Library, MSS 10,116, file 11 (testimonials), 5570, p. 613 (Fishmongers' Ledger). Cf. the disputes between rival masters at Hillingdon, Middlesex, in 1693, Lambeth Palace Library, MS VX 1A/12, no. 19, and at Norwich in 1699, Cambridge University Library, MS Mm.6.57, fos. 181v–187.

43. Nedham, *A discourse concerning schools*, pp. 3, 4, 10.

44. Guildhall Library, MS 10,116/1, file 1. A. Macfarlane, *The family life of Ralph Josselin* (Cambridge, 1970), pp. 37, 39.

45. Carlisle, *Endowed grammar schools*, vol. 1, pp. 131, 157, 516, 599, vol. 2, pp. 647–8, 759, 806. Schoolmasters' salaries are discussed in Vincent, *Grammar schools*, pp. 153–71, and in Holmes, *Augustan England*, pp. 58–64.

46. Nedham, *Discourse concerning schools*, p. 4.

47. Carlisle, *Endowed grammar schools*, vol. 1, p. 491.

48. Orpen, 'Schoolmastering as a profession', p. 186.

49. Guildhall Library, MS 5570, p. 685a. C. L. S. Linnell and A. B. Douglas, *Gresham's School, history and register, 1555–1954* (Holt, Norfolk, 1955).

50. Holmes, *Augustan England*, pp. 58, 59.

51. H. W. Saunders, *A history of Norwich Grammar School* (Norwich, 1932), pp. 112, 243, 244, 247. Holmes, *Augustan England*, p. 59.

52. Peacham, *Truth of our times*, pp. 19–20. Fuller, *Holy state*, pp. 98–9.

53. Nedham, *Discourse concerning schools*, p. 3.

54. Orpen, 'Schoolmastering as a profession', pp. 188–92.

55. East Suffolk RO, MS GB5/A8/1 (Wenhaston School Accounts).

56. R. Feyerharm, 'The status of the schoolmaster and the continuity of education in Elizabethan East Anglia', *History of Educa-*

tion, vol. 5 (1976), p. 108.

57. Norfolk RO, MS SUN/4. Essex RO, MS D/ALV 2, fo. 153v.

58. Feyerharm, 'Status of the schoolmaster', p. 106. Holmes, *Augustan England*, p. 49.

59. Sources as in note 21 above; discussion in Cressy, 'Education and literacy', pp. 154–6.

60. *Constitutions and canons ecclesiastical* (1612), quoted in Cressy, *Education in Tudor and Stuart England*, p. 67.

61. Greater London RO, MSS DL/C 335, fo. 188, DL/C 309, fo. 72v, DL/C 334, fo. 190v. Norfolk RO, MSS VSC/2, VIS/6; Macfarlane, *Family life of Ralph Josselin*, pp. 17, 34.

62. N. Lindop, 'Educational studies and professional authority', *British Journal of Educational Studies*, vol. 30 (1982), p. 160. Cf. Eric Hoyle, 'The professionalization of teachers: a paradox', *British Journal of Educational Studies*, vol. 30 (1982), pp. 161–71.

6

The Estate Steward

D. R. Hainsworth

The origins of the English estate steward are probably as ancient as the history of English land ownership. In Ely cathedral a rude stone monument commemorates Ovin, steward to the eighth-century queen, St Etheldreda. Stewards were a part of the English social scene throughout the succeeding centuries. In fourteenth-century Gloucestershire several estate stewards prospered sufficiently to found gentry families of their own, while in Cheshire in the same period gentry families served as stewards of manors on the Duchy of Lancaster estates. The much resented love affair and eventual marriage between Margaret Paston and her father's steward, Richard Calle, a melodrama familiar to readers of the Paston letters, illuminates social relations between lord and steward in fifteenth-century Norfolk.[1]

Stewards as a group have been largely ignored by historians of sixteenth- and seventeenth-century England. It is not simply that the topic of stewardship has not been analysed in publications of monograph or even article length, but that those useful indicators of awareness, the subject indices of more general works, are silent.[2] The lack of interest shown by historians of the sixteenth and seventeenth centuries in a category of person of great importance to the workings of English society seems to have been matched by contemporary writers. A popular seventeenth-century literary form was the 'character book', of which one of the better known is John Earle's *Micro-cosmographie* (*c.* 1627), which contains 77 essays, most of them devoted to well-known 'characters' — 'A Younger Brother', 'A Mere Alderman', and so forth. There is no essay on 'The Mere Steward', however. A similar work by Sir Thomas Overbury and his friends is equally silent, as is Fuller's collection of essays, *The holy state and the profane state*.[3] Of almost 1,000 titles mainly from the Elizabethan and early Stuart periods published in facsimile in 'The English Experience' series, not one concerns the duties of a steward, although several are devoted to navigation, the arts of the apothecary, to surgery, to surveying and map-making, to gardening and the practice of husbandry, and to the profession of arms.[4]

Before considering the implications of this literary neglect we must distinguish between three different meanings of the word 'steward' used by contemporary landowners. The first, 'estate steward', is the concern of this chapter. The second, 'household steward', of which Malvolio in *Twelfth Night* is a memorable literary example, was responsible for running his master's household, provisioning it, managing the indoor servants, keeping household accounts, paying wages, and paying the bills of merchants, tradesmen and skilled artisans. If the householder was a nobleman a household steward might well be a member of a minor gentry family, or even a kinsman of the householder himself. Nevertheless the office of household steward in the early seventeenth century was doomed to a gradual decline in status. The occupational descendant of the Elizabethan household steward was that formidable but plebeian figure, the Victorian butler. During the seventeenth century, as landlords began more and more to live in London, only occasionally visiting their estates (the exact reverse of earlier practice), the household steward tended to shrink in significance as the household he supervised shrank in size. (London households were smaller than rural households not least because they were much more expensive to maintain.) This decline in the significance of the household steward was counterbalanced by a corresponding rise in the significance of the estate steward who had been left behind in the country as his master's viceroy.

The third usage of 'steward' was 'steward of court'. Such a steward presided over manorial courts leet and baron, and was usually a lawyer fee'd for the purpose by the estate steward, although the latter would sit with the lawyer and keep a record of proceedings. Being a steward of courts was simply a branch of ordinary legal business, and many London-based lawyers fulfilled this function, at least for manors in the home counties, and sometimes for manors more distant. At least 190 members of the parliaments of Elizabeth I had been or still were stewards, and while some of these were estate stewards, a substantial proportion were unquestionably lawyers who regularly served as stewards of courts for particular manors.[5] Further afield provincial lawyers served in this role. For example, William Adams regularly fee'd a prominent Marcher lawyer, Sir Francis Manley, to keep Lord Cholmondeley's courts at Nantwich, Malpas and Bickley, Cheshire, for a fee of £10. Of course, where the estate steward was himself a lawyer there was no need for a separate steward of courts, and the two functions combined.

The literary neglect of the steward and of stewardship by writers of the early modern period is odd. Perhaps because stewards came from a diversity of backgrounds, or because the scope of their responsibilities varied widely from estate to estate, or even because they wore no distinctive dress, they seemed harder to pin down in a neat, immediately recognisable characterisation than 'the schoolmaster', 'the apothecary' or 'the clergyman'. Certainly at all periods of which we have knowledge some estate stewards were men of great prestige, although part of their status was a reflection of the status of the noblemen they served. Were they perceived as a profession? Indeed, how appropriate is it to classify stewardship as a profession? Professor Geoffrey Holmes believes that estate stewards had 'staked their claim to professional standing' by 1730. The steward was then omnipresent, omnicompetent, handling increasingly complex duties, and possessed of a status more distinguished than stewards had enjoyed in earlier times.[6] This implied change is here placed sixty or seventy years too late and, moreover, what Holmes perceives as a rise in the significance of stewardship as a profession was rather a great increase in the number of those stewards who were charged with heavy and complex responsibilities. Certainly his description of the steward of George II's reign could be applied equally well to a large number of stewards in Charles II's reign. Indeed it would have served to describe Richard Marris, steward to the future Earl of Strafford in the 1630s, or to the Trevors of Trevalyn in Elizabeth's reign, or to Sir John Thynne, famed as the builder of Longleat, when he was steward to the Earl of Hertford during the reigns of Henry VIII and Edward VI. At all times stewardship provided a career open to talent for a restricted number of fortunate and able men. During the seventeenth century, however, for reasons examined below, the opportunities for such careers greatly increased, and the diversity and complexity of the functions which a steward could be called on to discharge also expanded.

Does this amount to the emergence of stewardship as a profession? Holmes writes that 'a hallmark of the professional man in eighteenth century England was that he was entitled to nothing less than the prefix "Mr"', and that, in favourable circumstances, he might enjoy the rank of 'esquire' or at least 'rough social parity with esquires'.[7] This appears to say both too little and too much. There would have been few apothecaries, clergymen or schoolmasters who could claim social parity with esquires, and in the later seventeenth century there would have been few stewards who could not. As for 'Mr', any bailiff whose functions were merely to collect rents and ensure tenants' appearances at the manorial court could aspire to that. Stewards were *sui generis*: while their status tended to be high, their claim to be professional men appears at first sight to be insubstantial. Stewards served no formal apprenticeship, were members of no professional organisation, were never examined to test their mastery of any discrete body of knowledge. On the other hand, they usually commanded a very wide and diverse body of knowledge useful to the task of running an estate, and had the ability as well as the delegated authority to mobilise the skills of other professional men, such as lawyers, surveyors, architects, landscape gardeners, interior decorators or engineers, when their own knowledge and experience proved insufficient. They had to be able to negotiate with, and even confront, men of every degree from dukes to labourers whose interests or activities impinged on those of their master. As negotiators and mediators on behalf of their master they needed to be skilled in the arts of persuasion as well as able to mobilise the sanctions of authority. They also possessed the ability to transmit their knowledge and the fruits of their varied experience to others, although I suspect that this ability was rarely exercised except on behalf of some close relative whom they designed to step into their shoes at their death or retirement.

Like other professional groups in the seventeenth century,

stewards came from diverse social backgrounds. Younger sons of country gentlemen, former army officers, traders in provincial towns, yeomen farmers, country attorneys, sons of deceased or retired stewards who inherited their father's office, men whose fathers might have been husbandmen and men whose grandfathers might have been noblemen, were all to be found managing estates. The list emphasises a contrast between this profession and others in the same period: men did not pass from youthful education directly into stewardship. While all stewards had been educated at least to the point where they could read and write with reasonable fluency and keep accounts, they had then moved on to some other occupation. Some had been surveyors; some had been involved in such business enterprises as milling, mining or commerce; some had had experience of military service. Others had been and still were lawyers or yeomen farmers or gentlemen farmers. All were men of experience, although their experience of life differed. Young gentlemen with no business experience or knowledge of husbandry, and with little more knowledge of life and affairs than were to be acquired in the hunting field or at the gaming table, were not likely to be appointed to manage a concern worth several thousand pounds a year. Estate management was England's largest collective business, pervading not merely the lives of the vast majority of countrymen but stretching its tentacles into most industrial and commercial undertakings: money-lending, mining, quarrying, wool and textiles, timber, urban house-building, trading voyages, shipbuilding and shipowning, marsh drainage and other forms of land reclamation. The estate steward was a crucial figure in all this myriad activity, and it required a man of wide experience and managerial skill adequately to discharge these increasingly complex duties.

The stewards augmented their varied early experience by their practice of pursuing a variety of other activities after their appointment. Thomas Tickell, steward of St Bees-Whitehaven for Sir John Lowther from 1666 until his death in 1692, had been a Newcastle customs officer in the early 1640s, a royalist officer in the Civil War, and was involved in lead mining near Keswick with older relatives in the late 1640s. After Lowther appointed him steward he long sought, and his master's influence finally secured for him, the post of Surveyor of Customs at Whitehaven. He was also involved in collieries on his own account and farmed land leased from Lowther on favourable terms.[8] His successor, William Gilpin, was a member of a junior branch of a minor gentry family, and a practising lawyer. When Lowther appointed him to St Bees in 1693 Gilpin had a crown appointment as 'Steward of their Majesties' Courts Upon the Borders', and had had experience as a crown prosecutor at Carlisle assizes. After his appointment he may have abandoned his prosecution work, but only belatedly and reluctantly withdrew from his royal appointment (or was ousted by a rival). He continued to practise law with the full consent of his employer. Gilpin was probably induced to move to Whitehaven by the expectation that his master's influence would secure him a profitable position in the Custom House.[9]

The over-steward of Sir Richard Grahame of Netherby in north-east Cumberland was a local clergyman, Charles Usher of Kirkandrews-on-Esk. However, he was probably not a properly salaried steward with a detailed responsibility for the day-to-day running of the estate.[10] William Adams was a more typical example. Born to an armigerous family with a small estate at Longdon, near Shrewsbury, Adams was a leading surveyor in his region prior to appointment by the first Viscount Cholmondeley in 1679 to be chief steward of all the family's estates in Cheshire, Shropshire, Flint and Somerset. Adams seems to have inherited Longdon some time before his appointment, for it was his home throughout his service with the Cholmondeleys and his wife lived there permanently. Adams, however, normally lived at Cholmondeley, with board and lodging for himself and a servant. He also regularly visited Longdon, and throughout his career combined the very onerous duties of managing the Cholmondeley estates whilst being a local squire himself.[11]

These examples may prompt the question: were seventeenth-century stewards only part-time agents? They were 'part-time' only in the sense that they devoted part of their time and energy to personal concerns. Indeed it would be anachronistic to attempt to draw precise distinctions between 'part-time' and 'full-time', for that is not how their employers viewed their terms of employment. They were content for their stewards to have supplementary sources of income, for then they need not pay as high a salary as the position might appear to deserve. Moreover there could be other advantages.

For Thomas Tickell to be a senior customs officer in the port his master owned, and through which his master's customers annually exported thousands of tons of coal, and through which his master and his associates imported valuable cargoes of tobacco and naval stores, was potentially a highly advantageous situation. Too advantageous, perhaps, for the Customs Commissioners to continue to swallow, for they never allowed his successor the same combination of posts. The first Viscount Cholmondeley would have been able to reconcile himself to his steward's absences at Longdon for a more subtle reason. There appears to have been an interregnum between stewards at Cholmondeley during which the estates were administered by bailiffs. These bailiffs were not gentlemen of property but substantial tenants with the interests of a tenant rather than of a landlord. Shortly after his appointment Cholmondeley complained to Adams that when he had delegated the fixing of rents to the bailiffs they had 'effected to beat down my estate, and not improve it, being against their interest', but he expected better from Adams, who, as a gentleman, would 'affect the gentlemen's interest' and 'scorn' that of the 'clowns'.[12]

The employers' readiness to permit their stewards to engage in business on their own account, and even encourage it, is demonstrated by their practice of letting them land, or even whole farms, on favourable terms. While some stewards profitably sub-let such land, others kept them in hand to fatten cattle, graze sheep or take stock on agistment. Thomas Crewe, steward at Trevalyn, Flintshire, for Sir John Trevor in the 1630s, leased his master's mills at Marford, the profits of which augmented his salary.[13] There was, then, no formal division between the periods of time a steward had to devote to his master's affairs and other periods to be devoted to his own. So long as his multifarious duties were effectively discharged, how a steward spent his days was very much his own affair. This in itself emphasised the superiority of his status over that of other salaried employees.

Inevitably, where personal business competed with a master's affairs for limited resources of time and energy, difficulties arose. This was particularly true when the steward was a substantial farmer on his own account, for at certain times of year he could not leave his own business to tend his master's. The pressures produced by such competing demands eventually drove Arthur King to resign from Lord Fitzwilliam's service.[14] Other difficulties that could arise involved conflicts of interest, although these show up only rarely in stewards' correspondence, either because they were rare or because they were concealed. Where a steward also had a law practice his appearance on behalf of one of his master's tenants against another might adversely affect his master's interests by promoting factions and disturbing the harmony so necessary to the smooth running of the estate. His appearance on behalf of a local gentleman, perhaps involving him in some local feud, might prove injurious to his master's political influence.[15] Conflicts of interest could also arise where the steward was a large-scale farmer or grazier. Friends of Sir Thomas Isham of Lamport, who kept an eye on his estate during his prolonged 'grand tour', sometimes suspected that his steward, John Chapman, was lax in letting land, preferring to keep much of it in hand for his own advantage.[16]

The growing significance of stewards, with their functions and duties becoming more elaborate, more demanding of skill and experience, was due to a growing absenteeism amongst the landlords. When landlords lived permanently on their estates, the steward was only an adjutant. But when landlords spent most of their adult lives in London or abroad, the steward became a viceroy. Absenteeism became much more marked during the seventeenth century, and noblemen and the greater gentry in the second half of the century spent longer in London than their fathers or grandfathers had. London, with its social life, the palaces of Westminster and Whitehall, the law courts, its money market of scriveners and goldsmiths, became increasingly a magnet. Indeed Charles I's government had sought to check absenteeism by ordering landlords back to their estates and by fining the recalcitrant. It is significant of the social transformation which occurred later in the seventeenth century that such a policy, however partial and ineffective, would have been unthinkable during the reign of William III. It is possible that the Civil War, by cutting off some landlords from their estates (especially parliamentarian landlords in London) and in taking other landlords into the royalist or parliamentary armies, or into exile during the interregnum, may have helped this process. However the war probably held still more landlords on their estates who would otherwise have spent at least part of every year in London.

Certainly the restoration marks a convenient watershed. After 1660 long and regular parliaments, the expansion of the civil service, the army and navy, London's growing significance as a business and social centre for the ruling class, all combined on an unprecedented scale to persuade great and moderate-sized landlords to occupy London lodgings or even houses for at least part of every year.[17] Some landlords lived in London for years at a time, and when they visited their estates their stay was often more a tour of inspection than a lengthy sojourn.[18] They thereby became absentee landlords and their protracted absence threw a heavier burden of responsibility on the shoulders of their stewards.

The fact that landowners continued to own and acquire estates widely scattered across different counties also ensured employment for stewards, or at least under-stewards. Lord Cholmondeley's chief estate was centred in southern Cheshire, but he also owned properties in Shropshire, Flint and Somerset. Lord Fitzwilliam had estates in Norfolk as well as Northamptonshire. The Earl of Northampton had major estates in Warwickshire as well as Northamptonshire, an estate in Somerset and lesser properties in four other counties. Sir Thomas Thynne, subsequently first Viscount Weymouth, through his marriage, through inheritance and by purchase accumulated properties in Gloucestershire, Warwickshire, Staffordshire, Herefordshire and Ireland. On the unexpected death of a childless cousin he inherited the west country estate based on Longleat. Spending much of his time in London, making Longleat his rural base, Weymouth rarely, if ever, visited his other properties, preferring to rely on the reports and advice of a bevy of highly articulate stewards. These stewards might regret his protracted absence; judging by their frequent clamour for his presence, and even reproaches at his absence, they often did.[19] Nevertheless their isolation could only enhance their status as their lord's representative within his domains.

It is true that seventeenth-century stewards do not seem to have been very comfortable in their enhanced but lonely positions. By the nineteenth century, as Eric Richards has demonstrated, stewards had long grown used to the situation. They ran the estates, took frequent initiatives, made all the day-to-day decisions and also framed the long-term policies. Their employers tended to be remote rentiers who took little or no interest in detail so long as income was sustained, or better still, increased.[20] In the seventeenth century the position was very different. Stewards were afraid to use their initiative, and constantly besought their masters for firm instructions, permissions and decisions. Sometimes the matter was trivial, often it was routine. It made no difference. Although the steward would find tenants for land, purchasers for timber, contractors for fencing or building, sources of millstones for his master's mills, and millwrights to install them, no agreement would be signed, no lease sealed, nothing concrete would indeed occur until the lord sent his written approval. The early eighteenth-century steward who pursued his master with letters across Europe seeking permission to fell a tree for timber to repair a badly needed hay wain was only an exaggerated, not an untypical, example.[21] Conversely seventeenth-century absentee landlords differed from their nineteenth-century counterparts in maintaining a close interest in the detailed running of their estates. Absence of body did not mean absence of mind. Moreover, all landlords used their stewards as a source of local intelligence on a wide range of topics. For example, all expected political intelligence, particularly during a parliamentary election. The stewards were their masters' eyes and limbs and bitter would be the reproaches if those eyes were not constantly alert and those limbs ever active.

However inhibited their decision-making might be, stewards were seen by their neighbours, and especially by the tenants, as men clothed in great authority, 'viceroys' for their powerful master. They were bathed in reflected glory, for their status was strongly influenced by that of their employer. The steward of a duke would naturally have greater prestige than the steward of a baronet. However, although the prestige might vary from steward to steward, all were men of status. The fact that stewards often resided in their master's mansions, those potent symbols of rank and authority, and were sometimes charged not merely with their maintenance but even with their redesign and rebuilding, simply underlined their vice-regal status. Landlords, of course, saw their stewards from a different perspective. Generalisation is difficult because there are subtle shifts in attitude from master to master and even from steward to steward of the same master. The icy detachment with which Sir John Lowther contemplated the familial aspirations of Thomas Tickell, even while trying to further them, can chill the reader of the correspondence even today. The second Lord Cholmondeley's temper ranged between the testy and the volcanic in his relationship with William Adams. Complaints, abuse, even threats of dismissal pepper his letters, although Adams rode out these storms for a quarter of a century, apparently as unsinkable as a cork. In contrast, Lord Fitzwilliam's letters to Francis Guybon, chief steward at Milton, are charged with warm affection, and, as Guybon ages in his service, with concern for his health and wellbeing.[22] Of course, the survival of archives is haphazard, and most collections of estate correspondence are one-sided, often containing only the steward's letters. It is difficult to judge the attitude of the master by reading the letters from the man. However, it would seem that the lord's regard for the steward was largely determined by his own nature and personality, and, more importantly, by the social status of the steward at the time of his appointment. If Sir John Lowther remained icily detached from Mr Tickell (albeit a conscientious patron of both his steward and his family), he was warmer, even quite respectful, to his successor, William Gilpin, but Gilpin belonged to an old gentry family, and all such families in what is now Cumbria tended to be, at least distantly, interrelated.[23]

It might be thought that the salaries stewards received would reflect the status they held in the eyes of their master. In fact status and salary bore little relation to each other. Significantly both Tickell and Gilpin received the same salary, £40 a year. This salary was determined by Lowther's notion of what he could afford to pay for the duties involved, not by his concept of the worth of the occupant of the post.[24] It is possible that some men's salaries were influenced by their social background. William Adams, who received £100 a year, a very high salary for a seventeenth-century steward, was attractive to his employer, as we have seen, because he was a gentleman with a gentleman's interests. However, Adams was a very hard-worked chief steward with several bailiffs or under-stewards to supervise, along with a staff of grooms, gardeners, warreners, keepers, etc., and was eventually responsible for the remodelling of Cholmondeley Hall. His salary was barely commensurate with his wide responsibilities. Salaries are deceptive for this period, because, aside from the private earnings which stewards were prone to enjoy, their salaries were augmented by a variety of perquisites: for example, land rented on generous terms and fees from tenants signing new leases or renewing old ones.[25] There were also potentially profitable perquisites of more dubious propriety. The problem is to trace these in records which were mostly generated by the culprit himself. If it was difficult then, it is often impossible now. Thomas Gape, a lawyer to the Duchess of Somerset, reported that her late steward, Richard Beardesley, was worth only £1,000 on entering her employment yet died worth at least £30,000, 'but the man is dead, I shall make no inference'.[26]

One illicit perquisite was profitably to agist other men's cattle on the master's deer park or other pasture, or graze beasts of his own there. However, no doubt the most common and the most profitable perquisite was earnings from the master's funds lying in the steward's care. Significantly, stewards who died suddenly were often discovered to be heavily in debt to their masters for money received but not paid over, and yet these arrears were not in the steward's strongbox.[27] Whatever their salaries, and however honest or dishonest their proceedings, it was a commonplace among country folk to suppose that a long stewardship was a high road to affluence, and the death of a steward could arouse intense interest among his likely heirs.[28] Of course, among the rewards of stewardship we must number the psychic rewards of the sense of power and prestige which stewardship conveyed, although these can usually only be inferred.

The duties of a steward in the seventeenth century could be very diverse, but tended to vary in their number and complexity from estate to estate. There was a basic core common to all estates large enough to require the services of a steward. These were well set forth by Sir John Lowther of Whitehaven in 1680 when he appointed a steward for his isolated Westmorland manor of Waitby. He chose a local lawyer, George Fothergill, and gave him power of attorney to receive, sue for and recover all rents, debts and services due to Lowther from his tenants, and appoint a bailiff to collect the rents. Fothergill was to keep the manorial court, sign legal documents in his employer's name, issue receipts and acquittances, keep accounts, and pay surplus receipts to Lowther in London at regular intervals. Fothergill, in brief, was to 'exercise the place and office of a steward' and 'to perform as fully in every respect . . . as I myself might or could do I being personally present'.[29] Waitby was only a small manor, which could be looked after as part of the ordinary business of a country attorney.

Fothergill's power of attorney highlights the fact that stewards did not normally collect rents. That duty was relegated to an under-steward or bailiff. Bailiffs were men of less economic and social consequence than the stewards but on a large, and especially on a scattered, estate were an essential link in the administrative chain. The Victorian custom of all the tenants arriving at the manor house at Lady Day and Michaelmas to pay their rents to the steward across a great oak table and receive a convivial glass of beer or wine may only date, as a common practice, from the eighteenth century. Seventeenth-century tenants rarely paid on time, and the bailiffs or 'collectors' were charged with the task of dunning for and receiving rents on behalf of the landlord which they were then to pay over to the steward. In practice, since bailiffs so often collected rents in arrear regardless of date or season, but tended to account for it to the steward at particular dates (or when strongly pressed to do so), they also tended to have money lying profitably on their hands. As with their superiors, when they died in office they were often heavily in debt to their master and the steward would be castigated for permitting such a financially hazardous situation to arise.

The terms 'bailiff' and 'steward' were sometimes used almost interchangeably in the seventeenth century, and this confusion can extend to the twentieth-century historian because some bailiffs were more than mere rent collectors. Such men were really 'deputy stewards' , with delegated powers from their chief steward to find tenants for vacant farms or land, and even to negotiate rental agreements (subject to their lord's approval). It was this type of bailiff which Lord Cholmondeley had had to rely on, to his deep dissatisfaction as we have seen, prior to the appointment of William Adams in 1679. On the other hand, Lord Fitzwilliam found such an under-steward for the outlying Northamptonshire properties increasingly useful when Francis Guybon became too old for long journeys on horseback in all weathers. However, the more usual bailiff was a man clothed in very restricted authority, and that delegated by the steward, who spent little of his time in this service, received only a small salary, and devoted the rest of his time to some other occupation, such as innkeeper, storekeeper or farmer.[30]

The duties of the steward of a large or at least complex estate could be very rich and diverse, far removed from the bucolic simplicities of Mr Fothergill's Waitby. This is reflected in William Adams's power of attorney drafted by himself in 1679. In it 'William Adams of Longdon . . . Esquire' was appointed Cholmondeley's 'agent, steward and overseer' for his estates in Cheshire, Shropshire, Somerset and Flint; he was to let the properties to his master's 'best benefit', and from time to time to call Cholmondeley's 'bailiffs, rent gathers [*sic*] and under-agents' to account for all receipts from the tenants in rents, fines, heriots, services, sales of timber, etc., and issue receipts and acquittances. Adams had authority to oversee the under-agents for the better management of those parts of the estate committed to their care; to pay wages to them and to all other estate servants (including the household at Cholmondeley Hall) and reimburse their expenses. Adams was to account for all profits and expenses of the estate, and return the surplus to Cholmondeley in London. An enabling clause covered all unspecified matters: 'and in all other things relating to and concerning my said estate to behave himself in such sort as shall be most to my advantage, and as I shall from time to time order and direct'. Thus Adams was given a general authority to care for a very large estate, comprising mills, forests and salt-works as well as pastoral and agricultural farms, a mansion, several manor houses and at least one deer park, yielding an income of between £6,000 and £7,000 a year.[31]

Powers of attorney, however framed, are no more than a skeletal framework to the substantial body of a steward's duties, functions and responsibilities. To that body we must now turn. The bulk of a steward's duties concerned tenants and tenancies. Since the vast majority of English men and women were either landlords or tenants (and some were both), and since stewards were the vital link between them, stewards as a group could not fail to be of great significance to the effective working of English society and the English economy. To discharge effectively the onerous functions involved in this linkage required a cool and experienced head and a capacity for diplomacy. Nevertheless, stewards, however able, were always seeking to reconcile the irreconcilable. The landlords wanted high rents paid promptly; the tenants wanted low rents paid at their convenience, that is, late or (ideally) never. Finding the middle ground and persuading both sides to accept it was no light task. A fundamental duty of the steward was to find tenants for vacant farms, held on leases for lives or for a term of years. Landlords had a horror of having land 'in hand'. However, an absentee lifestyle in London was very expensive, and so they would always wistfully hope that a new lease might bring an increased rent. The stewards, at the sharp end of the battle, had lower aspirations: they hoped to obtain the former rent. The tenants aspired to a lower rent.

Significantly, of these competing aspirations it was the last which was likeliest to be gratified, at least in the second half of the seventeenth century. From the 1660s to the end of William III's reign stewards' correspondence from most regions is full of requests that the lord will consent to 'abate' the rent of a property the steward is trying to let, or 'be kind' to a prospective tenant, for otherwise the land will stand unlet. The euphemism 'be kind' meant either a straightforward reduction in rent, or a reduction of the rent actually to be paid in the short run, whilst the nominal rent on the rent roll, and in the lease, remained as before. Landlords compelled to charge lower rents by the exigencies of hard times or an inadequate supply of suitable tenants did not wish to see their property permanently devalued once those temporary exigencies had disappeared. The 'fall of rents' was a phrase in common currency among contemporaries during and after the post-restoration decade, but the phenomenon it described can also be discerned during the 1680s and 1690s.[32] Ironically this depression of rents, which filled so many landlords with gloom and made the steward's labours so difficult and frustrating, was blamed in part on absenteeism among landlords. Their living in London was said to drain money from the shires, thereby depressing regional economies, whilst their absence from their estates threw more demense lands on to a market in which too many farms were pursuing too few tenants.[33]

The long struggles to maintain leasehold rents demonstrate that the hegemony of the landlord could be successfully challenged. This made still more difficult the steward's thankless task of trying simultaneously to gratify his master's short-term appetite whilst seeking to promote the harmonious running of the estate to its long-term advantage. This was a hard task indeed where his master's absences were long and his grasp of local realities slight. Francis Guybon had, in Lord Fitzwilliam, a most sympathetic and understanding master, who was also a flexible, and even generous, landlord, and even he found it difficult. Charles Browne, steward of the Earl of Northampton's Somerset estates, found it impossible. Northampton was misguided and inflexible. Browne was stubborn, opinionated and tactless, poor qualifications for a mediator. The earl kept insisting in 1700 and after that the Somerset farms must be let according to an inflated valuation drawn up in 1692. Browne could not bridge the gulf between the rent his master demanded and the rent prospective tenants would agree to pay. In the end he was replaced, but his successor could do no better and the returns from the Somerset estates continued to fall.[34]

The role of the steward as mediator between lord and tenants was one of his most significant functions. Here the steward was not only his master's representative: he was also the representative of the estate, in the sense of those who lived on it or were connected with it. For example, acting through Lord Paget's chief steward, John Swynfen, the town of Rugeley (of which Paget was lord of the manor) obtained the revival of a long defunct annual fair.[35] This example reminds us that the activities of stewards were not confined to the countryside, but followed the meandering boundaries of their masters' estates into provincial towns and boroughs. Here the 'ambassadorial' role in an urban setting is most obvious when one considers the role of the steward as the maintainer of his master's local political influence, and (where his master or a member of his family was a parliamentary candidate) of election agent. It was a most important function of the steward to nourish and sustain his master's 'interest' at all times, and to mobilise that 'interest' at a time of county or borough elections. This involved the steward in maintaining close if respectful contacts with local gentlemen, and of being a channel for gifts or other favours from his master. One of the means employed to maintain friendship was through warrants (or licences) to hunt deer in forests which the lord might not own but in which he had a transferable right to hunt a specified number of deer each year. Another was through gifts of haunches of venison from his own deer park. Sometimes the lord selected the recipients, sometimes this was left to the steward's discretion.[36]

At election time the landlord might not interrupt his long absence even where he himself was a candidate. Sir John Lowther was a member for Cumberland in successive parliaments from 1665 to 1699, but his infrequent visits to Cumberland were not timed to coincide with elections. At elections, therefore, his stewards became 'postmen' charged with delivering (with suitable oral compliments) Lowther's written requests for support to all the leading gentlemen, who would in turn, Lowther hoped, mobilise those freeholders who were tenants on their estates on his behalf. Stewards at elections would also be ordered to direct their masters' tenants to cast their votes where his finger pointed. This naked exercise of landlord hegemony was not always effective. In 1701 Lord Cholmondeley decided to intervene on behalf of Sir Roger Mostyn and Sir George Warburton, candidates for Cheshire, instructing Adams to see 'that all my interest appears for 'em', and to inform him the names of any ('if such there be') who failed to comply with this 'reasonable desire'. This would-be autocrat was soon humbled. Only a week later he is complaining fretfully that a 'considerable interest' against his candidates is being made amongst his tenants, and Adams must promise that all who vote as he wishes 'shall hereafter have their expenses allowed'.[37] Threats against the possibly recalcitrant have been replaced by bribes to the potentially obedient. This was an old story for Adams, who had acted in elections for Cholmondeley's father. At a fiercely contested county election in 1681 he had instructed Adams to 'take notice who of either my tenants or friends shuffle in this service, that I may set a mark upon them for time to come'.[38]

If the county election could prove a source of anger and frustration to both landlord and steward, the borough election was normally even stormier. Sir John Lowther was never once opposed through all his county candidatures, so that he could safely be represented by a proxy on polling day. It was a very different matter when he sought to have his younger son, James, elected for Carlisle in conjunction with the Howard interest in 1695 and 1698. The 1695 election cost the anxious father more than £500, most of it spent 'treating' the Carlisle guilds and numerous other thirsty voters, and generally influencing leading Carlisle aldermen on young Lowther's behalf. In 1698, with 'treating' banned, the expense was less but the anxiety greater for all William Gilpin's diplomacy could not lure the principal clergy of the Carlisle diocese from their allegiance to the Musgrave interest.[39] In Tamworth in 1688 Lord Weymouth's steward, John Mainewaring, had to contend with a peculiarly humiliating situation: the powerful local leader of the anti-Weymouth interest was Mainewaring's predecessor as steward, the Welshman Captain Morgan Powell. As Mainewaring stumped about a town in which so many householders (and voters) were his master's tenants he must have been chagrined to discover that many who claimed to be loyal dared only say so in a whisper. Powell was now the mayor, and as a strong Jacobite was much involved in the negotiations with James II for a new town charter. His power was such that while, as Mainewaring angrily reported, 'he now declares (to the commonality) they shall have a public election . . . he never designs it for he has said that choose who they will, he will return none else' than the candidates he favours. Tamworth seems to have had a wide franchise, rather to Mainewaring's distress, for he observed at a later election: 'I believe we are sure of the best of the town and most of the magistrates, but the rest are biased by ale. Without that nothing can be done'.[40]

As an election agent the steward had to steer a difficult course between the Scylla of spending too much on the voters and arousing his master's wrath at the expense, and the Charybdis of spending too little to the loss of the election which would have angered his master even more. Once again the steward's vital qualifications are shown to be sound judgement based on experience, a prodigious memory, a knowledge of human nature and close attention to detail. Diplomatic skills could be important assets for a steward even in an election in which his master had decided to adopt a neutral stance. It would then be the steward's role to offend neither side, a difficult exercise when in fact his master's instructions firmly forbade him to support either.

The steward had also to mediate between his master and the local assessors and commissioners of taxation. He had to ensure that his master paid as little as possible, and certainly no more than any neighbouring landowner with an estate of comparable size. In 1693 William Gilpin was outraged by the discovery that, inadvertently, his master was being taxed as if he were a recusant, and successfully protested.[41] Some interventions by the steward were of dubious propriety, and some were downright tax evasion. In October 1689 John Mainewaring disingenuously persuaded the local assessors that the heavy expenses Lord Weymouth had been compelled to meet in his manor of Drayton Bassett should be set off against the income of the estate in assessing the tax owed. Subsequently when he was reprimanded by the chairman of the county commissioners, Sir Richard Newdigate, for putting forward such a specious argument for tax reduction, he hastily assured the commissioners that he had been acting entirely on his own initiative without any such direction from his master.[42]

It is usually impossible to know whether stewards pursuing such tax-evading policies were acting without the knowledge of their masters, although in view of stewards' general refusal to act on their own initiative this would seem highly unlikely. However, Lord Fitzwilliam left damning evidence against himself. Writing to Guybon in 1697, he observed that it was rumoured that the county commissioners would be very severe, and so they must conceal how much rent the tenants paid. Guybon must instruct the tenants to 'deny' their rents by a fourth or a fifth. They could not be punished for this deception, but the lord could be fined triple the tax if the steward was shown to have lied on his behalf. Therefore, if they sent for Guybon to bring his rent rolls he must pretend to have forgotten to bring them with him. If questioned about individual rents he must plead a bad memory, 'pretend you are ancient . . . let them tax what they will we will own nothing'.[43]

There was a range of activities which similarly show the steward in the role of a representative or as a mediator. Prominent among these was the duty to maintain his master's rights within his estate, since tenants were adepts at evading the incidence of tithes, boons, various services and heriots. Where these feudal rights bore harshly on widows, minors or indigent heirs the steward had a subtle intermesh of functions in which he was simultaneously a protector of the lord's rights within the estate, ever wary of inadvertently establishing damaging precedents to which tenants might appeal in the future; yet also serving as a channel for the lord's charity, and as an instigator of that charity, and determining who deserved to receive it. This was particularly true where a tenant died leaving a widow burdened with debts. The responsible steward, whilst ensuring that his lord's share of the debts was secured, would do what he could to protect the widow from other creditors, try to ensure that she was not left homeless, and where she had children of suitable age might seek to have them apprenticed to some 'honest mystery'.[44] Defending the feudal privileges of an estate was not always a simple matter. Records were often incomplete, incoming stewards would often have to make intensive and not always successful searches for old court rolls, whilst lords would frequently instruct their stewards to consult the 'ancient men' about the customs of the manor. Sometimes this advice had to be sought outside, as when Lowther of Whitehaven's tenants were prepared to go to law with their landlord, claiming that in West Cumberland heriots were payable only when a widow inherited. Tickell was instructed to discover the custom on neighbouring manors as a check on this claim, whilst Lowther's lawyers sought to prevent the matter being determined in the county court for fear (one must assume) of the likely result.[45]

A conscientious steward would make a point of regularly riding the bounds of his master's manor. The facts that the seventeenth century was a great age of map-making and surveying and that these arts were increasingly being applied definitively to map particular estates did not halt this practice. The steward was an ambassador who must seek to maintain good relations with the lords of neighbouring properties, particularly those whose bounds marched with the estate in his care, and to prevent situations arising which could lead to expensive and damaging lawsuits. In 1709 Ralph Gowland, steward of the Duke of Newcastle's Durham properties, discovered that a tenant of the Earl of Carlisle was ploughing some intake moorland which lay within the duke's boundary. Gowland's authority for deciding this to be an encroachment was a survey of 1576 and the recollections of aged tenants of earlier boundary ridings. Unhappily an under-steward had carelessly permitted such encroachments for some time. The duke, through his receiver, observed that 'the negligence of agents do often occasion both charge and trouble to their master', but on the other hand 'sometimes good stewards do accommodate and prevent differences'. Therefore, if Lord Carlisle had a 'prudent steward', Gowland should negotiate with him, but if Gowland was unable to persuade the earl's servant of the encroachment then Gowland must write to the earl himself in the duke's name, 'which you can do much better than we can here'.[46]

One problem the stewards constantly faced was how to transfer rural profits to London purses.[47] London banking was in its infancy, provincial banking almost unborn, the easy transfer of credit from provinces to London through branch and central banks undreamed of. The movement of specie was extremely hazardous. The roads fanning out from London were infested with highwaymen, and more distant arteries were scarcely more secure. Stewards were always in quest of 'returns', that is, means of paying money in the country to persons who could repay it in London either directly or through correspondents. Some of the methods employed seem remarkably cumbersome to modern eyes, but they were necessary and, within limits, they worked. The stewards of such Welsh families as the Trevors of Denbigh or such north-western families as the Lowthers and the Musgraves made great use of the cattle drovers during the 1660s and 1670s. Drovers received cash from the stewards in exchange for bills drawn on the drovers in favour of the steward's master. The steward then sent this bill to their master through the post. Meanwhile the drovers took the cash received from the steward to the great Welsh or Scottish cattle fairs, bought cattle, drove them to London, sold them at Smithfield, and redeemed their bills from the landlord for cash. Thus the squire's income travelled slowly but securely to London on the hoof. There were long delays in this imperfect system, and one large family of drovers, the Elletsons, went sensationally bankrupt in 1678 allegedly owing £30,000, which indicates the scale of their operations. Nevertheless, absentees like Sir John Lowther preferred irritating delays to the insecurity involved in sending money by road.[48]

Cheshire landlords like Lord Cholmondeley used cheese in the same way, their stewards 'purchasing' bills from cheese factors and cheese makers locally while the cheesemongers in London honoured the bills when presented either by the landlord or his goldsmith. Lord Fitzwilliam sometimes received sums of money in quite small amounts from his tenants who had brought livestock or other produce for sale in London. When his needs were more than usually desperate he would ride out to the fields around Islington to see if any of the flocks of sheep or herds of cattle arriving at these fattening paddocks belonged to tenants or neighbours charged with paying his returns.[49] Stewards of estates nearer London would obtain returns from market gardeners and suppliers of fodder. However, the topic of 'returns' is vast and complex, penetrating into many areas of English economic life, and here space will permit only this passing glance.

Stewards whose charge was a complex estate which included resources of mineral wealth, significant river navigation or a sea port needed a far greater range of skills and experience than the steward of a simpler estate. The St Bees-Whitehaven estate under Thomas Tickell and still more under his successor, Gilpin, involved collieries and salt-making, mills, the planning and development of a sizeable town and the operation, maintenance and development of an important port. Since Lowther tended to take shares in voyages to the Baltic and Virginia, as well as selling his coal to the locally based fleet of colliers plying to Dublin, his stewards were involved in commerce as well as in land and tenancies. Gilpin sought to launch a local vitriol works, and helped to execute Lowther's plans for local textile, glass and leather works.[50] Lord Cholmondeley owned salt works and, while these were often leased, they were at other times directly worked under a local manager. There survives in William Adams's handwriting a set of accounts for these works, with a preamble setting out exactly how they were to be kept.[51] Similarly such Cornish landlords as Barbara, Lady Arundel, were substantial investors in tin mines, and such families as the Trevors of Denbighshire and Flintshire required stewards with a knowledge of mining, whether of coal or iron.[52] Great landowners like Lord Cholmondeley, Lord Weymouth, Lord Fitzwilliam, Lord Halifax and his successor, Sir George Savile, were great exploiters of forests, and their archives are as vital a source for understanding the operation of the timber industry as the Lowther archives are for the coal industry. Lead mines, copper mines, slate and mill-stone quarries could all come within the experience of the estate steward, together with manufacturing enterprises derived from them such as smelting.

To these rich seams of experience must be added those associated with building. While tenants often rebuilt farm buildings at their own charge, although with materials supplied by the landlord, other buildings had to be contracted for by the steward. More elaborate buildings frequently became his responsibility. Lord Weymouth's new church at Minsterley, Shropshire, which still stands as that unusual phenomenon, a completely new church dating from the reign of Charles II, was supervised from foundation to completion by an estate steward.[53] Stewards frequently had to supervise the renovation and sometimes the reconstruction of their masters' mansions, although here they often brought in local experts to help them. For example, the clergyman at Dyrham church supervised the construction of William Blathwayte's mansion of Dyrham Park with the general co-operation of Blathwayte's general steward.[54] As with the mansion, so with the surrounding grounds: landowners commonly bombarded their stewards with advice to transmit to their gardeners, sending seeds they had imported or obtained from fellow enthusiasts, and plants, shrubs and infant trees purchased from London and Wise's Brompton nurseries.

This brief survey of the steward's functions is by no means exhaustive. The more estate correspondence one consults, the richer the variety of functions and responsibilities one discovers. Some were peculiar to particular topographies.[55] Some were peculiar to the type of employer.[56] Whatever the variety or limitations of the duties of individual stewards, however, there can be no doubt that stewards were figures of crucial importance to the social structure of early modern England. Without their labours in very corner of the country landowners would have had to neglect government, Parliament, public and military service, where their services were vital to the machinery of the state, or see go to ruin the estates which were the basis of their rank and the chief source of their livelihood.

Notes

1. N. Saul, *Knights and esquires: the Gloucestershire gentry in the fourteenth century* (Oxford, 1981), pp. 64ff; M. J. Bennett, *Community, class and careerism: Cheshire and Lancashire society in the age of Sir Gawain and the Green Knight* (Cambridge, 1983), pp. 72–3; H. S. Bennett, *The Pastons and their England*, 2nd edn (Cambridge, 1968), pp. 42–6.

2. For example, J. Thirsk (ed.), *The agrarian history of England and Wales, Vol. IV, 1500–1640* (Cambridge, 1967); L. Stone, *The crisis of the aristocracy 1558–1641* (Oxford, 1965); M. St Clare Byrne (ed.), *The Lisle letters* (6 vols, Chicago, 1981), vol. 6. For works relevant to stewards in the seventeenth century see: D. R. Hainsworth (ed.), *The correspondence of Sir John Lowther of Whitehaven 1693–1698: a provincial community in wartime*, Records of Social and Economic History, new ser., vol. 7 (1983), which largely comprises the letters of the stewards William Gilpin and John Gale; D. R. Hainsworth, 'The essential governor: the estate steward and English society 1660–1714',

Historical Studies, Australia and New Zealand, vol. 21 (1985); H. D. Turner, 'George, Fourth Earl of Northampton: estates and stewards, 1686–1714', *Northamptonshire Past and Present*, vol. 4 (1966–7), pp. 97–105; H. W. Saunders, 'Estate management at Rainham in the years 1661–1686 and 1706', *Norfolk Archaeology*, vol. 19 (1917), pp. 39–66; Sir Thomas Barrett-Lennard, 'Two hundred years of estate management at Horsford during the seventeenth and eighteenth centuries', *Norfolk Archaeology*, vol. 20 (1921), pp. 57–139; M. G. Davies, 'Country gentry and payments to London, 1650–1714', *Econ. Hist. Rev.*, 2nd ser., vol. 24 (1971), pp. 15–36; M. G. Davies, 'Country gentry and falling rents in the 1660s and 1670s', *Midland History*, vol. 4 (1977), pp. 86–96.

For the eighteenth century see G. E. Mingay, 'The eighteenth-century land steward' in E. L. Jones and G. E. Mingay (eds), *Land, labour and population in the industrial revolution* (1967), pp. 3–27; and 'Estate management in eighteenth-century Kent', *Agricultural History Review*, vol. 4 (1956), pp. 108–13. See also E. Hughes, 'The eighteenth-century estate steward' in H. A. Cronne, T. W. Moody and D. B. Quinn (eds), *Essays in British and Irish history* (1949), pp. 185–99; J. Martin, 'Estate stewards and their work in Glamorgan, 1660–1760: a regional study of estate management', *Morgannwg*, vol. 23 (1979), pp. 9–28; H. M. Thomas, 'Margam estate management, 1765–1860', *Glamorgan Historian*, vol. 6 (1969), pp. 13–27; P. Roebuck, 'Absentee landownership in the late seventeenth and early eighteenth centuries: a neglected factor in English agrarian history', *Agricultural History Review*, vol. 21 (1973), pp. 1–17; J. Wake and D.C. Webster (eds) *The letters of Daniel Eaton 1725–1732*, Northamptonshire Record Society, vol. 24 (1971). The writer is currently completing a monograph on the estate steward in the structure of seventeenth-century society.

3. John Earle, *Micro-cosmographie*, facsimile of autograph MSS (1966); W. J. Taylor (ed.), *The Overburian characters*, Percy Reprints xiii (Oxford, 1936); T. Fuller, *The holy state and the profane state* (1841).

4. 'The English experience' series (Da Capo Press, New York, 1968–79).

5. Courtiers and officials holding crown sinecures have been excluded; count based on P. W. Hasler (ed.), *The history of Parliament: the House of Commons 1558–1603* (1981).

6. G. Holmes, *Augustan England: professions, state and society 1680–1730* (1983), p. 24.

7. Ibid., p. 9.

8. See Cumbria RO, D/Lons/W, Lowther–Tickell letters, 1666–92 (approx. 1,800 items); for Tickell's mining experience see Leconfield Archives, D/Lec/81.

9. Hainsworth, *Lowther correspondence*, pp. 3, 29, 661, 675.

10. Usher's few surviving letters are in a group of uncatalogued stewards' letters at Netherby Hall, Cumbria; I should like to thank Sir Charles Grahame for granting me access to his archives. By contrast the Rev. George Plaxton was chief steward of Lord Gower for many years: see his letters in Staffordshire RO, Duke of Sutherland (Leveson-Gower) Papers.

11. For Adams as surveyor see E. G. R. Taylor, *The mathematical practitioners of Tudor and Stuart England* (Cambridge, 1970), p. 276.

12. Cheshire RO, Cholmondeley DCH/K/3/1, 18 and 29 Nov. 1679.

13. Clwyd RO, D/G/3272, 3273, Crewe–Trevor Letters 1630–9.

14. For King's difficulties with these competing demands, and his plaintive requests for a replacement, see Northamptonshire RO, Lord Fitzwilliam of Milton Papers.

15. Cf. John Gale to Lowther, 1 May 1697, Hainsworth, *Lowther correspondence*, pp. 380–1.

16. Northamptonshire RO, Isham IC 1089, Gilbert Clerke to Sir Thomas Isham, 25 May 1678.

17. See F. J. Fisher, 'The development of London as a centre of conspicuous consumption in the sixteenth and seventeenth centuries', *Trans. Roy. Hist. Soc.*, 4th ser., vol. 30 (1948), pp. 37–50.

18. Sir John Lowther visited Whitehaven only nine times in 32 years. Cholmondeley visited Cheshire during most summers, but Fitzwilliam was absent from Milton, Northamptonshire, for years at a time.

19. See Samuel Peers's complaint to Weymouth, 1686, Longleat House, Thynne Papers, vol. 22, fo. 290.

20. E. Richards, 'The land agent' in G. E. Mingay (ed.), *The Victorian countryside* (2 vols., 1981), vol. 2, pp. 439–55.

21. Cited by Roebuck, 'Absentee landownership', p. 4 and n.

22. For example, Fitzwilliam to Guybon, 8 Feb. 1705 (Northamptonshire RO, F(M)C 1378).

23. See Lowther to Gilpin, Hainsworth, *Lowther correspondence*, p. 431.

24. Ibid., pp. 430–1.

25. It may be that as salaries improved in the eighteenth-century licit perquisites declined in significance. Certainly William Elmsall, in 1711 the newly appointed steward of Sir George Savile's Yorkshire estates, assured his master that he would eschew all perquisites as 'pernicious': Nottinghamshire RO, DDSR 211/2 (15 Apr. 1711).

26. HMC, *Bath*, vol. 4, p. 266.

27. For a steward's death with rents in hand and his heirs' attempts to frustrate the lord's recovery of them, see William Whitehead to Lord Gower, 24 Jan. 1707, in Staffordshire RO Duke of Sutherland (Leveson-Gower) Papers, D/593/Add 4/1.

28. See Thomas Guybon, nephew of steward Francis Guybon, to Lord Fitzwilliam, 18 Sept. 1710, referring to 'the expectation of the rest of the relations running pretty high from the common report of my uncle dying very rich': Northamptonshire RO, F(M)C, Box 22, unnumbered corr. 1710–44, no. 85.

29. Cumbria RO, D/Lons/W, Commonplace Books (List 5), untitled notebook, *c* 1661–1680s, fo. 25.

30. A classic example was Lowther's bailiff at Whitehaven-St Bees who was charged with collecting rents and market dues, was paid £2 a year for this, and whose full-time occupation was 'bankman' at his master's principal colliery: Hainsworth, *Lowther correspondence*, index,

under ' Branthwaite, Lancelot'.

31. Cheshire RO, DCH/M32 Misc. Gilpin's power of attorney, without such an enabling clause, is outlined in Hainsworth, *Lowther correspondence*, p. 7.

32. For an interesting analysis of the rental decline, see Davies, 'Country gentry and falling rents in the 1660s and 1670s', pp. 91ff.

33. This complaint is not persuasive. Had landlords lived on their estates, farming their demesnes, living off their own produce, they would have needed to purchase little from their neighbours and their own surplus would have competed with their tenants' crops in the market place. Moreover, when the landlord came to spend some months on his estate his steward would be commissioned to purchase great stores of grain, hay, beef cattle, sheep and locally brewed ale. Finally, the highly profitable London market for the produce of tenant farmers would have been depressed if the wealthy households of London had been thinned by the permanent absence of the landlords.

34. Turner, 'George, Fourth Earl', pp. 101–3.

35. Swynfen's mediation is of unknown date but prior to the sixth Lord Paget's death in 1678. Swynfen to Paget, *c.* 1683: Staffordshire RO, Paget D603/K/3/4.

36. Fitzwilliam's letters to Guybon are studded with references to the use of venison or warrants to maintain 'friendship', e.g. North-amptonshire RO, F(M)C 970.

37. Letters of 20 and 27 Nov. 1701, Cheshire RO, Cholmondeley DCH/L/49.

38. Letters of 20 and 24 Feb. 1681 (together with 26 Jan., 8, 12 Feb.), Cheshire RO, DCH/K/3/4.

39. Hainsworth, *Lowther correspondence*, pp. 631, 633, 634, 637, 638. For the steward as election agent in the north-west see the analysis in Robert Hopkinson, 'Elections in Cumberland and Westmorland 1695–1723', unpublished PhD thesis, University of Newcastle upon Tyne, 1972.

40. Mainewaring to Weymouth, 25 Sept. 1688 and 8 Feb. 1689: Longleat House, Thynne Papers, vol. 28, fos. 236, 266.

41. Hainsworth, *Lowther correspondence*, p. 113.

42. Longleat House, Thynne Papers, vol. 28, fo. 239.

43. Northamptonshire RO, F(M)C 981.

44. E.g. Cumbria RO, Lowther–Tickell Letters, 10 Sept., 5 Oct. 1666; Northamptonshire RO, F(M)C 467; Longleat House, Thynne Papers, vol. 28, fos. 253, 265, 278. When the Irish war drove scores of refugees to Whitehaven in 1689 Lowther charged Tickell with distributing government funds provided for their relief: Hainsworth, *Lowther correspondence*, p. xxxv.

45. Lowther–Tickell Letters, Dec. 1672–April 1673, *passim*.

46. Nottingham University Library, Portland Papers, PW2/523a.

47. See the seminal article by Davies, 'Country gentry and payments to London, 1650–1714', pp. 15–35.

48. The Lowther–Tickell letters (Cumbria RO) 1665–75 are a particularly rich source for the use of cattle drovers. For the Elletsons'

'breaking', 19 and 26 Jan. 1675; see also Hainsworth, *Lowther correspondence*, index, under 'returns of money', 'Dixon, Thomas, drover'. For a later example (1710), Joseph Graham, drover, to Jeffrey Beck, steward at Edenhall: Cumbria RO, D/Mus/A/1/1.

49. Cf. Northamptonshire RO, F(M)C 1348, 24 Sept. 1704.

50. Hainsworth, *Lowther correspondence, passim.*

51. Cheshire RO, DCH, 'Salt Accounts'.

52. Letters of John Cocke of Redruth to Lady Arundel, various dates 1706–16: Nottingham University Library, Galway 12,322.

53. Longleat House, Thynne Papers, vol. 23, fos. 338, 364, 377; vol. 24, fos. 7, 15, 27.

54. For Dyrham and the Rev. Samuel Trueman, see Gloucestershire RO, Blathwayte of Dyrham, A23, A24, E239, E241.

55. E.g. the surveying and maintaining of levees and dykes in the fenlands, and organising their defence against floods and storms: see Northamptonshire RO, F(M)C 486.

56. E.g. Lowther as a Commissioner of the Admiralty after 1689 employed Tickell as a collector of Irish intelligence and of maritime intelligence concerning the Irish Sea and its approaches: Hainsworth, *Lowther correspondence*, pp. xxxiv–xxxviii.

7

The Profession of Arms

Ian Roy

The profession of arms is something of an oddity, and consequently difficult to categorise, when the whole body of the professions is considered as it emerged in the early modern period. There will be cause, as we examine the position and progress of the officers of the armed services during the sixteenth and seventeenth centuries, to emphasise their exceptional character, their particular prehistory, their anomalous position. The armed services do not fit easily into any schema which is based upon the well-known emergence and the recognised status in the period of the three classic professions — the law, medicine and the ministry. The emphasis — on suitability of the candidates for the vocation, of their entry qualifications and their professional training, of their devotion to the calling and their deriving from its acquired skills and high status the economic worth and social esteem they enjoyed — will mostly be irrelevant or marginal until late in the period under discussion, or confined to only some part of the profession of arms as a whole. Many of the features which distinguished the lawyers or the doctors as a professional group were largely absent among the soldiers or the sailors. The latter were, if anything, in a conservative age and among a conservative group of professional men, the most marked by their history, by their memory of their past — often a quite distinct entity from their actual history — and their concern to uphold those cherished ideals which the past had sanctified. They would be most anxious to preserve and if possible increase the privileges their special position had obtained for them in bygone days, to maintain their ancient ideals and special calling, rather than to carve out for themselves, through the imposition of extra qualifications or a more arduous training, or the demarcation of a supposed body of skills and a professionally exclusive association of practitioners to preserve it, a new place, at a higher level in society, than their predecessors. The established practitioners of the art or science of war, as a consequence, appeared very often to fear change; their most respected models of behaviour belonged to a bygone era and were increasingly irrelevant in an age of rapid technological and political change; but the pressures on them to perform their skills adequately were as great as ever. The very survival of the state depended on their competent execution of the tasks in warfare allotted to them; they, more than most, had their ability tested, at times, in the most 'absolute' conditions afforded by man's relations with man — the crucible of war; and failure in those conditions, however excusable or unmerited, could be catastrophic, not only for the immediate participants, but for the society they were defending. Nothing was more demanding than success in war, the competent maintenance of the defences of the realm under the pressures of external threats throughout the period for England. Nothing was worse for society as a whole than the possible results of the overthrow of those defences, and as a consequence those responsible in the armed services could suffer a terrible fate if found guilty of incompetence. In other callings a man could be dismissed for dereliction of duty or unprofessional behaviour in our period; only in the profession of arms could he be condemned to death. Here as in other respects the warrior occupies a special place.

That special place was the result of a long process — developing over many centuries before we take up the story in the middle of the sixteenth — whereby the association of military virtue and success in war with the reward by the crown in land and position was firmly established in feudal England, as elsewhere in western Europe. The warrior class was that which was closest to the King and his court, and was most intimately identified with the possession of landed estates. While the actual feudal relationship — military services performed for the lord in return for his continuance of the title to the land he had granted in the first place — decayed in the course of the later middle ages, there was still an assumption in the years which followed that the ruling elite, the landed aristocracy and greater gentry — the equivalent of the nobility in comparable European nations — were distinguished above all by their actual or potential leadership in war, at the side of the King, the commander-in-chief of the armed forces of the realm. Their position was next to the King; if the country was at war they first were called upon to defend it in arms; they were above all a military elite, even when knight's service by a king's tenant-in-chief could no longer be performed. A territorial magnate, and many of his gentry retainers, like the King himself, was expected to find his truest and most honourable vocation in arms, to be most fittingly occupied when at the head of his troops in war, and in peacetime in those activities which best imitated the warlike state: the skill in horsemanship and the display of courage which hunting in the field required, or — for the grandest of the ruling landed elite — the single trial by combat in the tiltyard.

The tournament, and the code of behaviour associated with it, leads naturally to a discussion of the other important inheritance from the medieval past which remained influential in the later period — chivalric ideas. The code of chivalry was the theoretical superstructure built on the foundations of the feudal military relationship, providing a justification for the military pursuits of the members of the landed elite, and a recognised body of beliefs they could live by, and which outlasted its territorial/military base. It has recently been argued that, in the hands of the heralds and the contributors to its popular literature, it had a vigorous and useful life of its own, when the original justification for its existence was a fading memory.[1] When the feudal host was a thing of the past, and the Tudor landowner was happy to pay the military rate instead of serving in arms personally, the legends of the court of King Arthur and his knights, and the tales of Amadis de Gaule remained popular fare. Many a gentleman's library contained copies of the *Morte d'Arthur* and other popularisations of knight errantry as well as printed testimony to the advance of the military science in the manuals of modern warfare, books of engravings of scientific fortifications and up-to-date accounts of recent wars on the Continent.[2] The Court of Chivalry still existed in England to resolve disputes over matters of honour, between gentlemen. The emphasis, in the chivalric code, on the winning of honour, which was distinct from material advantage or preferment to office and which required a certain form of behaviour, led to the continuation into modern life of a set of principles which was separate from and often at variance with the ordinary rules and regulations of normal life. The most common, and for those charged with keeping law and order the most worrying, manifestation of this independent code of honourable behaviour among gentlemen was the duel. From the beginning to the end of our period, and in most places, duelling was condemned by the authorities in church and state. But, especially among the officers of the armed forces, where the rules of honour were felt to be most relevant, there continued to be resort in the settlement of quarrels to the arbitrament of the sword or pistol. A grievance in this field could not be righted by the actions of the civil courts.[3]

The time-honoured beliefs that leadership in war was the peculiar preserve of the English aristocracy, that a nobleman never stood higher than when armed for battle at the head of his followers, and that, despite all the changes which the waging of war and military organisation were to undergo in the period, the field of arms was especially the celebration of aristocratic values, codified in the laws of honour rather than the laws of the land, would profoundly influence, well into the eighteenth century in Great Britain, as elsewhere in Europe, the way army and navy officers would view their profession, and the way the rest of society viewed them. This would resound, like the echo of a remote past, long after the physical presence of most members of the aristocracy was no longer actually required on the battlefield, and the task of command in war had passed to those better qualified by training and merit than by birth alone.

But at the start of our period theory and practice more or less still coincided. An English nobleman living at the end of Henry VIII's reign might well have had amongst his earliest memories the death or maiming of his father in the last wars fought on English soil in which the aristocracy had played the leading role. Most of the lords of military age in England in the second half of the fifteenth century had taken part in the Wars of the Roses; it has been calculated that some 37 of 62 noble families suffered casualties during the conflict.[4] It did not, however, contrary to popular belief, profoundly weaken the peerage and its role in political and social life thereafter. When Henry VIII came to play, once again, the traditional role of a young English prince in the lists in France, he would obtain a positive response from his noble followers when he called them to arms. In periods of popular disturbance the crown would depend on the loyalty and military skills of its most prominent supporters in the regions affected. The system of indentured retainers was tolerated by the sovereign for the good reason that he had no other force to uphold the King's Peace and ensure that his writs were obeyed in the more remote provinces of the kingdom.

But a long period of peace and of government parsimony in military expenditure would inevitably work a change in attitudes, as well as in social realities. The younger and more adventurous members of the peerage might turn out for Henry's foreign expeditions eagerly, reasonably well equipped, and with some hope of winning that precious commodity, honour, at the cannon's mouth. But in the following hundred years the opportunities for such activity were fewer, the chances of gaining honour were diminishing, and warfare itself was changing in ways which no longer permitted the easy entry of a body of noblemen largely untrained in modern skills and unregenerate in outlook; or if it was still politically prudent for such men to be given commands their general usefulness was in decline. They faced a situation in which the conduct of war had become expensive and complicated; the mounted arm, the traditional preserve of the chivalrous gentleman, was no longer queen of the battlefield; modern firearms required a period of training and some expertise, and the development of siege artillery had reduced the importance of the ancient castles of the nobility. Insofar as military skills, now elevated in some quarters to a science, which might be viewed as part of the new learning and the humanistic outlook of the age, could be considered novel, the old aristocracy would be at a disadvantage. Renaissance attitudes, with their fashionable emphasis on education and reform, weakened the claims of the ancient nobility to military command, if those claims were based solely on high birth, traditional habits of command and sheer familiarity with horse and sword.[5]

Domestic developments aided the process whereby the greatest in the land were weaned from their devotion to war. Of 118 Tudor years 77 were reckoned 'peaceful'.[6] The threat of domestic rebellion was receding throughout the century.

Baronial castles of the old type were not only now indefensible, costly and uncomfortable, they were no longer needed. In the great rebuilding of the time the houses of the landed class shared in the general move to lighter, airier, more comfortable and less cramped accommodation. An ancient and massive keep such as Raglan castle was transformed by the Herberts into a stately Elizabethan house. The greatest men at court built prodigy houses, fit to receive the Queen on her progresses or provide the setting for the meetings of the local gentry magistrates over whom the owner would preside. The progress of civility among the aristocracy was marked too by the building of town houses, the better to facilitate visits to London in pursuit of legal redress, office at court or the latest fashions. It has even been argued that this new concern for manners led to a reduction in duelling, at least in its most barbarous form, the 'killing affray'.[7] Certainly the taste for warlike pursuits was subsiding. 'The most part of gentlemen', wrote a contemporary at the start of Elizabeth's reign, 'are and have been of late days brought up so daintily and in such vanities that they can little skill of the service of their country'.[8]

At the same time the Elizabethan government reduced its dependence on baronial retinues by introducing the lieutenancy and the trained bands; placing military government in the shires in the hands of its greatest supporters, usually members of the privy council or other major figures at court, each assisted by deputy lieutenants drawn from the greater gentry and JPs of the county, and reducing the general obligation of the rest of society to a select few in each locality who would be trained for arms and be expected to turn out when invasion threatened. The actual number of paid troops in direct government employ remained small; the monarch's personal guard was, by Continental standards, tiny, and tended in any case to become aged, unmilitary and just another set of sinecures in the prevailing spoils system. Scattered among the garrisons and forts of the rest of the country — over a hundred of them in the sixteenth century — there were perhaps 2,000–3,000 men, as each contained a handful of soldiers and gunners. Little of this provided continuous honourable employment for gentlemen, and most of the 'governments' were sought by local gentry families as a useful adjunct to their other offices in the county. The Dering family, prominent in Kent, obtained the governorship of Dover castle, strategically very important, and were disappointed that they could not make a profit from it.[9]

In these circumstances, which may be said to have held good — with the exception of the civil wars and interregnum — until the end of the seventeenth century, we might expect army service to have freed itself from the attentions of part-time gentry amateurs and to have developed some of the attributes, when military opportunities offered, of a distinct occupational group. Such attributes could include its own status, derived from the competent exercise of its vocation — its function — rather than its association with the landed elite, its own career structure, its own internal regulation — 'the laws of war' — and some regard for itself as an honourable calling — what might be called its *esprit de corps*. But this, as we shall see, would be true only in part. The wars at the end of Elizabeth's reign, and the foreign expeditions of the 1620s, forced a reluctant government to increase military expenditure and the size of the military establishment. These were formative years in the development of the officer corps in England, for native soldiers were brought into direct contact with European armies and military practice, Continental experts were imported into England, there was an upsurge of interest in matters military at home, and the continuance for a lengthy period of Englishmen in arms aided the emergence of permanent ranks and the definition of function among office-holders. In place of the nebulous 'bands' led by individual captains, by 1600 there were regiments on the European pattern, with a hierarchy of commissioned ranks, from the ensign of foot or cornet of horse at the lowest rung to the colonel at the top, and promotion patterns established.[10] Manuals of all kinds — very often translations from the Italian or Spanish or, later, French — helped to define the role of each, and the qualifications needed.[11] The terms employed, both for units and ranks, were also adopted from foreign practice: the French 'coronel', for example, being replaced by the Italian 'colonel' in the early seventeenth century.[12] Regiments varied in size, but at the fullest — ten companies (Foot) or troops (Horse) — would require about thirty officers. Above the regimental level there was less certainty; the brigading of regiments was in its infancy, and 'generals', variously described, were usually appointed for a particular service only. The permanent status of the different field commands was a later development.

Land service and sea service were in some respects inter-changeable. It had long been the practice for English govern-ments — historically the Admiralty, to which was later added the body of civilian administrators, the Navy Board — to recruit its small naval forces, in time of war, from the merchant marine. There had been no rigid distinction, in an earlier period, between the warship and the cargo vessel — in this respect the Atlantic differed from the Mediterranean — and most ocean-going merchant-men carried cannon. The permanent officers of these ships, usually styled standing or warrant officers, were the master and his mate, the purser, the boatswain and so on. Over them, for the duration of the conflict only, the Admiralty placed temporary commissioned officers, who carried the same ranks and were often the same men, as those of the land forces — captain and lieutenant. They came on board to 'fight' the ship, leaving the sailing of it to the mariners. Further to confuse land service with sea service, it was not unusual for the King's ships to carry a complement of soldiers, to board the enemy, to take part in amphibious operations, or to help police the vessel. Even late in the seventeenth century army officers found opportunities to serve afloat, and sea captains to command land forces.

The development of heavy, ship-destroying guns, carried broadside in larger, purpose-built ships, and the tactics of accommodating the new 'off-fighting', where ships bombarded each other at longer range, rather than grappled and boarded, would in the course of time require men in command who were properly trained, had served an appren-ticeship in ships of the line — so called once warships developed 'line-ahead' formations, the better to deploy their formidable armoury — and were solely at the disposal of the lords of the Admiralty. But this time was not yet. While England's battle fleets grew larger they continued to rely on converted soldiers, or merchant skippers, who were in commission, 'in post', only so long as the King's ship was, and returned to their former occupations thereafter. Even when a body of trained, regular sea officers had been formed, they were only employed when they were 'in post'.[13]

The co-operation between the merchant marine and the Admiralty in financing, manning and officering fleets designed for war was best demonstrated in some of the armed expeditions of Elizabeth's reign. Organised on a profit-making, joint-stock basis and enjoying political patronage, gentlemen, along with soldiers and seamen, could adventure themselves as well as their financial stake in the voyage. Where commissioned officers were so few they were useful, said Drake, 'for government's sake', to help discipline the crew, who, then as later, were mostly press-ganged, usually described as the dregs of the seaports, and whose wretched existence on the lower deck required constant surveillance and the frequent brutal punishment of offenders. Drake insisted, however, that the gentlemen without command must be prepared to draw and haul with the common mariners; the danger was that, being inexperienced, self-financed, often quarrelsome and prone to duel, and lacking command respon-sibility, such men could not be brought to accept military discipline themselves. If well connected at court they might bring with them the factious spirit and rivalries of their patrons.[14]

The privateering voyages of Hawkins and Drake, as well as the Leicester expedition to the Netherlands, Essex's to Ireland or Buckingham's to France, many of them involving close co-operation between the naval and the military arm, may be taken together as providing the necessary employment and furnishing the experience for thousands of potential officers: perhaps 3,000 in Elizabeth's reign.[15] Who seized these oppor-tunities in late Tudor and Stuart times? As warfare remained of great political importance, and was viewed as a noble vocation, leading courtiers, and the members of their entour-ages, would play a significant role. Several ventures were led by court favourites in person; their supporters and clients followed where they led, in pursuit of honour and profit. A career in soldiering could lead to rapid social advancement: if a man was not a gentleman before becoming an officer he became one after. Attachment to a great political figure in time of war might pay more and speedier dividends than in time of peace. Essex was notorious for promoting men of little breeding and less wealth. 'A knight of Cadiz' became a term of contempt, as he knighted so many of his lowly dependants on that expedition; another, so honoured for his services in Ireland, was described as a 'base captain and rascal'.[16] Most recruits, however, seem to have been drawn from the ranks of the minor gentry, often impoverished, the younger sons and brothers of those well connected at court, those with mercantile interests — especially in the privateering voyages — and the offspring of middle-class parents who had little inclination or aptitude for civilian life and employment. The lawyer James Whitelocke said of his brother William, who served in more than one of Drake's expeditions:

> He was brought up with the rest in learning, but had no mind to it, and therefore was bound apprentice to a merchant in London, but when the Portugal voyage was undertaken, he left master and thrift and all, and put himself into the action, and so fell from that civil course to a martial life . . . He followed that course of life, until at the last, going forth in a ship of war from London to the Indian seas, he lost his life in a conflict with the Spaniards. He was a very tall young man, strong of body, flaxen hair, fair of complexion, exceeding wasteful in expense, and careless of all worldly matters that tended to thrift. He was about the age of 27 years old when he died.[17]

There is a mixture of family pride, sorrow and strong disapproval in the puritan judge's comments on an errant brother.

William Whitelocke had decided in the end to 'follow the wars altogether'. The trade of war was emerging as a separate occupation, which bred its own devotees, who were distinguished from, and — as we have seen — on occasion deplored by, their fellow citizens. Although often titled, and well connected in political terms, the most successful soldiers of the period were those who committed themselves to the military life, gained the necessary experience and, by breaking free of the shackles of political clientage, were able to survive the fall of favourites. The Norris brothers of Rycote, Oxfordshire, began their careers as Cecil protégés; they won fame and fortune in the Netherlands wars, rose to be generals and governors of important towns, and entered Parliament.[18] Viscount Wimbledon, the most celebrated soldier of James I's reign, was a Cecil by birth, but as a younger son could hope for little in the way of inheritance: he carved out his own career as an infantry officer and was ennobled following the 1625 Cadiz expedition.[19] the family of Vere, though one of its branches possessed an ancient earldom, was obscure and almost penniless when its male members set out for the Dutch and

German wars. Most had no other occupation than soldiering; at one point the heir to the earldom 'had scarce any means to live but on a captain's place in the United Provinces'.[20] But the cousins were talented and mutually aided each other in their rise to the top; Sir Horace Vere (later Lord Vere of Tilbury) and his brother Sir Francis became the greatest generals of their age, and the central figures in the group of English officers associated with the wars of the first half of the seventeenth century.[21] Military command, overseas if necessary when home postings were scarce, was becoming settled in certain families and officers began to develop their own political connections. The Anglo-Dutch brigade for much of the seventeenth century provided continuous employment when all else failed, and an apprenticeship in arms for many young hopefuls; or indeed for several black sheep. So rigorous a training was it that anxious heads of 'good' families in England would buy commands in the force for spendthrift, shiftless sons or nephews, in the hope that a spell under military discipline, away from temptation, with regular pay, might prove character-forming. The young George Goring was sent out to save the family's fortune from further depletion. Others sought in military service abroad refuge from the long arm of the law: George Monck, Richard Grenville and Thomas Lunsford, all famous Civil War commanders, began their army careers in this manner.

But whatever their motives, those who made good in the European wars, alongside or fighting against the best soldiers of the age, took in this period an undoubted pride in their craft. The polite disdain of the comfortable citizen for the hazardous, primitive and often shameless life of the soldier was heartily reciprocated by the seasoned veteran, confident of the rightness and honour of his calling. A good Christian, even a puritan, could become a soldier. As well as honours and riches he might win a good reputation, on the pattern of the Arthurian knights, Old Testament warriors, the heroes of Homeric legend or the less fanciful models that a reading of classical texts provided. John the Baptist allowed the soldier's calling, deploring only the abuses. 'Solomon . . . held such as were men of war to be more honourable than to be employed in servile work.' The soldier was, or could be, a pious Christian knight, valorous for the Gospel and the Divine Law, wrote one of their number.[22] The influence of Ancient Rome continued into the seventeenth century: the well-known first- and fourth-century military manuals remained in translation and popular in England, as elsewhere; the thoroughly workmanlike Francis Vere, the 'compleat captain' of his day, modelled his memoirs, as did the famous French marshal, Monluc, on Caesar's commentaries; the most successful English commander in Ireland, Lord Mountjoy, named one of his sons Scipio. There was a general recognition, in the literature of the time, that the contemporary soldier had not only to equal the heroes of the past in courage and chivalrous behaviour, but master a wide range of modern skills, from mathematics, military engineering and pyrotechnics to the command of foreign languages.[23]

War was almost continuous in seventeenth-century Europe; only three years were reckoned peaceful. At the same time Britain's permanent armed forces remained weak, with the exception of the interregnum, until almost the end of the century. The opportunity existed, before the Civil War and after the restoration, for the experienced commander, whose knowledge and skills could be applied equally successfully in almost every theatre of war, to offer his services to any foreign power prepared to pay handsomely for them. English Catholics debarred from holding office, impoverished Scots lairds, Welsh gentlemen of little estate, Irish squireens, all flocked abroad in search of military employment, having little to detain them at home. Some 6,000–8,000 Scots, under their own commanders, served Gustavus Adolphus in the Thirty Years War. Wallenstein, it will be recalled, was murdered by Irish and Welsh officers in his own entourage. A younger son of the famously puritan family, the Barringtons of Essex, sought a captain's place in the Venetian or Swedish service, which would make him self-supporting.[24] For soldiers of fortune — the term was coming into use in the 1660s — the continuity of career, the regularity of pay and promotion, as well as incidental rewards such as the spoils of war, the winning of titles and estates in a foreign land, justified the setting aside of national ties or political or religious loyalties. It was, however, a 'base maxim', according to Sir James Turner, one of their number, that 'so we serve our master honestly, it is no matter what master we serve'.[25] Many Protestants scrupled to serve Spain or the Empire; others left their commands when their sovereign declared war on the prince who employed them. But many felt it was better to serve the Turk than not to serve at all. Turner himself schemed to join the Persian forces as a military adviser; Scots mercenaries were also to be found in the Polish–Turkish campaigns in leading positions, and in the Muscovite state. Sir Arthur Aston, the Catholic mercenary soldier of Cheshire gentry stock, passed from Russian, to Polish, to Swedish service in the 1620s and 1630s, before becoming a leading Royalist commander in the civil wars.[26] Such men brought the latest Continental practices into England and formed the officer cadres around which, as the need arose, new English forces could be built.

These men and their colleagues in arms from foreign service were able to show their mettle in the wars, in the British Isles, or that Britain waged overseas, in the period 1638–60. They made an important contribution to the rapid re-education in the methods of modern warfare which their fellow countrymen underwent during these years. Several hundred took leading positions in the Scots Covenanting army, the English and Scots forces in Ireland, the Irish Confederate army, Charles I's armies, and the earlier Parliamentarian armies under seasoned campaigners like Essex, Waller and Poyntz. They competed for these posts, however, with gentlemen volunteers in 1642, for the outbreak of the English Civil War witnessed a remarkable reassertion of the aristocratic prerogative of leadership in war. Although the participation of the peerage alone was not on the scale of the wars of the fifteenth century, and the schooling of the gentry was now at university or inn of court rather than the jousting field, they rallied to the defence of their sovereign; even compared with the casualty figures for the Wars of the Roses it is still remarkable that 13 peers and 42 baronets and knights died on the field of battle for Charles's cause.[27] On the other side half the infantry regiments raised by Parliament at the beginning of the conflict were commanded, at least nominally, by members of the House of Lords. As the war progressed, however, these gentry commanders tended to be replaced on both sides by more expert soldiers, usually trained abroad, like Aston or Monck, or those with a greater political or religious commitment to outright victory, like Cromwell and Ireton.

The 1640s and 1650s were, like the closing years of Elizabeth's reign, a formative period in the history of the British armed forces and their leaders. The needs of war created the first standing army and an enlarged navy; and their continuation on a war footing in the 1650s, at a high level of preparedness, brought about lasting changes. For the first time a regular army of 50,000 was kept up, its maintenance guaranteed by the constitutions of the Republic, permanently garrisoned throughout the British Isles; its land settlement in Ireland, its fortifications in Scotland were to remain after Cromwell's death and the restoration. A requirement of 1,500 army officers was easily met. Monck's chaplain may be believed when he asserted that the Cromwellian army in Scotland attracted 'men of good parts and learning', who were able to save money out of their pay.[28] For the Cromwellian officers, under their proven commanders, soldiering was a serious, professional and profitable occupation.

The changes were no less marked in the Republic's navy. Parliament had taken over Charles I's ship-money fleet, added to it, purged its officers and gone to war with the world's greatest sea power, the Dutch. The opportunities for new men in the service were great: perhaps as many as 600 posts to be filled in twenty years. The Commonwealth's naval commanders were drawn from a wide spectrum of society, comparable in background to that of many army officers. The long years of war, and the political revolution, allowed talent to be recognised, and men who had learned their trade by practising it, whatever their social origins or previous military experience, rose to the top. The 'generals-at-sea' of the 1650s were, typically, competent soldiers — but very often with some seafaring connection — drafted in to fill the gap left by departing gentlemen commanders: Robert Blake, the puritan hero of two Civil War sieges, was a Somerset MP of merchant stock; Richard Deane, 'once a hoyman's servant' according to one Royalist report, had made his name as an artilleryman in the Civil War; George Monck, a career soldier who changed sides, and Edward Mountagu — later Earl of Sandwich — a puritan squire turned colonel of foot, were summoned to the sea service by Cromwell and left their previous posts.[29] The captains of the interregnum survived to fight for Charles II; over two-thirds of the naval commanders of 1660 were old Cromwellians. Lely's portraits of the flag officers at the battle of Lowestoft (1665) show them in their prime: most were 45 or more, with upwards of twenty years' service. Ten of the 13 had served the Commonwealth, and of these 6 were of non-gentry birth, mostly from coastal, seafaring communities, which were geographically dispersed from Yorkshire to Bristol. They did not avoid danger: 4 of the 13 officers would be killed in action.[30] Those who had been promoted from the lower deck retained the respect of their men. Pepys, Clerk of the Acts (secretary of the Navy Board), was astonished, as well he might be, considering the evil reputation of the ordinary seaman at the time, when a dozen of Sir Christopher Myngs's men volunteered at his funeral to avenge his death at the hands of the Dutch.[31] The first fighting instructions issued to the commanders, and the evolution of line-ahead tactics, date from this period. The English navy met de Ruyter and the Tromps, the finest admirals of their day, on equal or better than equal terms. Several engagements in the Anglo-Dutch wars showed the superior gunnery, discipline and morale of the royal navy. 'The English are now masters of us, and consequently of the sea,' one of the Dutch admirals confessed publicly in 1653.[32] From the mid-century onwards the growth of Britain's world-wide colonial empire, and the massive and continuing expansion of her mercantile marine, brought the nation into conflict at sea with old and new commercial rivals, and ensured that, even in years of peace, the strength of the navy would be maintained. The basis was being laid of Britain's later naval mastery, whatever changes there might be on the political scene.

The restoration was such a change, which particularly affected the evolution of the officer corps of both the navy and the army. Charles and James were both passionately interested in the sea, and, despite lapses, had no intention of markedly reducing the size of the navy. Pepys, the reforming administrator, worked under the patronage of James as Lord High Admiral and later as King. None the less, the first impact of the return of the King, and the hordes of needy hangers-on who followed him home, as recorded by Pepys, was alarming. The history of the previous twenty years had shown the dangers of having military power in the wrong hands; it was now crucial to place in the most important posts those who had best demonstrated their loyalty. In the 1660s young and ardently Royalist gentlemen and courtiers sought by their personal example to expunge the memory of the years of defeat and dishonour; they crowded into the King's ships as they did into the newly established guards regiments around the palace.

Monck's wife — 'the damned Duchess' — complained that her husband was sent to sea with 'gentlemen captains with feathers and ribbons', instead of 'the old plain sea-captains that he served with formerly, that would make their ships swim with blood, though they could not make legs as captains nowadays can'.[33] There was an inevitable loss of efficiency, and a rising tide of indiscipline. The fears of a courtier at the battle of Lowestoft led the Dutch to escape; in the following year Pepys heard that all the sober commanders, the 'bred seamen' of an earlier era, now nicknamed 'tarpaulins', cried out against the newcomers, whose 'ill government' permitted 'swearing and drinking and whoring, and all manner of profaneness quite through the whole fleet'.[34] The gentlemen not only introduced into the fleet the morals of the restoration court, they reproduced there its notorious rivalries and factions. At the higher level few captains would co-operate willingly with Prince Rupert; among his subordinates the corrupt and buccaneering Holmes, though a dashing commander, was frequently involved in duels with his opponents or threatening to resign his commission on a point of honour.[35]

Pepys and his successors as Navy Board administrators recognised that, in the world of restoration politics — or that of Walpole later — the navy, now the biggest and the biggest-spending department of state, was too important to be insulated from prevailing social trends or to be kept politically neutral. The rough-hewn virtues of the tarpaulins were insufficient on their own to withstand political interference or parliamentary criticism and financial cutbacks. The navy would inevitably be open to the exercise of influence and 'interest', so long as it sought friends at court and its admirals seats in Parliament. The navy needed both the skilled tarpaulin and the well-connected gentleman. Unfortunately, as Macaulay put it: 'There were gentlemen and there were seamen in the navy of Charles II. But the seamen were not gentlemen and the gentlemen were not seamen.' Pepys, as we shall see, hoped to bridge this gap by educating the tarpaulins and making them politically acceptable, while subjecting the well-bred recruit to some form of sea apprenticeship. But the division in the service was to persist into the eighteenth century.[36]

The restoration worked an even more important change in the army. The Cromwellian army, like the Cromwellian navy, had brought back the Stuarts, but for political and financial reasons it was largely disbanded once the King was settled on his throne. There was even some argument as to whether a standing army should be continued at all: the example of the interregnum was one to be studiously avoided after 1660. But Britain now had colonies to be garrisoned, military installations in Scotland and Ireland to be maintained, and a royal family to be protected against domestic disturbance: this lesson, at least, from the civil wars, was well learnt. It was decided to create a small force, of 6,000 men, which was styled, to allay criticism, 'guards and garrisons'. Cromwellian officers and regiments were sent to distant parts of the British Isles, and remote overseas stations, where they did not need to be included in the English establishment and were in consequence less visible to parliamentary critics of the standing army. Career soldiers, and returned soldiers of fortune, as we shall see, could make their way there. But the centre of political attention, and the focus of social aspirations, would be the small force around the court, the newly created guards regiments, whose officers would stand or fall in public esteem thereafter.

It was a new force, unencumbered by existing office-holders with prior claims; its duties were light, and, in peacetime, not dangerous; it offered honourable, paid employment, close to the sovereign: hardly surprisingly, commissions in Charles II's army were hotly competed for. They soon commanded a price. The continuation of a standing army opened up a new and attractive field for the marketing of offices under the crown, a practice familiar to Englishmen over a long period before the Civil War, and to returning Royalists who had spent some time in France, where the sale of office was an important institution. The purchase of an army commission could be viewed as a business proposition, comparable to the financing of the earlier privateering expeditions: those who bought a stake were entitled to an officer's place and a share of the profits. The hope of financial gain was genuine; officers, unlike their men, were paid in full, if not always promptly, and it was calculated that, after anything from four to seven years, they would have received in pay a sum equivalent to the cost of the commission. They handled the pay of their own regiments or companies and could pocket the difference between the paper and actual strength of the unit. Profits could be made out of clothing and lodging allowances, levy money and the sale of commissions to subordinates. There was always an element of peculation, whenever the government was lax.[37]

These considerations were, however, probably subordinate to the other, unquantifiable, attractions of the service. The right to wear the King's coat, to follow the colours, to serve him personally, was much coveted; the high status of the household cavalry reflected this close association between the monarch, the commander-in-chief of the armed forces of the realm, and the officers of his horse guards. The old ideals of aristocratic virtue remained alive; birth and upbringing in a landed household, familiarity with horses and horsemanship, swordplay, the ordering of servants, still seemed the best qualifications for command. The opportunities for honour and glory outweighed any economic calculation. Many officers, particularly in the most fashionable and expensive regiments, were to find that in practice their expenses were greater than their pay, and they came in effect to subsidise the service. Poor men, even if they borrowed money to buy a commission, could not afford to live in the style thought appropriate in certain units. With the many defects of organisation and finance which characterised the armed forces of late Stuart and early Hanoverian England, rich officers were essential for the smooth running of the service.

The claims of birth and wealth, allied to political loyalty, were strongly reasserted at the restoration, and remained important for over two hundred years. The officers of the six standing regiments, based in England, were drawn from the political and social elite of the day. Monck and the Duke of York controlled patronage in the early years, promoting young men of old Cavalier family, like the Legges, Gerrards of Brandon, Trelawnys and Kirkbys. James II, both before he became King and after, took as close an interest in the army as he did in the navy. Many of those holding military posts were considered merely pensioners of the court and government; many were members of Parliament. Of 188 officers of Charles II's reign, serving in the six regiments whose careers have been studied, 89 had seats at some time. In all, from 1660 to 1690, 181 (compared to only 18 sea officers) were MPs. As a group they were overwhelmingly of noble or gentry stock; only 10 per cent were not, and, unusually by later standards, contained within their number a high proportion of eldest sons. The core of the army was an exclusive club, for entry to which 99 per cent of the population were ineligible. The claims of new wealth were not ignored, though often disguised. The paymaster general of the forces, Sir Stephen Fox, was able to buy commissions in the guards for the husbands and sons of his daughters, who had married into the aristocracy. He rescued their impoverished estates by subsidising their military careers thereafter.[38]

Officers who had purchased their places, and were in effect proprietors of their units, enjoyed a great deal of independence. Their privileged background and status, their possession of arms, and their idle and undemanding lifestyle equally ensured that, like the gentlemen volunteers of old, they would not bear disciplining easily. Their drunken frolics fill the pages of Pepys's diary. Two killed a footboy in Covent Garden, but were too well connected to suffer for it. Young Legge, an MP, was convicted of manslaughter. Two killed fellow officers in duels. The most notorious duel of the age involved, predictably, Rupert's crony, Holmes, and another officer. A veteran of the civil wars lamented in print the revival of the image of the 'deboshed (= debauched) cavalier', and the debasement of the old ideal of selfless military service. The disparaging view of the military held by polite society, which has already been noticed in the opinion of Judge Whitelocke, was powerfully reinforced by the riotous behaviour of some army and navy officers, and the 'vicious and dissolute' conduct of their men. Pepys admired their finery on the parade ground but doubted their military efficiency.[39]

Fortunately the survival of the nation did not depend on the small force maintained for home defence. Overseas, in England's first colonial outposts, in pacifying Scotland or holding down Ireland, as sea soldiers or marines, or in officering the regiments raised for foreign expeditions — in other words wherever active soldiering was to be found — there were career soldiers more committed to the profession. Many could not have served at home; although in terms of social class they were nearly comparable to the guardsmen, they tended to come from poorer families, who lacked political connections; and some were ex-Cromwellians. They sought posts, even in foreign service, where they could find them. Pepys saw in Tangier the best and the worst of them. Sir Palmes Fairborne, the governor, had been a soldier since boyhood; an impressive commander, he was mortally wounded successfully defending the almost indefensible garrison against Moorish attack in 1680. His family were to continue to serve with distinction in arms. He was succeeded at Tangier by a contrasting personality, but an equally professional officer, Colonel Percy Kirke, whose long service included a spell of soldiering in French pay. Tyrannical and corrupt, his name was to become a byword for oppression after Monmouth's rebellion. The commander in Scotland was another remarkable old Royalist career soldier, and soldier of fortune, who had waged war in Ireland and in Russia: General Tam Dalyell, his enemies alleged, employed barbarous Muscovite practices in suppressing the Covenanters. He went on to found his own regiment (the Scots Greys, i.e. Royal Scots Dragoon Guards), which has survived to the present day. If court patronage controlled entry to the guards in London, posts in garrisons abroad were reserved for professionals; this distinction was to remain and grow in the years to come.[40]

The reforms, which were to improve the conditions of service, and so better the quality of the candidates for office, came first in the navy. Pepys, as Clerk of the Acts, and then, under James, Secretary to the Admiralty, and his successor as Clerk for almost thirty years, Charles Sergison, built on the fact of the navy's permanence and importance, and their own access to leading ministers, to persuade good families 'to breed up their younger sons to the art and practice of navigation', by making the service more attractive. After mid-century the state was no longer, as it had been before, merely a minority shareholder in naval expeditions; the navy had world-wide obligations, its leading officers increasing responsibilities; it was the biggest employer in the country, if the dockyards are included as well as the 40,000 or so seamen required in time of war. In 1661 the Admiralty took the first of a succession of steps, each one minor, but cumulatively important, to regulate the service. Previously entry to the navy had been in the hands of the captains of warships, who had selected a number of hopeful youths to act as their 'servants' and in due course be promoted to lieutenants on their recommendation. Now at least one of these boys was to be selected, warranted and paid by the Admiralty, and this 'volunteer per order' or 'King's letter boy', as he became known, was marked for promotion above his peers. In 1677 an examination at the Navy Board for candidates for promotion to lieutenant was introduced, the first such test in the history of the British armed forces. Each candidate had to be over twenty years old, have performed three years' service at sea, one as a midshipman — this junior post was now appropriated in part for this purpose — and have obtained a certificate of competence in the service from his captain. The number of years' experience required would be increased later.[41]

A grave difficulty, as we have seen, in an earlier age, was the failure of the navy to provide continuity of service for its officers and men. Appointments were to posts on board particular ships; when they were taken out of service the posts lapsed. This might occur not only at the end of a war, but while the ship's wooden hull underwent its frequent cleaning and repair. The navy, as a result, and unlike the army, could not easily establish grounds of seniority for promotion, as officers were taken in and out of the service, placed in different ranks or no rank at all. Sea officers had less prospect of continuous service, constant pay and certain promotion than their army colleagues, and many would continue till the end of the century to combine sea with land service. John Churchill, later Duke of Marlborough, was a volunteer at the battle of Solebay; Admiral Herbert, Earl of Torrington and First Lord of the Admiralty in 1689, had spent time in command of land forces. Pepys and his successors introduced the concept of half pay, already well known in the army, to counter this major difficulty. At first confined to senior ranks, half pay was extended to all by the end of the wars in 1715. In that year 449 officers went on the half-pay list. When no longer 'in post' the officer would, as a result, still receive a proportion of his pay and be ready to serve when the opportunity again arose. The Admiralty would know how many experienced men were in reserve and available. This at least was the theory: until the introduction of pensionable retirement for senior officers in the middle of the eighteenth century many commanders, still on half pay after a long period of peace, would be too old for active service. Several admirals were in their seventies in the wars of the 1740s. Unlike their counterparts in the army they had not bought and so could not sell their commissions, and retire on the proceeds.[42]

A number of new posts were created at this time. The midshipman was often now an apprentice officer. From the

Dutch the title of commodore was borrowed for officers in charge of overseas stations or detached squadrons; and more flag ranks, which had hitherto been limited by the three traditional divisions — red, white and blue — to which all admirals had been assigned, were created. The bigger men of war were given more junior officers; after 1700 there would be up to five lieutenants in first and second rates, where the massive firepower — equal to that of a contemporary army — and the 800–1,000 crew had not previously been matched by the number of officers. Marine regiments, hitherto raised and disbanded at need, were also made permanent, adding to the manpower of the navy; small units of marines acted as a police force on men of war when, in the course of the eighteenth century, with great progress in the art of navigation, the King's ships were often at sea for years on end. These changes reflected the growing strength of Britain's navy and the greater scope and complexity of its mission. After 1715 she possessed naval bases overseas and fleets were kept more or less permanently in colonial or other distant stations, readied for action.[43]

More opportunities in wartime for promotion, greater flexibility in the career structure, improvements in pay and the allowance for officers' servants (part of which, at least could be pocketed), so that sea officers were rewarded on roughly the same scale as their counterparts in the army, all contributed to the increasing attractiveness of the service. But there were other important inducements. For much of the eighteenth century the royal navy met little serious challenge in its role as defender of British colonies and commerce, and sea officers could profitably exploit friendly merchants' need for protection. The link between the navy and mercantile interests was traditionally close. The Admiralty permitted captains to carry in their ships, or convoy, valuable cargoes, otherwise endangered by enemy attack, and to charge a percentage of the value for the service. Bullion was frequently transported in this manner, and freight money, as it was termed, could significantly augment naval earnings in wartime. More important still was prize money. Where the war at sea was carried to the enemy, and consisted in good part of commerce raiding, there were splendid opportunities for the capture of rich prizes. The value of enemy vessels and their cargoes was assessed, and the spoils distributed among the ships involved according to the rank of the participants, from the three-eighths of the captain to the two-eighths shared among all the ordinary sailors and marines. The distribution of prize money continued in the royal navy, although in different proportions, until the end of the Second World War. Some prizes, especially in the mid-century wars against Spain, were spectacular. The capture of the Spanish treasure ship *Hermione* in 1762 gave the principal flag officer over £40,000, the sailors each £485, equal to three years' pay. The sack of Havana in the same year made the fortunes of that rapacious pair of brothers, General George and Admiral Augustus Keppel.[44]

The lure of prize money reflected not only the success of the navy in its now world-wide role and the close association of profit and power in a mercantilist age, but the semi-piratical and freebooting origins of much naval enterprise in the past. There remained room in the navy of the Georges for the buccaneering spirit of Drake's day. But if most commanders put the hunt for prizes in enemy waters, or freight money in friendly stations, ahead of their orders from the Admiralty, naval efficiency and the maintenance of an overall strategy would suffer. While some MPs approved a self-financing war of piracy and plunder, their lordships could hardly permit the captains of their ships to view themselves as mere soldiers of fortune. They found that duties in remote tropical stations with high mortality rates, or in blockading enemy ports, where the risks were great and rewards few, were less popular than postings in fast cruisers to the sea roads where soft targets abounded: to compensate they offered special bounties for the capture of enemy warships, 'head money'. But it was still the case, at the end of our period, that, if Britannia ruled the waves, she enjoyed no monopoly of her servants' activities. Many captains resigned in 1740 rather than accept postings to the West Indies, and the Admiralty failed to get reluctant officers removed from the half-pay list, particularly those sufficiently astute to plead ill health and have their plea supported by someone of influence. Those officers wealthy or well connected enough not to have to obey their lordships' orders would continue to enjoy a good deal of freedom of action.[45]

A post on the quarter deck was clearly, at this date, one of honour and profit, which would attract the younger sons of good family as Pepys had hoped. In Queen Anne's war the merchant marine had still supplied recruits to the officer corps. The navy had been rapidly expanded — there were nearly a thousand posts available — and 44 per cent of the lieutenants commissioned were from merchant ships; 48 per cent were 'King's letter boys', an indication of the success of that device. That 'tarpaulins' were as numerous as the gentlemen who, in the Duchess of Albemarle's phrase, could 'make legs', may be inferred from the incident at the ball held at Barcelona in 1708 to honour the presence of the combined English and Dutch fleet. Out of a considerable number of officers attending, there was only one English officer who could dance! It was possible then for men of talent but obscure social origin to become admirals. Patronage was not exclusively a matter of aristocratic kinship: Shovell and Narbrough came from the same Norfolk village as Myngs. Sir Charles Wager was of low birth, but rose to be First Lord, after a successful career at sea, through Walpole's patronage.[46]

The navy remained a 'rough school', apprenticeship to which, even for the well connected, could be daunting, dangerous and humiliating.[47] Because it was entered into at an early age it precluded the normal gentry training at college or inn of court. 'A man of war was my university,' said one MP in the 1750s.[48] The midshipman's lot was an unhappy one; to accept it, according to one satirist in Queen Anne's reign,

> A youth of any tolerable hopes, and good parts, must have a wonderful stock of Christian stoicism, to choose to abandon the secure and standing advantages, which law, physic, divinity, trade, nay agriculture itself does propose to its followers; and venture their all, in so uncertain, and fluctuating a bottom as the navy, which at best, affords no better an annuity, even to a lieutenant, than any of the other professions can pick up in a month perhaps.[49]

Although he might be a future officer, he had no status with either the crew or his captain. The former were almost invariably the rejected of society, the scum of the seaports, unwilling victims of the press-gangs or the 'collected filth of jails'; the sea, it was said, like the gallows, refuses nobody. But the latter might prove to be even worse: the ship's commander, according to Tory scribblers in Queen Anne's war a 'mighty czar' in his own vessel, had the power almost of life and death over the young entrant to the navy on board his ship. He might be a petty tyrant, a drunkard or a mere incompetent. The midshipman had no right to complain, and on his captain's recommendation his future career would depend.[50] Some were unlucky, even when posted to the ship of a close kinsman. The eleven-year-old Augustus Hervey, of aristocratic family — he was the son of Queen Caroline's confidant and courtier, Lord Hervey — entered the service in an uncle's frigate; like many of his family he was intelligent and artistic, as his midshipman's logbook, which has survived, shows; with his name and background, and with friendly guidance at the hands of his first captain, his career might be considered to have started under unusually favourable circumstances. But his uncle turned out to be a cruel monster; even at that time, and even in the navy, his brutality caused comment, and he was later cashiered. How damaged was the young Augustus at the end of his first voyage? We do not know, and in any case his natural talents and family connections ensured that he rose to flag rank within a reasonable period of time. A lesser man, however, might scarcely have survived such a punishing experience at an impressionable age.[51]

Except for a wealthy and self-indulgent captain, who might fill his cabin with servants, cabin boys and creature comfort, life at sea was notoriously hard. Conditions were generally appalling; living space cramped, food scarcely edible, simple rules of hygiene ignored, the threat of mutiny among the brutalised crew ever present. As Dr Johnson said: 'No man will be a sailor who has contrivance enough to get himself into a jail; for being in a ship is being in a jail, with the chance of being drowned . . . A man in a jail has more room, better food, and commonly better company.'[52] The naval authorities were only beginning to come to terms with the mental and physical consequences for officers and men of the navy's ability to keep its ships at sea for long periods in the performance of its world-wide role during the eighteenth century. On average two-thirds of a ship's complement would perish of disease in the course of a two-year voyage. Many vessels foundered in storms; and in an engagement a man of war, raked by broadsides, would still 'swim with blood': gunnery, as well as navigation, was improved in the course of the eighteenth century.[53]

Nevertheless, as the century advanced, literary and other evidence suggests that the service was becoming increasingly exclusive. It may be significant that, as a form of recruitment, the King's letter was abandoned in the 1730s, and selection once again left to the captain, whose powers of patronage were thereby strengthened. The opening of a naval academy at Portsmouth did not alter this picture, for it did not flourish until much later. The carefully devised qualifications for entry and promotion were often not observed; baptismal certificates could be forged where the candidate was under age, records of sea service attested to by a friendly captain although he had not been to sea. Mere boys, with the right connections, had their names entered on the books while they were still at school. Young men who were nephews of sea lords or cousins of dukes were rapidly advanced and given the most profitable stations to serve in: young Hervey was 12 when he qualified as lieutenant; Augustus Keppel was a captain at 19, Rodney's son at 15. The navy became, in the words of its historian, 'a nearly perfect reflection of the political structure of the nation'.[54] Its senior posts would be dominated by those with influence, for the sea service was now too important to be left to the career sailors alone. Success at sea might bring honours and titles; it certainly brought fame and wealth. Some families, like the Boscawens and the Byngs, were able to establish naval dynasties. Some combined their commands with a seat in the Commons: 36 officers were MPs between 1747 and 1754. Others took care to have their cause promoted there. The upper reaches of the service became an aristocratic preserve: of the 23 First Lords of the Admiralty in the eighteenth century, 16 were peers.[55] The death of one of the last examples of a plain seaman, Sir John Balchen, may mark a point of transition. 'Of very obscure parentage', Balchen was apparently uneducated, and, lacking a powerful patron, his career had been painfully halting and dogged by misfortune. But when his flagship, HMS *Victory*, disappeared in a storm in 1744, as well as the 74-year-old admiral and the thousand crew, there perished 'upwards of fifty young gentlemen', 'some of them belonging to families of the first distinction', who were being apprenticed to him.[56]

Many of the developments noted in the case of the navy were to have an impact on Britain's army over the same period. As the fleets, and their personnel, were expanded in the wars at the end of the seventeenth and the start of the eighteenth centuries, so were the land forces. Under William and Anne

Britain became a principal combatant in full-scale, lengthy, and increasingly bloody wars in Europe and European colonies overseas. Her army was transformed in the process; tripled in size — by the time of Malplaquet the British contribution to the alliance against Louis XIV was some 70,000 men, and battles in Flanders were on a scale never seen before — it found senior and junior officers equal to the new and greater tasks now imposed upon them. The greatest of these was John Churchill, Duke of Marlborough, whose chequered career, as a professional soldier subject to innumerable political vicissitudes, reflected the turbulent course of events from the fall of James II to the accession of George I, in which Churchill had a significant part to play. His father's family were modest Devon gentlemen and lawyers, who had suffered in the civil wars for the King; his mother's claimed relation with Sir Francis Drake. The elder Churchill obtained minor legal and court office at the restoration, and both John and his sister were able to advance themselves at court: the first by favour of the King's mistress, the second by becoming the mistress of the King's brother. Churchill's first captaincy was probably purchased for him by his paramour. He was a career soldier rather than a courtier-officer, seeking action at sea, in the Tangier garrison and in the service of Louis XIV, under Turenne. He was one of an important and experienced core of professional officers around whom James II built his new army, and his defection to William in 1688 was a heavy blow to James.[57]

The existence of proprietorship among English officers was an impediment to any sudden political change imposed from above in the forces: a fact which later reconciled Marlborough, in the intense party strife of Anne's reign, to the continuation of the purchase system. Both James and William relied to a great extent on the wider British establishment to effect their purposes. Having failed to obtain a significant change among the officers of English regiments — only one-eighth were Catholic by 1688 — James turned to his Scottish and Irish forces and loyal elements among the troops in the Anglo-Dutch brigade. William, for his part, had a justifiably low opinion of English soldiers at this stage, and headed his invasion army and his later expeditions against Louis XIV's veterans, with Huguenot refugees, Protestant volunteers recruited from several nations, and the major section of the

Anglo-Dutch forces which had resisted James's blandishments. These seasoned troops remained thereafter the backbone of the British army heavily engaged in the wars with France. The Scots were described as 'the best men and best prepared for service'; they would make an increasing contribution to the army. Huguenot regiments and Huguenot officers in British units played a vital part in Ireland, Flanders and Spain, without which the nation could scarcely have discharged successfully its now extensive Continental and extra-European military obligations. Above all,the refugee French Protestants brought discipline and organisation, in both of which departments the native troops were badly lacking.[58]

In part these developments reflected not only the fact that Britain was fighting a major land war as part of a complex European coalition, and the poor state of English troops, but the political distrust of armed forces of any size in the nation as a whole. From the Bill of Rights to the parliamentary battles over the standing army in peacetime, from the sacking of Marlborough in 1692 to his fall in 1711, the army was at the centre of prolonged and at times bitter political controversy. A standing army was declared 'unlawful', and many of William's non-English troops were disbanded in 1698. Marlborough was accused by his critics of abusing his position as supreme commander — he was both Captain-General and Master of the Ordnance — for his own ends. The need for competent officers wherever they might be found brought into the forces under his command a wide range of talented individuals, of foreign and non-gentry origin, whose rapid advancement would be resented by English country gentlemen and taxpayers. Captain Robert Parker, whose memoirs of service are an informative source for the wars of the period, was typical: a poor man, born in Ireland probably of new Cromwellian and Protestant planter stock, he rose from the ranks in Irish, Williamite service. Although he had at first thought that 'carrying a brown musket was but a melancholy prospect', he became 'a solid, sober and reliable soldier whose whole life from 1689 to 1718 was intimately bound up with his regimental family'.[59] He was able to make a career out of the army, although as an officer lacking connection he could not rise very far in the service. The sale of his captaincy provided him with a modest pension at the end of the day. A succession of big battles and major sieges, in which, with the increased firepower of the armies of the time, casualties were heavy — a quarter of the 50,000 Allied troops engaged at the battle of Blenheim were killed or wounded — gave great opportunities to aspiring soldiers, in much the same way as 'tarpaulins' from merchant service had profited from the wartime expansion of the naval service.

Where the war aims of the Allies, and the high command of the British forces on the Continent, had become a matter of party conflict, military men and matters would be subject to continual political interference. Some 15 per cent of all MPs in the period were army officers; the more senior posts were the target of Marlborough's opponents while Anne lived, of George I and the new political establishment after his accession. Perhaps as many as twenty Tory MP-officers lost their places in 1715–16, after the abortive Jacobite rebellions had been suppressed. Under the Georges the most loyal elements in the country, Hanoverian Scots and Huguenots, whose fate depended on the maintenance of the Protestant succession, would continue to have an important role to play in the army. But that army, after the end of the wars, would be maintained on a much reduced basis. While the navy, to the nation's great advantage, was kept at sea to provide protection for England's maritime and colonial empire, the army was subject to continuing parliamentary criticism and control, despite the evident wish of the Georges — whose only talents were military — to field armed forces which would, if necessary, defend the electorate of Hanover and not besmirch the honour of the realm. All the Hanoverians attempted to keep control of the army; George I and George II were genuinely warlike princes, emulating their Hohenzollern neighbours: George II scrutinised the promotions list and no officer could be advanced beyond the rank of colonel without his knowledge and very often permission. If a commander-in-chief was to be appointed, he would be a prince of the blood, such as George's son, the Duke of Cumberland. When ill success forced his retirement there would be, his father hoped, no more captain-generals or commanders-in-chief: ultimate power would lie with the petty tyrant in St James himself.[60]

He disliked the purchase system, as detrimental to military efficiency, and he shared William III's low view of the military capacity of the English landed elite. He would have agreed with the great Lord Halifax's dictum: 'The port and style of a

nobleman of England did not accord with the life of a soldier.'
It was his bitter enmity which ensured that Byng, the son of a
First Lord of the Admiralty, would be shot on his own quarter
deck and that Lord George Sackville was publicly humiliated
throughout every unit of the army for his behaviour at
Minden.[61]

But the Hanoverians did not preside over a Hohenzollern
despotism. Through the secretaries of war and the paymaster
general, the annual budget and the Mutiny Act, Parliament
shared control of the armed forces. A German officer, called to
give evidence against Sackville, commented, when the court
martial's power had lapsed with the expiry of the current
Mutiny Act, that, in terms of military efficiency, 'a country can
have too many laws': in this regard England was 'a country with
many peculiarities'.[62] The eighteenth century witnessed in
England the maintenance and some have argued the recrudes-
cence of old aristocratic values. There was an urgent social
need for the dominant families to satisfy the demand from
their kin, dependants and clients to gain places of honour and
profit. The purchase system, and the proprietorship of
regiments, in a smaller peacetime army, and in a political world
of increasing exclusivity, ensured that rank and title, allied as
appropriate to new wealth and political influence, increased its
hold on the upper echelons of the army. Purchase was not
permitted in the technical arms, where some expertise was
obviously required, nor above the rank of colonel, but three-
quarters of the officers in the Hanoverian army had purchased
their places. The *Court and City Register* of 1769 lists 102
colonels of regiments; 43 were peers or sons of peers, 7
grandsons and 4 married to daughters of peers. Less active
posts, such as governors of garrisons, were equally an aristroc-
ratic preserve. The higher one penetrated into the top brass,
the more thickly clustered the offspring of the great landed
families of England. If 10 per cent of major generals were
peers, 27 per cent of full generals were. In each Parliament of
the period 1715–90 there were 50–60 army officers in the
lower house alone, a larger number than the navy — admittedly with only a quarter of the complement of officers — and
about 10 per cent of all MPs in the second half of the century.
The benches of the House of Commons in 1780, to take a year
at random, were adorned with no less than 23 generals; it was,
admittedly, a war year. For such men possession of the King's

commission was only a part of their wider role as leading members of the political nation; their many other responsibilities competed with army service for their attention. MPs could absent themselves from their units for long periods; others enjoyed largely titular command. Best of all were governorships in America, which were lucrative and conferred prestige on the recipient, but did not require constant attendance, at least in time of peace.[63]

There was little argument that such a situation was necessary and indeed desirable. If there were 'no sons of merchants among our generals' this was because it was felt that, by upbringing and aptitude, they were less suitable than those sprung from old landed families. It was commonly believed that the only or the most important military attributes could not be acquired by training or experience, but were most likely to be found amongst the possessors of wide estates, who had inherited, it was assumed, those sterling fighting qualities which had distinguished their forebears: John Charnock, the early historian of the navy, described Prince Rupert, for example, as possessing 'that impetuous gallantry which so frequently attends high birth'.[64] Developments in the military science did not wholly invalidate these assumptions; the era of the sword, spontoon and round shot had not yet been replaced by that of shrapnel and rocket; the life of the ordinary infantry and cavalry commander was not yet unduly complicated. The day-to-day management of the men could be left to the NCOs; in battle what was most valued appears to have been steadiness, discipline and coolness under fire. As a consequence many officers went out of their way to display reckless courage in front of their men; what was most damaging to an officer's reputation was not incompetent administration, or even corruption, but any doubt about his personal bravery. As modern-minded and militarily experienced a statesman as Frederick the Great preferred as officers those for whom any such doubt would be social death for themselves and their families, an indelible stain on their honour. The Duke of Cumberland's standing with his father suffered when it was rumoured that he had 'turned his head' at a moment of danger. If in the navy, to which Parliament gave priority and which had introduced, in the previous century, regulations governing entry and promotion, these regulations were, as we have seen, widely circumvented by young men of influence, it may well be imagined that in the army of the Georges, where no such tests were required, there was even less chance of the inculcation of a professional spirit among its officers. The purchase system, and the concept of the gentleman officer, continued to be defended long after the period under discussion. Palmerston, a former Secretary of War, argued in the 1820s that it was politically desirable that the army be identified in feelings and interests with the country's civil and political institutions; and that this was best achieved by ensuring that those who held military command came from the same stock as the ruling elite. As Henry Pelham said in 1744, English liberties were best preserved by putting the standing army under 'men of family and fortune'. The nation could not afford a military caste with independent ambitions; the memory of Cromwell (or even Marlborough) could be invoked. As late as 1869, on the eve of the abolition of purchase itself, this argument was still being seriously employed by experienced officers and military commentators.[65]

But of course this is not the whole picture. If senior posts in the army were reserved for the aristocratic, and were often in peacetime held by men with better things to do than attend to their military duties, junior officers were different. The Hanoverian army could hardly have discharged its many functions, in several areas of the world, had this not been the case. The home training of the army was not wholly deficient, though it was distracted by the need to aid the civil power over smuggling and the occasional grain riot.[66] It did not disgrace the name of Britain even alongside the formidable Prussians, and in North America it usually proved capable of dealing with colonial militias, 'yelling Indians and wild Canadians'. The evolution of effective musketry, the search for the optimum form of thin red line, the development of better quality field artillery — all indicate the presence in the armed forces of some well-trained and conscientious officers. We must recall that in the system of purchase most buyers of commissions were also sellers, and had to find only the difference in price between the rank held and that aspired to; that places made vacant by the death of the holder were not sold; that the artillery and engineering arms were not part of the system. Where senior officers were so often absent — all four colonels of regiments were not at their posts in Minorca when the French launched their surprise attack in 1756 — the survival of the unit might depend on the commitment and capacity of junior officers and senior NCOs, and the best of these were valued by the high command and the rank and file alike. There were greater opportunities for advancement by those lacking wealth and influence when war broke out, and new regiments were to be raised; some resulted from the process of 'raising for rank' by which wealthy, patriotic individuals undertook to provide new units at their own expense. Officers had to be found for these regiments. The onset of war brought other opportunities. Postings to distant, fever-ridden colonial stations, like those in the West Indies, would be unpopular with the well connected, who would prefer and could afford to stay at home; their place would be taken by more career-minded or impoverished officers. Those who went overseas, particularly to the tropics, risked a quick death. The appalling casualty figures in the Jamaica garrison, mainly due to yellow fever, led to the baleful comment: 'There is no God in Jamaica.' A war fought overseas and on Continental battlefields improved promotion prospects out of all recognition. Frustrated, long-serving junior officers raised their glasses to the toast: 'A bloody war or a sickly season!'[67]

Purchase and patronage played no part in the recruitment of the artillery and engineering arm, which was, of course, the responsibility of an independent department of state, the Board of Ordnance. Here private and political interest had to be subordinated to the needs of the service and the development of scientific skills. After several false starts, Britain founded a military academy for entrants to the artillery in 1741, at the same time as the Portsmouth naval school; it was the last major European nation (including Russia) to do so. Sited at Woolwich, long a centre of the nation's munitions manufacture, the Royal Military College, as it became known, had modest beginnings; only two masters (and those possibly deputised) taught forty or so cadets and young officers, aged from 12 to 30. From 1761 engineers as well as gunners were trained there, and in 1764 a public examination was introduced: there was later an entrance examination, with the result that in due course a number of unofficial preparatory schools sprang up in the locality. The college became famous for rowdiness and indiscipline, 'riots and drunken broils'. Woolwich itself was described as a 'dirty town', and no doubt the young cadets, 'not quite officers or even gentlemen', were subject to a host of evil influences. But in time the school, affectionately known as 'The shop', and its products began to acquire a better reputation. Michael Faraday was to be a professor there early in the following century, and if we consider the confidence with which the guns were run out in the battles of the Seven Years War, or later in the Peninsula, or by Captain Mercer at Waterloo, we can see that professional skills had been assimilated, and were being employed.[68]

There were therefore several different sources of officer recruitment and routes to promotion. The Scots and the Huguenots — or their descendants — would continue to play a disproportionately large role in the army throughout the eighteenth century. The example of General John Ligonier demonstrated that a penniless exile could rise rapidly in the army by his own efforts; it was said that he had raised the price of his first commission by his winnings at cards. He was later to show that a taste for under-age girls was no impediment to the holding of supreme command.[69] A different route to the top was taken by General William Roy, a typical Scottish 'lad o' parts' without family or political connection. A Lanarkshire civil surveyor, who had worked on the post-1745 Highland Survey, he was commissioned by the Board of Ordnance in 1755 and then kept in pay and steadily advanced as a titular infantry officer (in one of the new regiments raised in the Seven Years War), while serving the Board as an engineer and military surveyor. His death, in 1790, prevented him from supervising, and taking the credit for, the scheme which he had long planned, the Ordnance Survey of the British Isles.[70] Continuous service available in a standing army which was taking on such new roles aided the emergence of 'army families' like the Handasydes, Burgoynes and Wolfes, not necessarily aristocratic. The career of General James Wolfe is a good example of someone bred to the military life (his father was a lieutenant colonel), but rising by his own exertions and providing a military education for himself in the absence of a British military academy for future line officers; he learned mathematics in Glasgow, French at Paris. At one time he planned to go to cadet school in Lorraine, and his superiors were worried that, excellent young officer as he was, he would be tempted to leave British service altogether for the Prussian. Military skills were international in their application, and the soldier of fortune was not yet a thing of the past. Only after

1815, and the growth of nationalist feeling, was there a restriction on the free movement of military men seeking fresh fields to conquer. Wolfe stayed, but experienced endless frustration as a regimental officer. Refused leave by his absentee commanding officer, Lord Bury (George Keppel the later general), he complained that Bury 'desires never to see his regiment and wishes that no officer would ever leave it'. He was disgusted by the trifling of the senior ranks with the 'poor soldiery'.[71] Studies of Scottish junior officers, who were not rich and whose promotion ceiling was consequently low, reveal a similar picture; as years of service lengthened, and conditions did not improve, bitterness and frustration grew.[72]

A quarter of all regimental officers in the British Army in the eighteenth century were Scots, and mostly Lowland Scots, like Roy. There can be little doubt that most of them looked on their calling as a serious and full-time occupation; while none could have been trained at a British cadet school, for none such existed at the time, they no doubt educated themselves on the job, under the watchful eye of a veteran officer or NCO. There were no certificates of competence or attestations of experience to acquire, nor examinations to pass. The view was taken that these, like performance on the parade ground, or in peacetime administration, or in mock battlefield manoeuvres, were not necessarily accurate indications of military ability. Greater reliance was still placed, in the intimacy of the regimental 'family', on personal qualities. Even when, in the following century, the army acquired its first cadet school and formal qualifications, 'honour, courage and gallantry were rated above the acquisition of professional skills'.[73] In this sense the gentlemanly traditions within the armed forces, which have been traced in this essay, continued to exert a pervasive influence, long after the passing from the scene of the chivalrous knight at arms and his replacement by modern methods of warfare.

Notes

1. M. Keen, *Chivalry* (1984), Ch. 10–13.
2. Ibid., and S. Anglo, 'The courtier: the Renaissance and changing ideals' in A. G. Dickens (ed.), *The courts of Europe* (1977), p. 36. The earliest printed books in England were romances of this kind: M. J. D. Cockle, *Bibliography of military history up to 1642* (1900). See, for

the great popularity of Amadis, J. J. O'Connor, *Amadis de Gaule and its influence on Elizabethan literature* (New Brunswick, NJ, 1970).

3. L. Stone, *The crisis of the aristocracy, 1558–1641* (Oxford, 1965), pp. 245–7.

4. A. Goodman, *The Wars of the Roses: military activity and English society, 1452–97* (1981), p. 209.

5. J. R. Hale, *Renaissance war studies* (1983), Ch. 8. In Ch. 14 Hale challenges the conventional view that the introduction of gunpowder had much to do with the decline of chivalry.

6. C. G. Cruickshank, *Army royal* (Oxford, 1960), p. 190.

7. Stone, *Crisis of aristocracy*, pp. 245–7.

8. Richard Barkhede, 'A brief discourse . . .', cited Hale, *Renaissance war studies*, p. 248.

9. L. O. J. Boynton, *The Elizabethan militia* (1967); Cruickshank, *Army royal*, pp. 189–90; L. B. Larking (ed.), *Proceedings principally in the county of Kent* (Camden Soc., o.s., vol. 80, 1862), pp. xxxiv–xxxv.

10. C. G. Cruickshank, *Elizabeth's army* (Oxford, 1966), pp. 50–60.

11. The better known include L. and T. Digges, *Stratioticos* (1579), B. Riche, *Allarme to England* (1578) and T. Styward, *The pathwaie to martial discipline* (1581). Machiavelli was translated into English by 1560. See Cockle, *Bibliography*; Cruickshank, *Elizabeth's army*, Ch. 12; Hale, *Renaissance war studies*, Ch. 9; H. J. Webb, *Elizabethan military science* (Madison, Wis., 1965).

12. *OED*.

13. M. Lewis, *England's sea officers* (1948), *passim*.

14. Ibid.; K. R. Andrews, *Elizabethan privateering* (Cambridge, 1964); M. F. Keeler (ed.), *Sir Francis Drake's West Indian voyage, 1585–86*, Hakluyt Soc., 2nd ser., 148, 1981), pp. 12–23. Drake's view cited in *Oxford dictionary of quotations*, 3rd edn (1979), p. 193.

15. Based on the number of troops raised: Cruickshank, *Elizabeth's army*, Appendix 1.

16. Essex's expedition brought forth hundreds of 'green-headed youths, covered with feathers, and gold and silver lace': cited J. E. Neale, *Queen Elizabeth* (1938), pp. 339, 341; P. W. Hasler (ed.), *The House of Commons, 1558–1603* (1981), vol. 1, pp. 25, 35, 408.

17. Quoted from the *Liber familicus of Sir James Whitelocke* in K. R. Andrews (ed.), *The last voyage of Drake and Hawkins* (Hakluyt Soc., 2nd ser., 142, 1972), pp. 45–6.

18. Hasler, *House of Commons*, vol. 3, pp. 135–40; A. L. Rowse, *The expansion of Elizabethan England* (1957), pp. 144, 370–5, 381.

19. C. Dalton, *Life and times of General Sir Edward Cecil, Viscount Wimbledon (1572–1638)* (1885).

20. G. E. Cokayne, *Complete peerage* (rev. edn, 1910–59), vol. 10, p. 257; vol. 12, part II, p. 259.

21. C. R. Markham, *The fighting Veres* (1888). Portraits of their comrades in arms were in the possession of a descendant until dispersal this century.

22. C. Hammond, *The loyal indigent officer . . . which hath faithfully served his late Majesty* n.d. [*c.* 1675], p. 13; and his *The old English officer . . .* (1679).

23. Cockle, *Bibliography*, pp. xvii–xviii, 3–4, 16–17, 24–5. The earliest use of the term 'military profession' is G. Gates, *The defence of militarie profession* (1579), but the author was no doubt referring more to military skills than to a body of practitioners of those skills.

24. A. Searle (ed.), *Barrington family letters, 1628–1632* (Camden Soc., 4th ser., 28, 1983), pp. 41, 79, 101.

25. *Memoirs of his own life and times by Sir James Turner, 1632–1670* (Edinburgh, 1829), p. 14.

26. Copies of Aston's commissions are preserved in the British Library, Harleian MS 2149, fos. 148–50.

27. J. Prestwich, *Respublica* (1787), pp. 131–48. These are the figures used in *Complete peerage*, vol. 2, pp. 525–6.

28. T. Gumble, *The life of General Monck* (1671).

29. *DNB*; J. B. Deane, *The life of Richard Deane* (1870).

30. The portraits, completed by April 1668, now hang in the National Maritime Museum, Greenwich. See *The diary of Samuel Pepys* ed. R. Latham and W. Matthews (11 vols, 1970–83), vol. 7, pp. 102, 109; vol. 10, *sub nomine*.

31. Ibid., vol. 7, pp. 165–6.

32. C. R. Boxer, *The Anglo-Dutch wars of the seventeenth century, 1652–1674* (1974), pp. 10, 15.

33. Pepys, *Diary*, vol. 7, pp. 10–11.

34. Ibid., pp. 323, 332–3.

35. Ibid., vol. 4, pp. 83–4, vol. 7, p. 348, vol. 9, pp. 26–7; R. Ollard, *Man of war: Sir Robert Holmes and the restoration navy* (1969), pp. 136–7.

36. See the admirable discussion in R. Ollard, *Pepys. A biography* (Oxford, 1984), pp. 225–35, and Pepys, *Diary*, vol. 10, pp. 282–91.

37. J. Childs, *The army of Charles II* (1976); A. Bruce, *The purchase system in the British Army, 1660–1870* (1980); C. Clay, *Public finance and private wealth. The career of Sir Stephen Fox, 1627–1716* (Oxford, 1978).

38. Childs, *Army*, pp. 21–46; Clay, *Fox*, pp. 275–302.

39. B. D. Henning (ed.), *The House of Commons, 1660–1690* (3 vols., 1983), vol. 1, p. 101; Pepys, *Diary*, vol. 4, p. 217, vol. 8, pp. 140–1, vol. 9, pp. 26–7, 273; Hammond, *Loyal officer*, pp. 12, 16; Childs, *Army*, pp. 13, 43.

40. Ollard, *Pepys*, pp. 272–3; *DNB*.

41. Lewis, *Sea officers*; Pepys, *Diary*, vol. 10, pp. 282–91; Ollard, *Pepys*, Ch. 16; D. A. Baugh, *British naval administration in the age of Walpole* (Princeton, NJ, 1965), Ch. 3; D. A. Baugh (ed.), *Documents on naval administration, 1715–1750*, (Navy Record Soc., vol. 120, 1977), Ch. 2.

42. Baugh, *Age of Walpole*, p. 104.

43. J. Ehrman, *The navy in the war of William III, 1689–1697* (Cambridge, 1953), pp. 138–43, 451–61; R. D. Merriman (ed.), *Queen Anne's navy*, (Navy Record Soc., vol. 103, 1961), pp. 310–12.

44. Baugh *Age of Walpole*, pp. 108–18; M. Duffy, 'The foundations of British naval power' in M. Duffy (ed.), *The military revolution and the state, 1500–1800* (Exeter, 1980).

45. Baugh, *Age of Walpole*, pp. 116–17, 141–2.

46. Ibid., pp. 65–8, 97-8; C.R. Markham (ed.), *Life of Captain*

Stephen Martin, 1666–1740 (Navy Record Soc., vol. 5, 1895), p. 114. I owe this last reference, and that in note 49, to E. S. Turner, *Gallant gentlemen: a portrait of the British officer, 1600–1956* (1956).

47. Merriman, *Queen Anne's navy*, p. 317.

48. L. B. Namier and J. Brooke (eds), *The House of Commons, 1754–1790* (3 vols, 1964), vol. 1, p. 145.

49. B. Slush, *The navy royal: or a sea-cook turn'd projector* (1709), p. 15.

50. Ibid., p. 8; Ned Ward, in *The wooden world* (1707), offered similar criticisms of the captains of his day. Smollett later (*Roderick Random*, 1748) portrayed them as bullies where they were not fops.

51. D. Erskine (ed.), *Augustus Hervey's journal, 1746–59* (1953); British Library, Add. MS 12, 129.

52. *Oxford dictionary of quotations*, p. 274.

53. Ehrman, *Navy of William III*, p. 124.

54. Baugh, *Age of Walpole*, p. 126.

55. G. Holmes, *Augustan England: professions, state and society, 1680–1730* (1982), Ch. 9; J. Cannon, *Aristocratic century: the peerage of eighteenth century England* (Cambridge, 1984), pp. 118–20; R. Sedgwick (ed.), *The House of Commons, 1715–1754* (2 vols, 1970), vol. 1, introduction.

56. *DNB*; J. Charnock, *Biographia navalis . . .* (6 vols, 1794–8), vol. 3, p. 159.

57. D. Chandler, *Marlborough as military commander* (1973); J. Childs, *The army, James II and the Glorious Revolution* (Manchester, 1980).

58. Childs, *The army*, pp. 19–24; R. D. Gwynn, *Huguenot heritage. The history and contribution of the Huguenots in Britain* (1985), pp. 79–80, 144–59.

59. D. Chandler (ed.), *Military memoirs, Robert Parker and Comte de Merode-Westerloo* (1968), pp. xiii, 6.

60. R. Hatton, *George I* (1978); the portrait of George II that emerges from Mackesy's study of Sackville's 'crime' is distinctly unflattering: P. Mackesy, *The coward of Minden* (1979).

61. Mackesy, *The coward of Minden*. There was some sympathy for Byng, a poor officer who had consistently over the years exploited his position as son of the First Lord to evade his responsibilities as far as possible: Charnock judged that he should not be blamed, as he was '*naturally* incompetent to the task imposed on him': *Biographia navalis*, vol. 4, p. 179.

62. Mackesy, *Minden*, p. 213.

63. Holmes, *Augustan England*, Ch. 9; Cannon, *Aristocratic century*, pp. 118–20; Sedgwick, *House of Commons*, vol. 1, introduction; Namier and Brooke, *House of Commons*, vol. 1, introduction; J. Shy, *A people numerous and armed* (New York, 1976), Ch. 4.

64. Charnock, *Biographia navalis*, vol. 1, p. 124.

65. J. A. Guy, 'The standing army under George II and the Duke of Cumberland, 1727–1763. Command, regimental administration and finance', unpublished D Phil thesis, University of Oxford, 1982, p. 160; C. M. Clode, *The military forces of the crown* (2 vols, 1869), vol. 2, pp. 739–45.

66. J. A. Houlding, *Fit for service: the training of the British Army, 1715–1795* (Oxford, 1981).

67. Ibid.

68. Sir John Smyth, *Sandhurst* (1961); F. G. Guggisberg, *'The shop'. The story of the Royal Military College* (1900).

69. R. Whitworth, *Field Marshal Lord Ligonier: a story of the British Army, 1702–1770* (Oxford, 1958).

70. Y. O'Donoghue, *William Roy, 1726–1790. Pioneer of the Ordnance Survey* (1977).

71. B. Willson, *The life and letters of James Wolfe* (1909), p. 161.

72. J. W. Hayes, 'Scottish officers in the British Army, 1714–63', *Scottish Historical Review*, vol. 37 (1958); and the same author's unpublished University of London MA thesis, 1956, 'The social and professional background of officers of the British Army, 1714–63'.

73. E. M. Spiers, *The army and society, 1815–1914* (1980), p. 2.

Index

accountancy 2, 4, 15, 131
accountants 14, 70
accounts 158, 165, 175
Act for . . . Attornies and
    Solicitors 75
Act in Restraint of Appeals 37
Act of Six Articles 38
Act of Uniformity 133
actuaries 14
Adams, William 156, 160–7
    passim, 170, 175, 178n
administrators vii, 5
    see also civil service
Admiralty 188, 200, 206
Admiralty, Court of 65, 70
advocates 66–7, 74, 76, 79
advowsons 46
age qualifications 139–40, 141,
    201, 206
alcohol 103, 104–5
alehouse keeping 148
Alford Grammar School,
    Lincolnshire 143
alphabet, teaching of 132
America, governorships in, 211
America, North 212
anaesthetics 117
Anne, Queen 204, 206, 209
anticlericalism 33, 48–9, 57,
    60n
apothecaries 12, 66, 98, 100,
    124n, 155
    and food and drink trades
        103, 105
    and physicians 108, 115
    and tripartite structure 91,
        94, 95, 109
apparitors 72
apprentices 69, 127n
apprentices at law 66, 67, 79
apprenticeship 92, 112, 131,
    157, 172, 190
    in law 67
    in navy 196, 201
    in physic 97

in surgery 103
arbitration 70, 98
archdeaconries 61n
Arches, Court of the 9, 66, 76
architects vii, 4–5, 15, 157
aristocracy 3, 9, 20, 70, 155–76
    passim,
    see also armed services, elite,
        gentry
arithmetic 131, 132, 137
armed services
    and aristocracy 182–6, 193,
        198–9, 205–6, 210–11, 215
    conservatism of 181–2, 215
    growth of 18, 78, 162, 187,
        193–4, 202, 206–7
    interchangeability of 198–9
    see also army, military, navy
arms, profession of 5, 181–215
    passim
army
    Cromwellian 193–4, 196–7
    Hanoverian 206–15
    later Stuart 195–6
    officers *see* military officers
    parliamentarian 161, 192
    regiments 195, 197–9, 210
    royalist 161, 193
    standing 194, 197, 208
articles of religion 133
artificers 113
artillery 185, 186, 212, 213–14
artisans 155
arts
    liberal and mechanical 13, 14
    military and naval 13
assizes 65, 159
Aston, Sir Arthur 192, 193,
    217n
astronomy 132
attorney, powers of 165, 167
attorneys 9–11, 14, 15, 18, 19,
    66–85 *passim*
    and barristers, vocational
        spheres of 78–84

220

Index

Index